MW01007214

Book interior design by Zoe Donalson

Map of Historical Places of South Mobile
by Peter Palm, Berlin

Dedication

You know how it is. You pick up a book, flip to the dedication and find that, once again, the author has dedicated a book to someone else and not to you.

Not this time.

This one is for you.

The citizens of South Mobile.

SOUTH MOBILE

1699 - 2018

Susan Rouillier

CONTENTS

Part III: Places and Events (continued)

Foreword

"No one understands the tender feelings we have for this area."

There is just something wonderful about one's home dirt. When I was born, my parents were living on Bay Front Road just south of Mobile, Alabama. We spent years living and working in other places, but eventually returned to Mobile. To me we were like migrating hummingbirds, coming home to nest. I made my final nest on the very same road where many treasured memories were stored. I wanted to contribute to the community that I held dear. One night I attended a local civic meeting where Sgt. Ron Yokeley, the Mobile Police Department representative said, "I wish someone would write the history of this area." Six years and 1,146 files of text and images later, *South Mobile* is finished.

Sometimes the more neglected areas of South Mobile can obscure the fact that it has a history as rich and fascinating as the better-known parts of the Port City. I was advised by Chuck Torrey, historian for the City of Mobile, that it would be difficult to isolate the history for one geographical area because of many historical tangents that penetrate the borders into other regions. Even so, I decided to focus on the land area from Brookley Air Force Base, south of Mobile, to Dog River, from the time of Native Americans until today. Sometimes referred to as "off DIP" or "on Dog River" this book will refer to the area as South Mobile. Because South Mobile was annexed into Mobile's city limits relatively recently in 1956, its records were scarce and scattered, had never been assembled, and therefore required extensive searching.

I focused on the question, "What forces brought people to South Mobile?" The brief answer was for food, work, transportation, commerce, pleasure, and a warm climate. The Native Americans lived off the rich bounty of the bay and rivers, Civil War soldiers encamped on Dog River, and during WWII an Air Force base played an important role, bringing with it an influx of workers including fishers, boaters, manufacturers, farmers and night-clubbers. Thus, South Mobile lured a wide-ranging group to its rich bounty.

I interviewed many residents whose memories were the longest. The oldest, Rosa Boone, age ninety-eight at the time, told me that she arrived here after "The War" which she described as World War One! Many people told the same story: Life was simple and sweet in the twenties, thirties, forties and fifties. Long-term residents often referred to themselves as "poor" or living "in the country", because they had little money. But they were strong people and they enjoyed the richness of the land and close-knit friendships. They feasted on the abundant bounty of seafood from the waters, they rowed wooden boats they built themselves into the fish-laden Bay, hunted large stands of ducks in winter's cold waters, captured bushel-loads of crabs, and gigged flounders on moonlit nights. They searched barefooted on sandy shores for soft-shelled crabs, they worshiped in churches the community built, enjoyed music in night clubs, grew rows of satsuma trees and their own vegetables, rode horses to backyard movie shows with ten-cent admissions, left their doors unlocked, shared freshly caught fish with friends, built their own schools, and helped their neighbors. I literally found myself crying at some of the moving stories I was told. As one life-long resident, Mary McKeough said, "*No one understands the tender feelings we have for this area.*"

Our beloved region has a vibrant story as unique as a fingerprint, and as rich, detailed and colorful as a Rick Bragg narrative. Inhabited for more than ten thousand years, the history of South Mobile begins with its earliest inhabitants, the Native Americans, followed by the first European presence at King Louis IV's Warehouse on Dog River, and after that, the earliest settlers, the Rochon Family, successful entrepreneurs who lived at the mouth of Dog River. Other chapters in South Mobile's history describe African-American settlers who built their own school called the Race Track School, when there were no other schools in the area; William Cottrill's Magnolia Racetrack and stables where an 1884 Kentucky Derby winner, Buchanan was bred; a popular night club, The Radio Ranch, where Elvis sang; Garland Goode's Cotton Factory located on a tributary of Dog River; a Civil War Encampment on Dog River including letters written from its commanding officers to wives back home; swimmers who won the Fairhope to Grand View Park Race; A veneer factory that supplied wood for R.C.A. Victrolas; one of most unusual yacht clubhouses in the world; and many iconic businesses. The final section contains interviews and stories of individuals who graciously revealed their life experiences and shared their images.

What is most important to me is that this history is recorded for posterity and not be lost forever. I hope you enjoy reading *South Mobile*.

Susan Rouillier

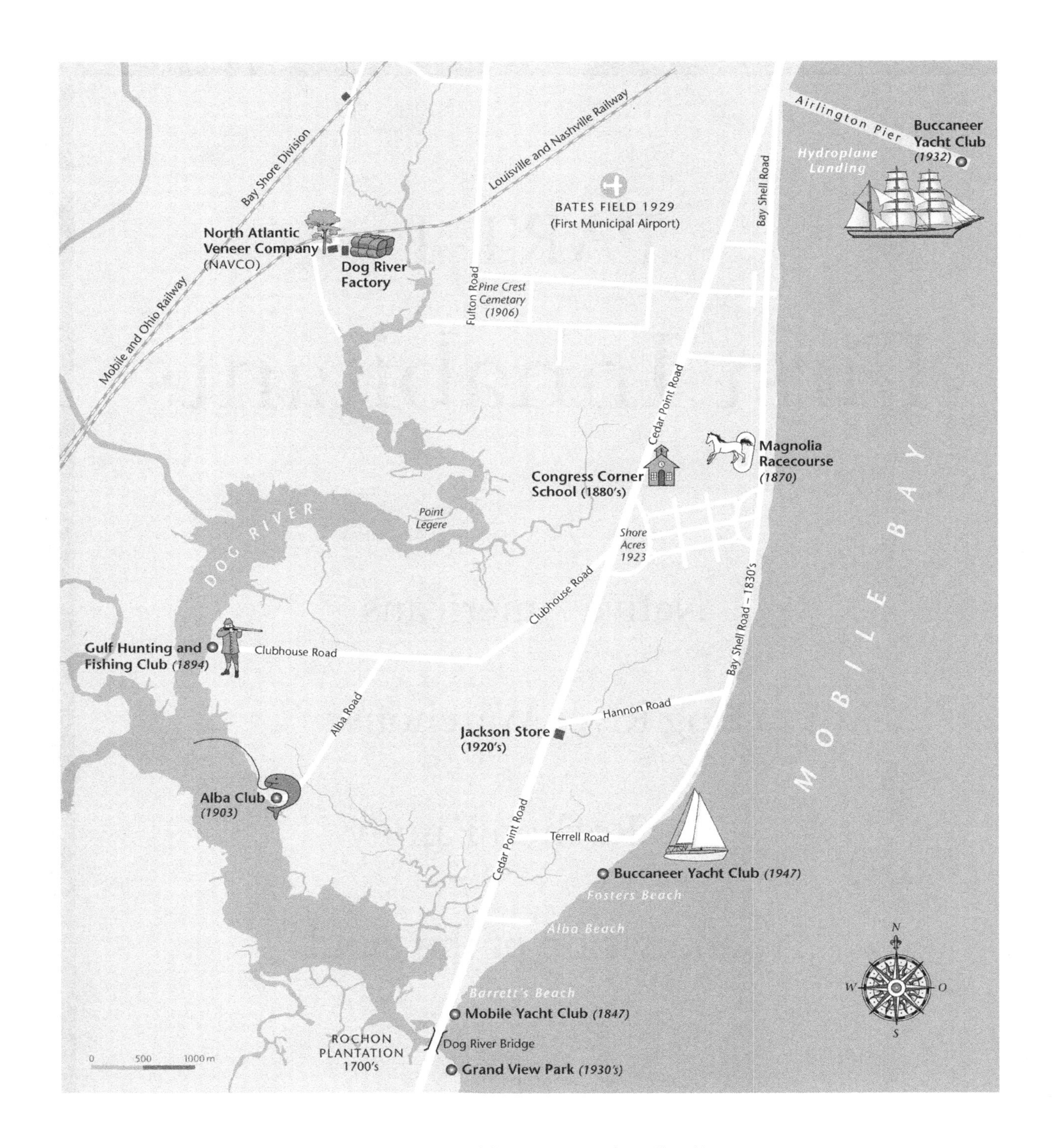

Map created by Peter Palm, Berlin

This map illustrates locations of historical focal points of South Mobile before 1930.

PART I
First Inhabitants

Native Americans

Dog River Warehouse

The Rochon Family

Subdivision of the Land

Chapter 1
Native Americans

Their dugout canoes ghosted on the misty waters
as copper toned people navigated their sacred places.
Bob Grubbs, poet, Dauphin Island

Traces to the earliest people in our area are still here, hidden in their artifacts that have washed ashore and in our local names. The word Alabama is from a Choctaw name meaning "thicket-clearer" or "vegetation-gatherers." Mobile is a derivation of a local indigenous group that means "paddler", or "trader". Other connections can be deduced from the artifacts that have been unearthed from South Mobile's sandy beaches and from the work of archaeologists.

Mrs. Linda Kennedy Jones has collected Native American artifacts for over thirty years on Alba Beach, just north of Dog River. It is not known if all the artifacts originated here or if they were washed in by hurricanes over the decades. What is known is that the first humans to occupy our area were prehistoric hunting and gathering people from the Asian heartland who crossed the Bering Land bridge connecting Siberia and Alaska twenty to thirty thousand years ago gradually occupying the Americas. They may also have entered the Americas along the Pacific west coast feeding on kelp and seals. Within the borders of Alabama, thousands of locations were occupied by Indian societies for about 12,000 years, long before the first Spanish Conquistador, Alonzo Alvarez de Pineda met the Indians when he explored Mobile Bay in 1519, looking for wealth. The people were described as "well made both men and women," with coppery skin and long black hair. The Indian nations of the South were agricultural people who lived in permanent villages, but some were nomadic. Some were mound builders. Their diet consisted of "the three sisters", corn, beans and squash. Beans ran up the corn stalks while squash grew in between. They ate seafood including oysters and left refuse piles called middens in many places around Mobile Bay. Andre Penigaut, a ship's carpenter for Iberville, kept a detailed journal for twenty-four years in his "Annals of Louisiana from 1798 to 1722" as they explored the region from Mobile Bay west to present-day Louisiana and into Spanish territory in what is now Texas. He described a delicious type of bread that local Native Americans made from a reed similar to oats found along the riverbanks. Pénigaut notes that they also used this grain in a soup called sagamité, which included corn, beans, and meat, and was popular among the French as well. His animal descriptions include mammals such as bears, buffalo, wild cats, and deer, turkeys, racoons and opossum; birds such as eagles, herons, wild geese (called bustards); and insects such as mosquitoes.

The stone artifacts Mrs. Jones found at Alba Beach are prehistoric according to Auburn University's Archaeology Department. Some of the pottery, dating from the last five hundred years is composed only of clay. Similar pieces from Dauphin Island contain many small pieces of shell mixed in with the clay. Pottery designs consist of bands or chains of triangles, arches, scrolls and spirals inscribed while the clay was wet. Some pottery pieces are part of vessels, and some have knobs. The pieces usually were decorated with stamped, punctuated, pinched, brushed, or incised designs of swirls, zigzags and circles. The artifacts belonged to ancient local Native American groups such as the Tomé, Naniaba, Mobilian, Apalachee, Choctaw, and Creek Indians.

The oldest objects found on Alba Beach are made of sandstone quartz and quartzite. Rock spear heads, some with lashing grooves were used by the prehistoric Native Americans as spearheads attached to sticks to impale the abundant fish and crabs off the shores. Few arrowheads were found but one very pointed one was found that was probably used to make holes in deer hides. Shards from spearheads were also found suggesting that they were made on site. Other stone implements that she found were probably used as crushers, carvers or hatchets. Perhaps these were used to skin animals, carve meat, or crush corn and beans that were grown on river banks.

One unusual artifact Ms. Jones found shows that the ancient culture played games. The round puck, or disc shaped stone was used as a moving target with players throwing spears in attempts to come the closest. The puck she found has a nick on it, showing that one person won the game that day. The many tubular French clay pipes in this collection were likely used for ritual and ceremonial tobacco smoking. A sandstone bead for adornment, a flint sinker for fishing, and a very unusual bird rim effigy head of a turkey were also found on Alba Beach.

Native Americans worked at the Rochon Plantation just across Dog River from Alba Beach in the early 1700s. Most left South Mobile after the Indian Removal Act law was passed by Congress in 1830, during Andrew Jackson's presidency, and were relocated into federal territory west of the Mississippi River in Oklahoma in exchange for their homeland, but some, like Gaines Frazier's ancestors remained in our area. Indians have always been expert net makers for fishing and used traps before they were used in other parts of the world. Mr. Peter Dais said that his great grandfather, Gaines Frazier, who owned the property now occupied by Gaillard school was of Native American heritage and learned how to weave and knot large nets for capturing fish and smaller ones for crabs from his ancestors. These knotting techniques were passed on the to the next generation and are still used today.

Native Americans lived here for thousands of years; their culture grew, developed and thrived. By comparison, Europeans have been here only three hundred years.

Gaines Frazier, Native American descendant and father of twenty-four, on his doorstep on Cedar Point Road (now D.I.P.) in 1943. Photo courtesy of Peter Dais III.

Linda Kennedy Jones: resident since 1942 with her Native American artifacts, collected over 30 years

French clay pipe pieces

Flint sinker used for fishing

Spear heads with lashings

Very rare turkey head effigy

Pottery with decorations

Pottery with decorations and knob

Rare Native American gaming puck with notch

CHAPTER 2
The King's Warehouse

Background

In 1988 the Alabama Department of Transportation proposed the replacement of old bascule-style Dog River Bridge but it was discovered that the south bank at the mouth of the river was an historically and archaeologically important site. For over two years, large areas of the Dog River Warehouse site at Bay Oaks were excavated by University of South Alabama archaeologists, Greg Spies and Michael T. Rushing as the bridge was being constructed. They found a sequence of human occupation there since 1701. The importance of this site must be emphasized because it was a focal point of activity for the first French colony in the Louisiana Territory, an equivalent to the British colony, Jamestown, Virginia. This was also the site of the subsequent Rochon-Demouy plantations. This poem below was written about the new bridge construction:

Now only scattered bricks are left where once a tiny fortress stood,
A Frenchman's wood hewn citadel twixt salty marsh and piney wood.
Then, cavaliers patrolled the shore. The King's Wharf spanned the muddy quay. But now, great creature-like machines efface the earth, dig to the Bay.
The dirt is heaved; a rusty sword falls, loathe to leave its resting place.
The site is razed steel hammers pound, and concrete fills the ancient space.
—IMOGEN INGE FULLTON

The Warehouse

By order of King Louis IV, the capital of colonial French Louisiana was chosen by French Canadians, Iberville and Bienville to be twenty-five miles north on the western shore of the Mobile-Tensaw River. Iberville and Bienville also wanted to trade with and have influence over Indian tribes: the Choctaw, Chickasaw and Alabamas. Moving colonists so far up river, and supplying them with goods and building materials would not be easy, so before the colony could be established, two ports were needed: A port was established on "Isle de Massacre" (Dauphin Island) where large ships with deep drafts could offload supplies. The supplies were reloaded onto smaller boats that traveled to a second port and warehouse on the south side of the mouth of Dog River called the Magazin de Roi (The King's Warehouse). The Dog River site was chosen because it was the only river emptying into the bay that had enough water to unload the "traversiers" from Dauphin Island close to shore, and because it was concealed and more easily defendable from raids. Here supplies were stored and reloaded onto yet smaller boats because the depth of large sections in the upper bay was only six feet. The supplies sometimes took six weeks to arrive up-river to the new colony. The Dog River warehouse site was completed before the new town was constructed in 1702. Sandstone foundation ruins were tentatively identified from the research as Iberville's magazin structure on the bluff at Dog River's mouth.

Other ruins discovered were the presence of frame structures that stood on the bluff within a walled post and plank area. One was a factory that used nearby pine trees as source material to create pitch and tar for preservation of naval wood and cordage. Another was a kitchen garden structure. "Clearly this was a relatively self-sufficient outpost from its inception, with the King's storehouse functioning as the supply center and locus of domestic and kitchen activities and the adjacent area used for the provision of food and manufacture of pitch and tar made for local use and export. Thus the enterprising LeMoyne brothers were probably the first European entrepreneurs to establish and maintain a manufacturing facility and port of trade on Mobile Bay, even as the colony at Fort Louis on the river struggled to survive:"[1]

Historical confirmation of the excavation data is provided by Jay Higginbotham in his book *Old Mobile* published in 1977. Citing Iberville's journal, he states that "Iberville had reached the mouth of Dog River, where he camped for the night, noting in particular the excellent position of the warehouse on the bluff of the stream's southern bank." This extraordinary and important site of King Louis' Warehouse remains unmarked and unprotected.

1 From Archaeological Investigations at the Bay Oaks Sites on Dog River, Mobile County, Alabama, Greg C. Spies and Michael T. Rushing. 1978.

Excavation Photos from the Dog River Plantation Site (1MB161), Mobile County, Alabama.. Gregory Waselkov, Bonnie L. Gums, George W. Shorter, Jr., Diane Silvia. Mobile, Alabama: University of South Alabama Center for Archaeological Studies. 1994.

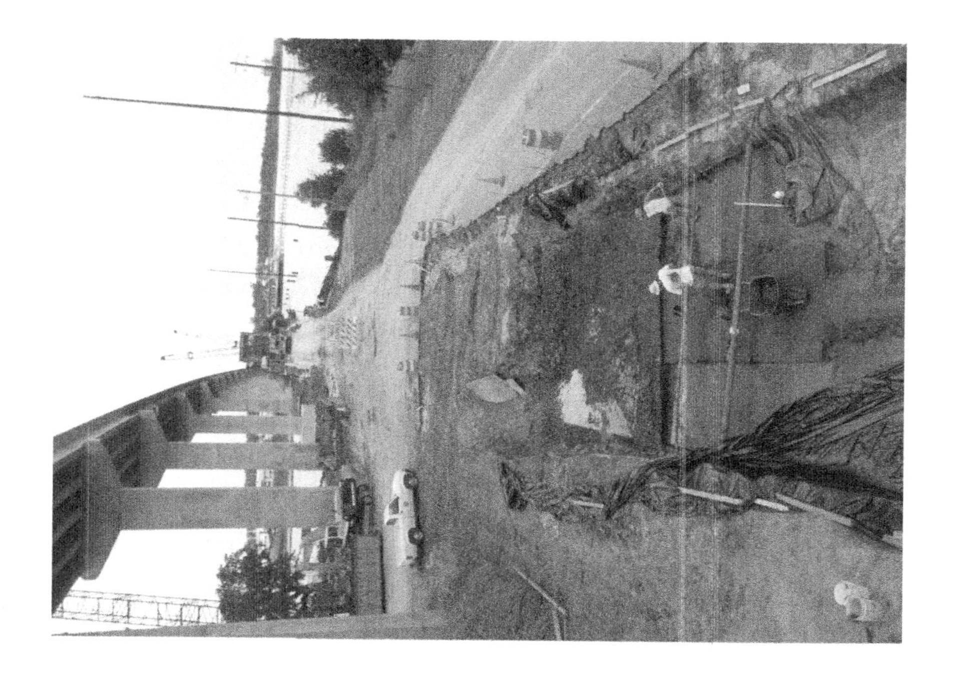

Excavation Photos from the Dog River Plantation Site (1MB161), Mobile County, Alabama.. Gregory Waselkov, Bonnie L. Gums, George W. Shorter, Jr., Diane Silvia. Mobile, Alabama: University of South Alabama Center for Archaeological Studies. 1994.

CHAPTER 3
The Rochon Plantation

The Rochon Family
Early Entrepreneurs
1704-1850

Charles Rochon, a French Canadian, traveled the Mississippi River exploring with Henri De Tonti. He also dealt in furs. He had drifted into Mobile where Bienville enticed him to stay and placed him on the King's payroll. After he was discharged, his first thought was to become a trapper again, but he was thirty-five, and a widower with one child, so he decided to stay and built a twenty-by-twenty-seven foot house with two other Canadians. He maintained ties with the LeMoyne brothers and became a successful exporter culminating in the acquisition of the highly desirable Dog River Property at the site of the King's warehouse on the southern edge at the mouth of the river, which later became the successful site of his son Pierre's military and naval supplies exporting business.

In 1704, while the colonists up-river at Twenty-Seven Mile Bluff were begging for supplies, Charles sent a small cargo of articles on the traversier "Preieuse", to customers in Veracruz "which they hoped to sell unobtrusively". Charles' plantation encompassed the majority of what is today known as Hollinger's Island. Chato and Apalachee Indians from Mississippi Valley tribes, a source of cheap labor, were cultivating his land, and Charles and his young wife Henriette, a half-Kaskaskian Indian were raising a family of eight children. But tragedy struck the Rochons in 1733. Within one month Charles, Henriette, and two children died of smallpox, leaving an orphaned young family headed by two brothers, 17-year-old Charles and 16-year-old Pierre. But the family survived and within a few decades the Rochons were prosperous citizens of Mobile.[1]

By the 1750's Pierre and a work force of black and Indian slaves at the Dog River plantation were raising cattle, manufacturing brick, lumber, and naval stores, and

1 Jay Higgenbotham, Old Mobile

building and repairing ships. He and his first wife, Catherine, had four children before she died in 1751. After her death, Pierre began a relationship with his mulatto slave named Marianne, who gave birth to six children. Around 1780 the plantation became the home of Pierre Rochon's neice Marie Louise Rochon and her husband Charles Orbanne Demouy. The plantation stayed in the hands of the family until 1848. Pierre's brother Louis Augustus, established a plantation on the eastern shore of Mobile Bay that became modern-day Spanish Fort.[2]

In 1780 the Spanish Military Governor Galvez led a force of 2000 men in an assault on British Mobile basing their operations on Dog River in the home of Don Charles Urbanne Demouy as the headquarters. After the Spanish takeover, the days of the Rochon exporting and contracting businesses were over. Today there are few Rochons in Mobile. But during the seventeenth century, this prominent and industrious family endured and prospered through wars, changes in government and the American Revolution.[3]

Charles Rochon has had a number of notable descendants: Hale Boggs, U.S. Congressman from Louisiana, House Majority Leader, Cokie Roberts, Television journalist, Barbara Boggs Sigmund, 1980's mayor of Princeton, and Connie Bea Hope, cook, television host and socialite in Mobile.

Adam Hollinger Jr. acquired two-thirds of the Dog River property in 1834. Within a few years he had a working sawmill on Dog River. His work force of nearly 200 slaves cut timber for the mill and labored at other plantation tasks such as tending cattle. Hollinger lost the Dog River land by foreclosure in 1848.

---

2 Rochon and Related Familes, David A. Sprinkle.

3 Archaeological Investigations at the Bay Oaks Sites on Dog River, Mobile County, Alabama, Greg C. Spies and Michael T. Rushing. 1978.

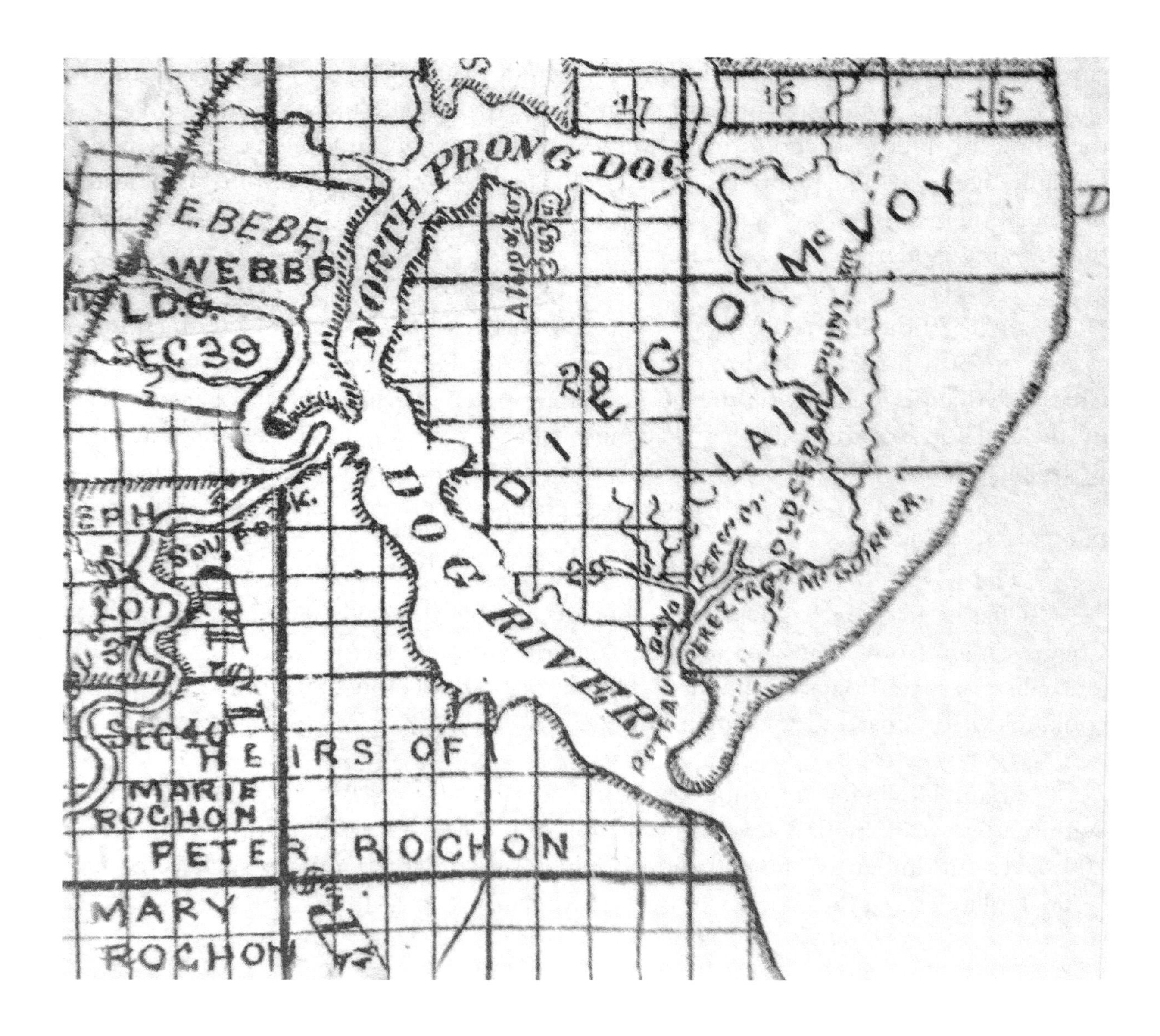

Hand drawn French map circa 1780 shows shows the large area of land on the south side of Dog River owned by the Rochon family and its descendants. Also visible on the map is the Diego McVoy tract of land, land owned by E. Beebe, land owned by Webbs, Perch Creek, and Aligator Bayou. Map courtesy of Mobile Municipal Archives.

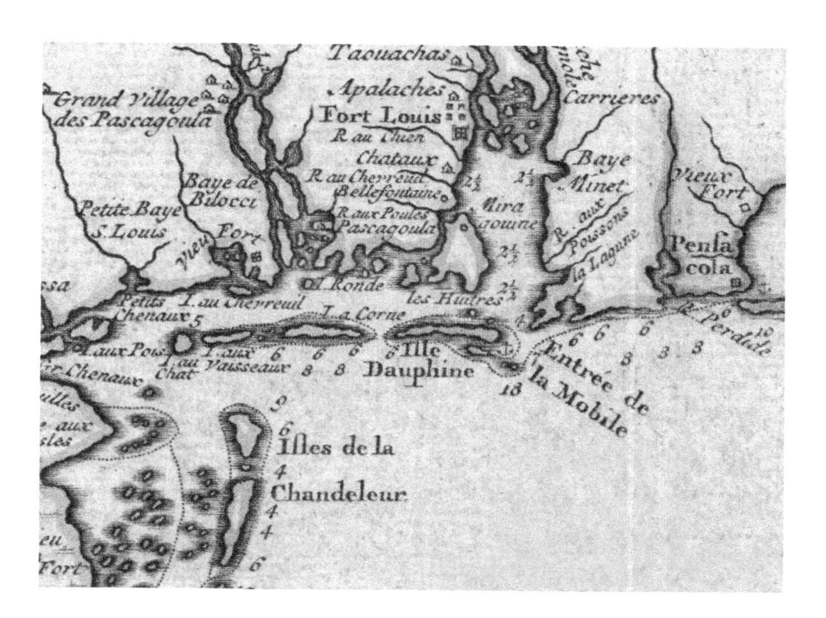

Dauphin Island is clearly marked on this section of a 1718 French map as "Ille Dauphine," The map was created by famed French cartographer Guillaume Delisle (1675-1726) and became the definitive map of the Gulf Coast and Mississippi River region because of its accuracy. Photo courtesy of the Library of Congress.

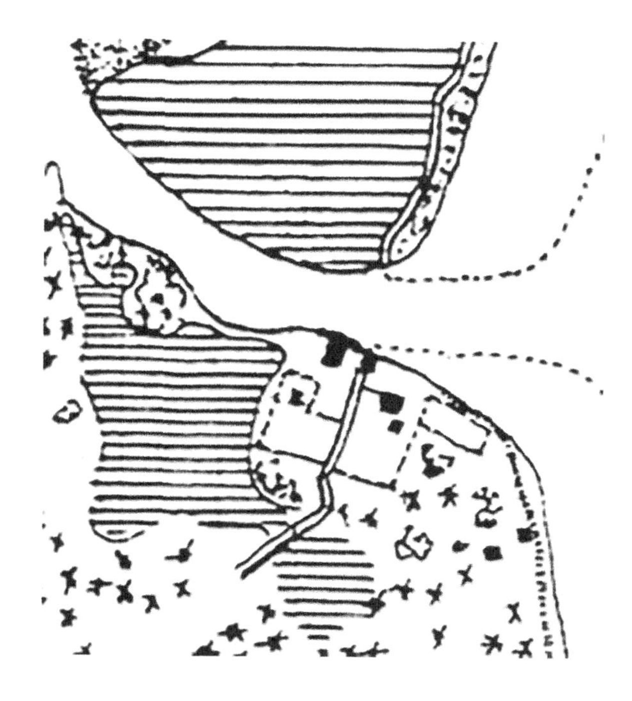

A hand-drawn 1775 British map shows two small structures, perhaps a kitchen and warehouse, and the main house at Hollinger's sawmill plantation.

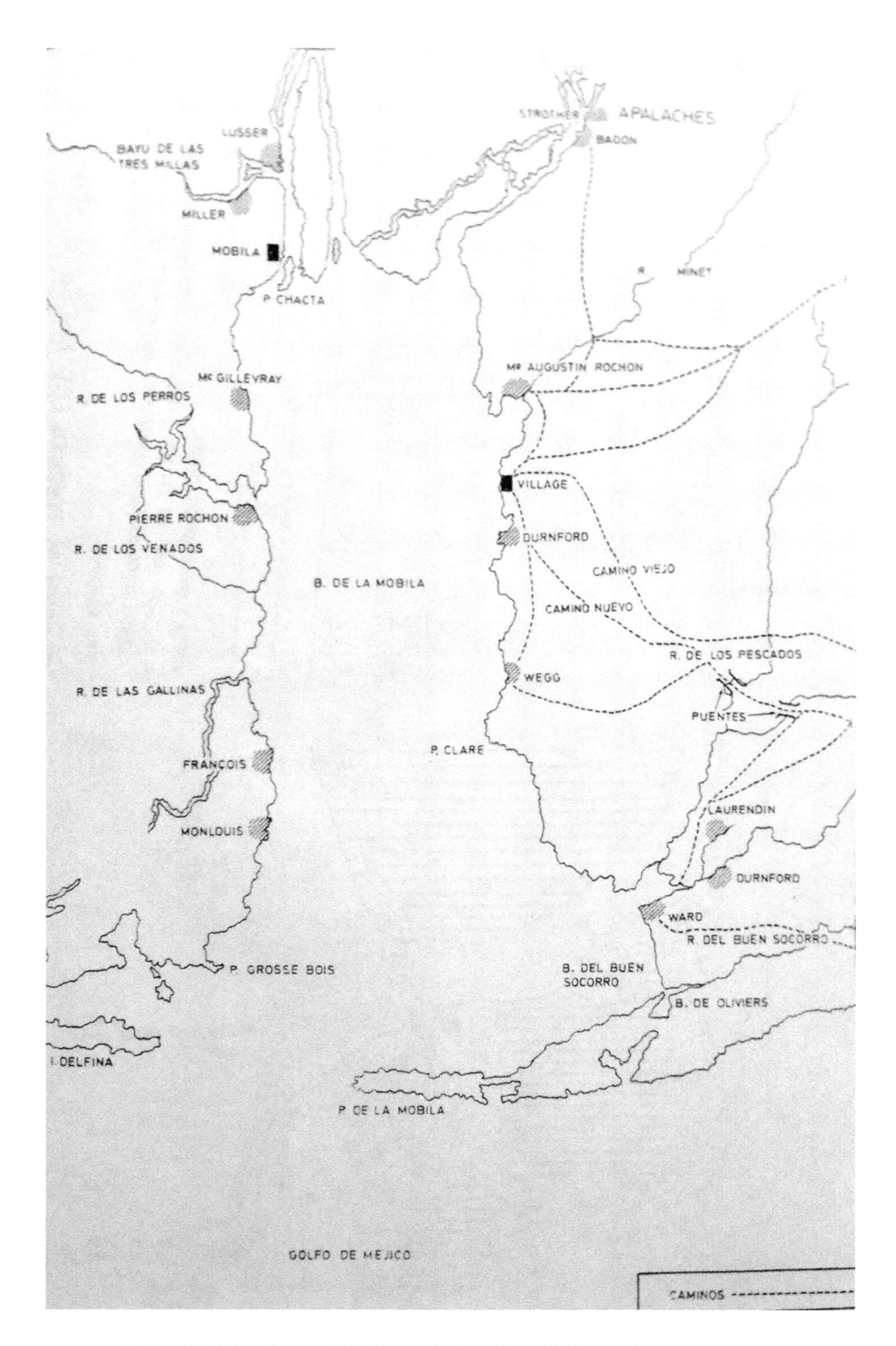

A Spanish Map from 1790 shows the location of the Rochon Property.

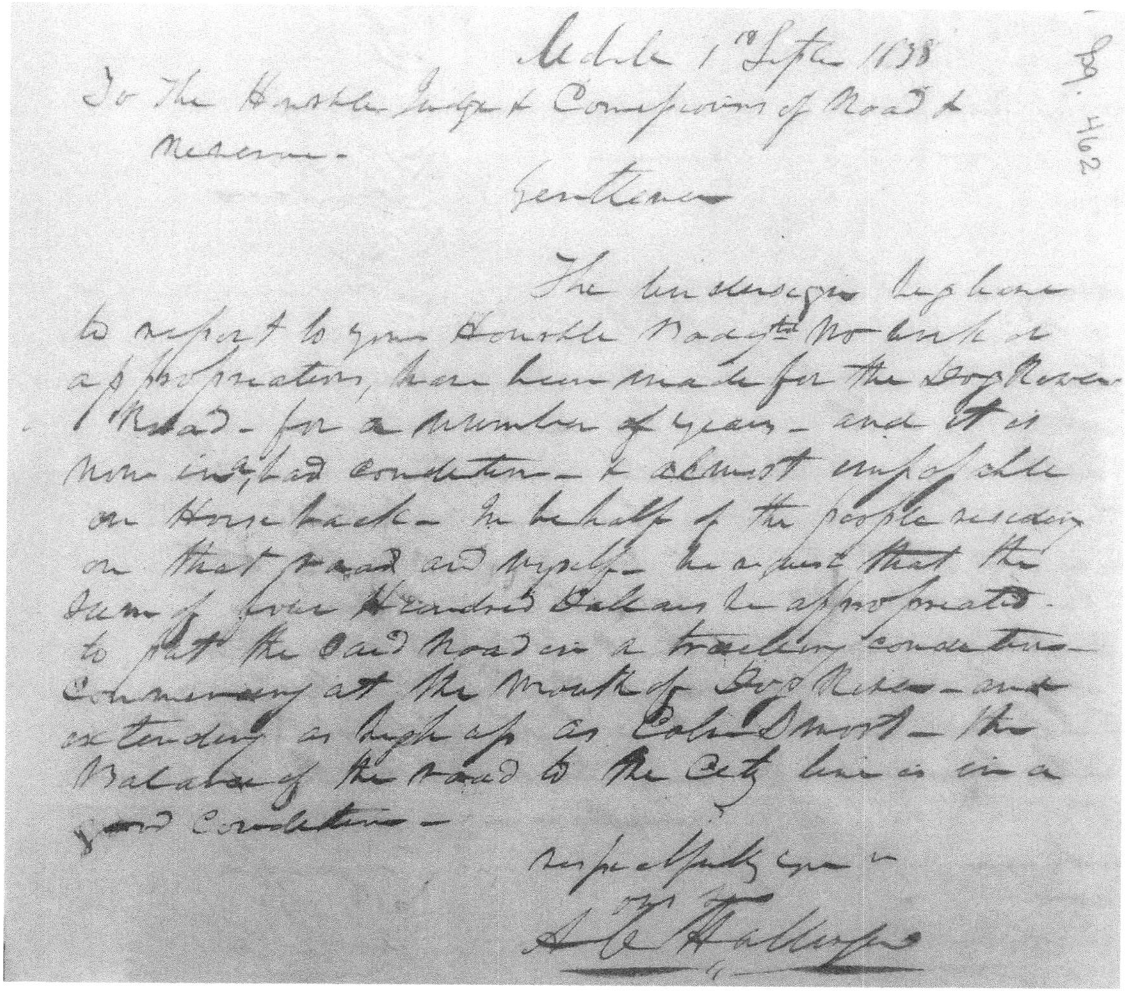

(Transcription:) To the Honorable Judge and Commisioners of Road and Revenue
Mobile 1st September 1838

Gentlemen

The undersigned begs leave to report to your Honorable Body no work or appropriations has been made for the Dog River Road for a number of years and it is now in a bad condition and almost impossible on horseback. In behalf of the people residing on that road and myself we request that the sum of five hundred dollars be appropriated to put the said road in a travelling condition commencint at the mouth of Dog River and extending as high up as Collin Smoot. The balance of the road to the city line is in a good condition.

Respectfully yours,
A.C. Hollinger

1° une terre à désert, située sur la Rivière des Tensaws de quatre cents vingt et trois arpents, estimée à la somme de 425.

2° une terre située à la Rivière aux Poules de huit cents soixante six arpents de superficie, estimée à la somme de 400.

3° une habitation située sur le bord de la baye, avec toutes ses édifices, à trois lieues de la Mobile, estimée à la somme de 3500.

$ 11439.50

Montant transporté de l'autre part

Inventory of Marie Rochon's properties. 1. Land situated on the River Tensas (Tensaw River) 2. Land situated on the River Poule (Fowl River) 3. Her home or habitation situated on the Bay of Mobile, or Dog River. 1813. Courtesy of the Mobile Municipal Archives..

221. PIERRE ROCHON

On 4 October 1717 was born Pierre, the legitimate son of Charles Rochon and Henriette Colon, his wife. On the next day he was supplied the ceremonies of Baptism by me, the undersigned performing his function as Curé of Fort Louis of Louisiana. He was baptized at birth because of feebleness. Godparents were Pierre Le Sueur, resident of Fort Louis, and Catherine Christophe.

Le Sueur — Catherine Christophe

Rochon

Alexandre Huvé, Priest

Baptismal record for Pierre Rochon from the Sacremental Records of the Roman Catholic Church of the Archdiocese of Mobile, Volume 1, Section 1, 1704-1739.

Chapter 4
Subdivision of the Land

Ownership and Subdivision of the Land 1783-1927

Cornelius McCurtin owned most of the land from Dog River's western side to Mobile Bay from the original Spanish Permit granted him in 1783. He held 5,195 arpents which is roughly 6.86 square miles. The land was owned by very few people until around the 1930s, when population growth increased, and the land was subdivided. The following is a transcription of a Title Insurance Abstract from 1927 detailing the passage of land through inheritance and subdivision from the original large Spanish Permit given in 1783 to Cornelius McCurtin to the parcel purchased by Mrs. Gonzales in 1927.

Title Insurance Co June 9., 1927 Abstract of Title No. 14785
To Lots 17, 19, 3, first Division of the McVoy Tract

> In American State Papers vol 5, page 594 Duff Green's Edition under heading: No. 1 Abstract of claims to lands situated West of Perdido East of Pearl River and below the 31st degree of N latitude, presented to the Register and Receiver of the land office at St. Stephens, Alabama acting as Commissioners under the authority of the third section of the Act of Congress of the 2nd March 1829 entitled "An Act confirming the report of the Register and Receiver of the land office for the district of St. Stephens in the State of Alabama and for other purposes" we find the following:
>
> Claim No. 2. Present Claimants, Heirs of Cornelius McCurtin. Original Claimant Cornelius McCurtin, Spanish Permit, dated 20th December 1783, for a tract of land on the West side of Mobile Bay, area 5195 arpens, Possession 1790 to 1830. Signed by John B. Hazard Register and J.H. Owen, Receiver, March 7, 1832.

In 1807 Cornelius McCurtin's first wife, Margaret Liflou died and they had one child who died at 10 days old. His second wife Miss Euphrosyna Bosarge was left the entire estate in 1807 at his death.

Diego McVoy married the widow and at her death inherited the land in 1814.

In 1819 McVoy sold to Edward D. Hayden the land for $11,000. Description: "The following land situated in the County of Mobile on the West side of Mobile Bay containing 5195 arpens and 76 poles of 18 feet, bounded on the East by Mobile Bay, on the West by Dog River, and on the South by mouth of said River and north by land claimed by Samuel Garrow and formerly by Don Cayetano Perez. (Note: 6.96 square miles of land was sold for $11,000.)

In 1842 this land was subdivided into 7 lots and passed to Jane M McVoy wife of Diego.
In 1846 Diego and Jane M. McVoy sold lot 3 to Charles Le Baron.
In 1881 Charles Le Baron died left the land to his son William Alexander LeBaron.
In 1883 William A. LeBarron executed the will of Charles LeBaron and sold Lot 3 to Mary Emily Thrower
In 1895 Mary E. Thrower and her husband Fremont Thrower sold three pieces of the lot to Patrick Hannon for $260.00. "The three pieces contained 130 acres more or less"
In 1910 Patrick Hannon died.
In 1912 Father Eaton, Edward Faith and F.C. Scheible executed the will of Patrick Hannon and sold the land to William Syson for $10,000.
In 1912 Oliver Hume surveyed the land for W.K. Syson creating the River Division Shore Acres, being in lots 3 and 4 of the First Division of the McVoy Tract.
In 1921 W. K. Syson and his wife Bessie F. Syson gave 60 feet of land to "The Public" to make a road from the Gulf Hunting and Fishing Club to Cedar Point Road and 30 feet wide to make a road to the Alba Club.
In 1927 William Syson and his wife sold to Eleanor M. Gonzales lots 17 and 19 in Lot 3 of the 1st Division of the McVoy Tract in the River Division of Shore Acres for $5,000.

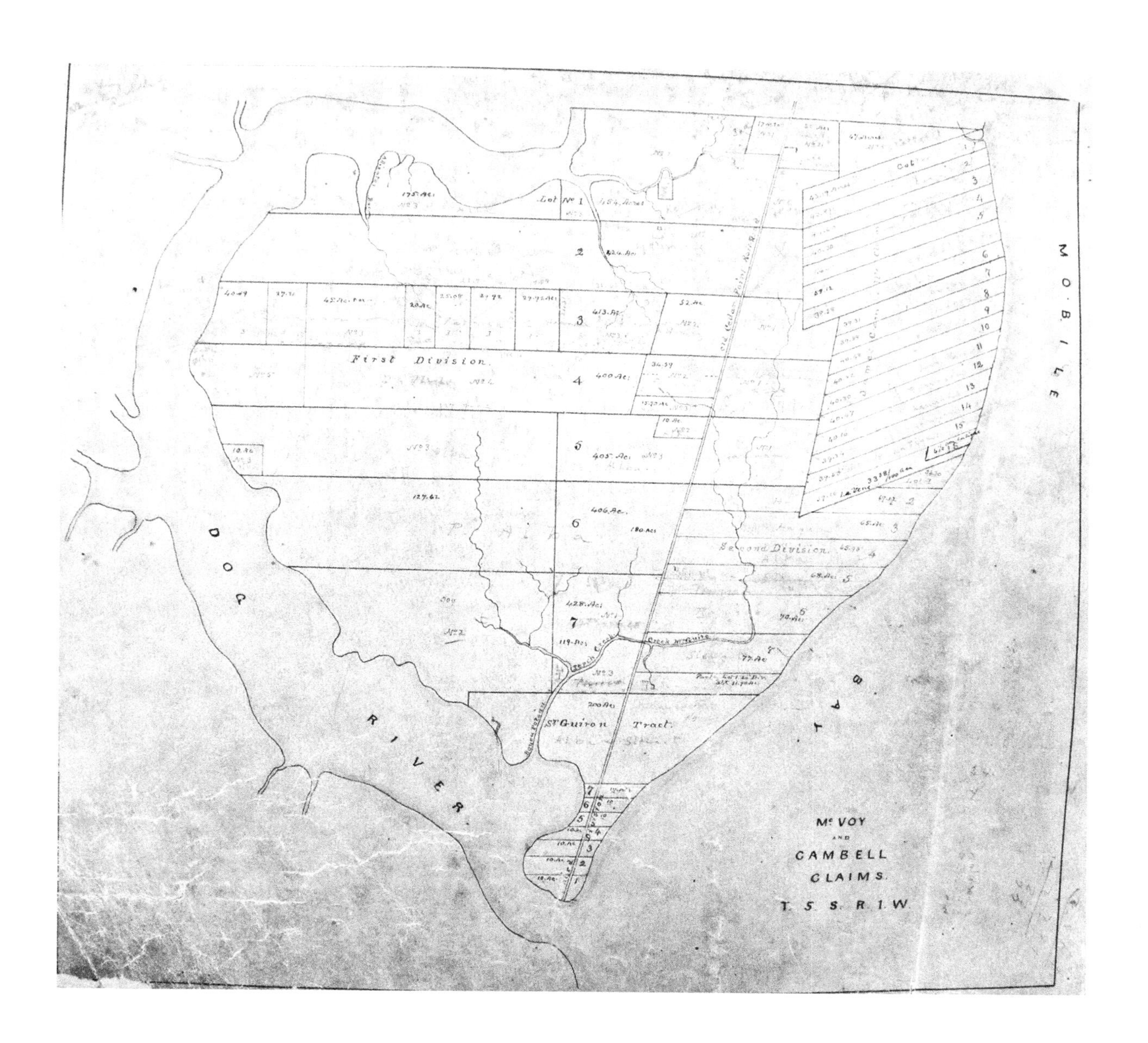

This calf velum map from the 1830's shows the first and second subdivisions of the land from the original Spanish Land Pzermit issued to Cornelius McCurtin in 1783, and inherited by Diego McVoy in 1814. Note the Cedar Point Railroad line on the map that ran parallel to Mobile Bay stopping at Dog River. Map image courtesy at Mobile Municipal Archives.

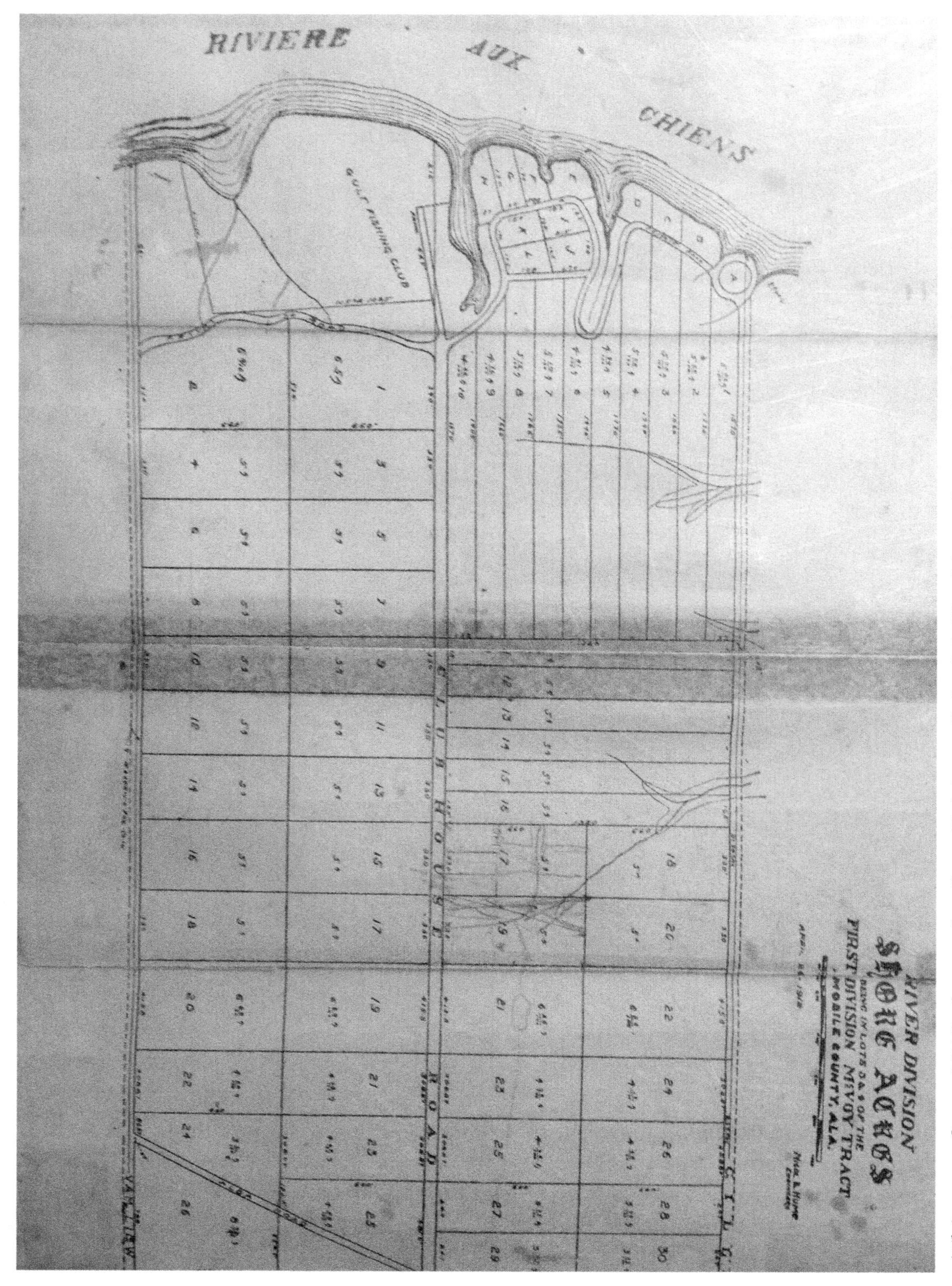

This map from 1912 shows the first division of the McVoy Tract that resulted in the Gulf Fishing Club. Map courtesy of Harriet Dykes' family's title search from 1927.

Portion of a map showing the first subdivision of the McVoy Tract. Note the northern boundary of the land owned by McCurtin. Map courtesy of Harriet Dykes' family's title vvsearch from 1927.

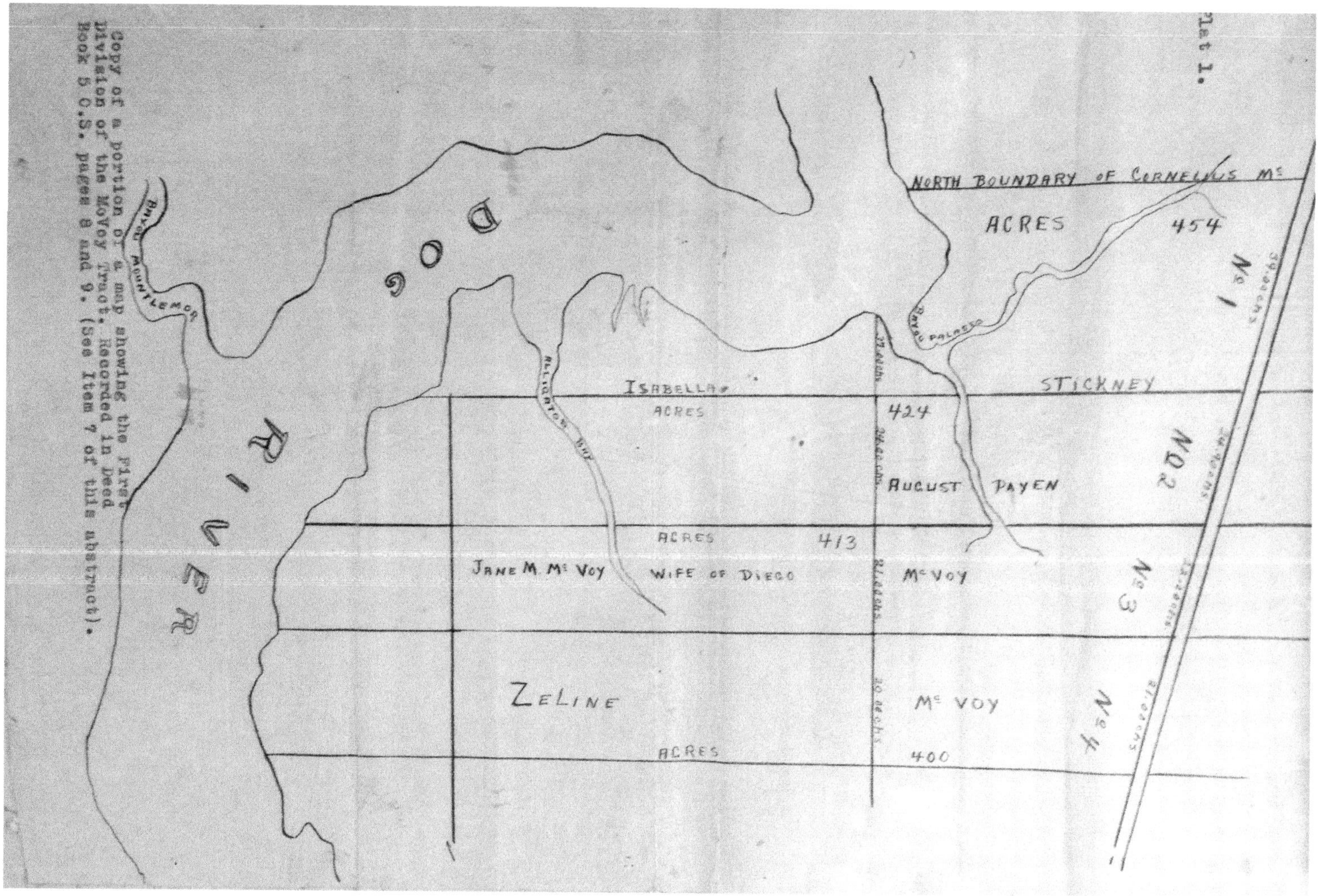

Plat 1.

Copy of a portion of a map showing the First Division of the McVoy Tract. Recorded in Deed Book 5 C.S. pages 8 and 9. (See Item 7 of this abstract).

PART II
The 1800s

Magnolia Race Track

Dog River Factory

Civil War Encampment

The Cedar Point Railroad

Chapter 5
Magnolia Race Track

Discovering the Location of the Magnolia Race Track

The first evidence came from resident, Fred Lorge, who spoke of an old horse-racing track in the 1930s near Rosedale Road when he was a young boy. "It was old then, but you could walk around it." The second hint came from an image of forty children on steps for their annual school photo taken near New Hope Church dated 1923. Although the name showing on the school said "Congress Corner School", it was nicknamed "Race-track" because it was located near the racetrack. The third and final confirmation came from a 1939 Corps of Engineers aerial map that clearly showed the outline of a large empty horse-track shaped area standing out clearly from the surrounding green treetops and matching a map of the track. After discussions with Charles Torres, Research Historian at the History Museum of Mobile, the location of the famous Magnolia Race Track, almost forgotten, was determined. Stereo-opticon images from 1870 and Mobile Daily Register articles, collected by Mr. Torres gave a clear picture of the history of this famous horse-racing track.

Captain William Cottrill
The Developer of Magnolia Race Course and Stables

English by birth, Cottrill came to Mobile in 1841 at age 26 and began working with his brother-in-law in the butcher business. Mobile was home to the Bascombe Race Course near Magnolia Cemetery and it wasn't too long before Cottrill came into the racing fold. In fact, Cottrill rode in the country's first hurdle race, which was run at Bascombe in the late 1840s. His involvement in the racing industry steadily grew as he turned his attention to buying and running Thoroughbreds.

During the Civil War, Captain William Cottrill was in command of a cavalry company and once the conflict had ended he purchased the Magnolia track near the corner of Cedar Crescent and Cedar Point (now DIP) roads. His interests turned to raising and training thoroughbreds numbering in the hundreds.

Cottrill is credited with reviving racing in the North in the years following the Civil War. In the late 1860s he found success on tracks in the north and east in such races as the West End Hotel Stakes at Long Branch (NJ), which he won three years running from 1869 to 1871. Expanding his reach even further in the racing world, Cottrill's horses began running at tracks in Chicago, St. Louis, Memphis, New Orleans, and elsewhere. The postwar reconstruction of New Orleans's racetrack, now dubbed the Fair Grounds, became Cottrill's turf, because his horses dominated the meets there from the track's reopening in 1872 until well into the next decade. The 1880s brought the Captain's greatest racing success with his best horse Buchanan's win in the 1884 Kentucky Derby. His previous attempt at winning the classic race resulted in a second-place finish for Kimball, behind that year's winner Fonso in 1880.

He was admired by fellow horsemen and after his death in 1887, was described as "universally esteemed for his many good qualities of head and heart; ...he was an ornament of the turf." (The Kentucky Live Stock Record, 1887). When he was approached to have a race named after him, he modestly declined. In 1872, the Alabama Stakes was named in Cotrill's honor by Saratoga officials and has been run every year since. Today the Alabama Stakes carries a purse of $600,000. Cottrill is buried at Magnolia Cemetery in Mobile.

The Magnolia Race Course and Buchanan

Located a half mile from Mobile Bay, (near the current Cedar Crescent Drive) the Magnolia Race Course could be reached by horse and wagon by traveling about three miles along Mobile Bay's shoreline on Bay Shell Road. The race course could also be accessed by water. Gamblers and visitors docked their boats at Magnolia's pier which led to the large Magnolia Hotel, where bets were placed on races at the two and a half mile-long track behind the hotel. Racing fever was always at red-heat and betting on horses was egalitarian: anyone could bet...men, women, Creoles, Indians, Officers, soldiers and people of color were all welcome. Many jockeys were African American. The Thoroughbred breeding farm and breeding sheds that gave life to spirited winning horses were on property behind the track. The most important Thoroughbred to emerge from Magnolia's breeding farm was Buchanan, who won the Kentucky Derby in 1884.

The following eye-witness account from an article in the Mobile Daily Tribune, March 23, 1870, reveals the exciting and furious scenes of the first two-mile hurdles races ever held at Magnolia Grove:

"Never before in the history of the turf was there a prettier day than yesterday for the inauguration of the Spring Meeting over the Magnolia Course. The heavens smiled most propitiously upon the occasion, and long before the arrival of the hour when the sound of the bell from the judge's stand called the contestants for the first race upon the track, the beautiful drive along our bay shore was threaded

throughout its entire length with visitors, anxious to witness the first hurdle race ever run under racing rules on the Magnolia track. Magnolia grove for hours together was alive with the moving throng and the many hot brushes made by fast roadsters gave a degree of life and animation to the panorama that strongly called to mind the antebellum days when the "old Bascomb" was a power in the land. The bay was calm and smooth, not a ripple disturbed its placid beauty, and yes, there were gentle breezes wafted through the air which gave an additional charm to the drive, and made it all the more exhilarating. Betting aside all high flown speeches, and coming down to plain talk, the attendance yesterday was the best that has been had since the war, and there was a good sprinkling of the fair sex."

"The first race was that which for its novelty and the additional fact that the two best hurdlers in America were known to be the contestants, elicited the largest interest. There was not a great deal of betting on Dr. Underwood's pools, for the reason that the opinion of outsiders did not coincide with the estimate placed upon the two horses. Lobella sold for two to one easily, and the result, as in the succeeding race, showed that the knowing ones were not wrong in their calculations."

"The start was a first rate one, Mitchell having rather the advantage over Lobelia and maintaining it, as will appear, pretty well. To say the first hurdle was cleared most elegantly will serve as an appropriate expression for all the rest. No deer could have bounded over a fence with more ease and grace than did these two beautiful specimens of horse flesh, and had the obstacles been a foot higher to all appearance the feat would have been no more difficult. The bushes were scarcely ruffled in a single instance of the eight that had to be overcome. The lead of almost two lengths taken by Mitchell was steadily held until nearing the third hurdle on the second mile, when the brown mare began to close the gap, and went over the last hurdle hardly half a second in the advance. The last quarter was fought with desperation. The whip and spar was freely applied by both riders, but it was of little service to Mitchell, for Lobelia passed the string about half a length ahead, having made the first mile in 1:57, the second in 1:59, the race in 3:56 and with one exception, when in New Orleans 3:52.5 was recorded, the best time known in the American hurdle calendar."

William Cottrill bred Buchanan, a Kentucky Derby winner in 1884 at his stables at the Magnolia Race Track.

1939 Aerial Map showing the outline of the old Magnolia Race Track and its relationship to Cedar Crescent and Cedar Point Roads. U.S. Army Corps of Engineers.

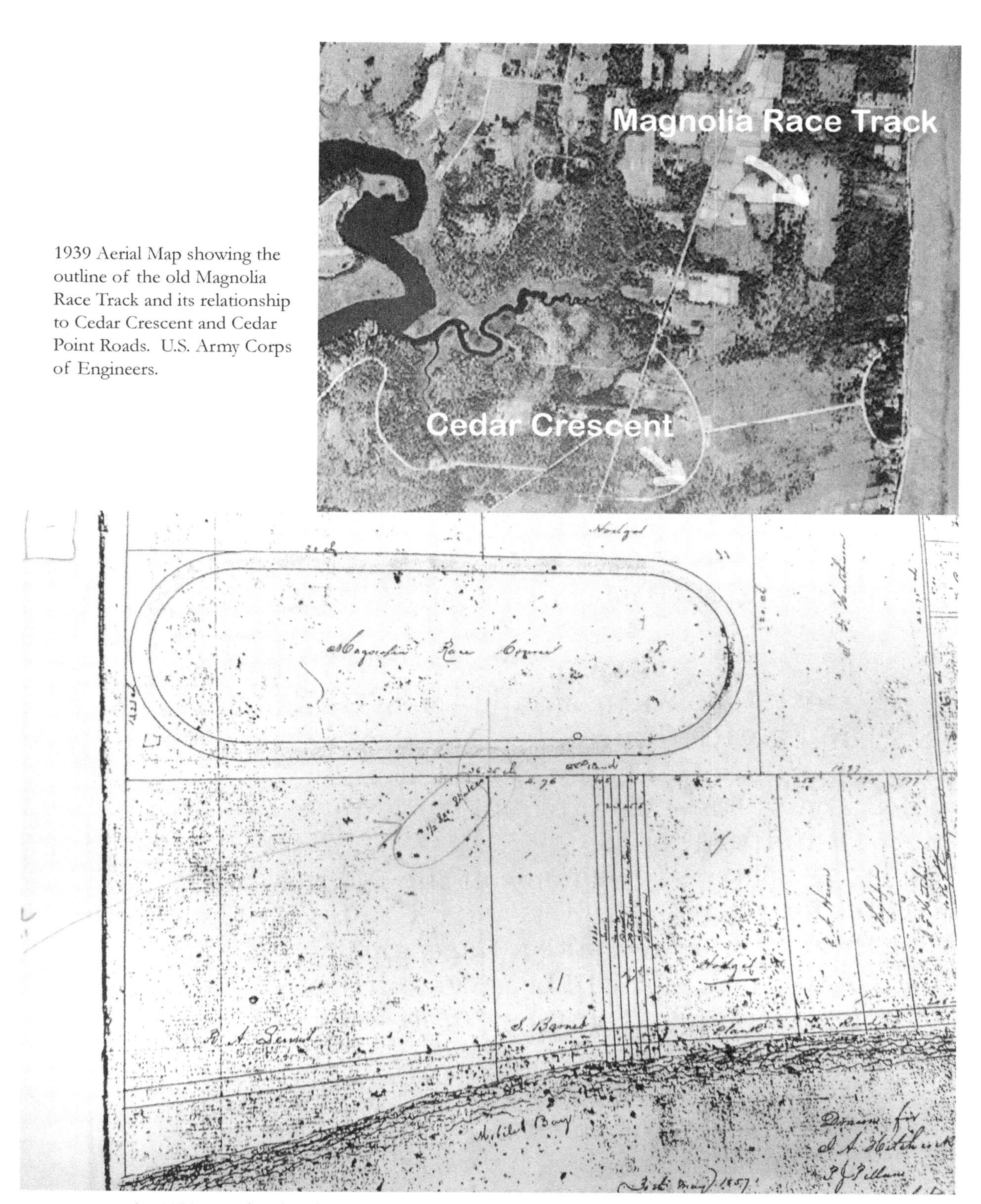

An 1858 map showing the location of Magnolia Race Track and its relationship to Mobile Bay.

THE TURF.

MAGNOLIA COURSE.

The SUMMER SPORTS will commence **July 15th, 1868,** with the following Purses:

FIRST DAY.

Purse of $150 for Running Horses—Mile Heats.

SAME DAY—Purse of $150 for Pacing Horses—Mile Heats—Three in Five to Harness.

SECOND DAY.

Purse of $100—Dash of One Mile—for Running Horses.

SAME DAY—Purse of $75—Free for all Trotting Horses owned in Mobile—Mile Heats—Three in Five to Harness.

THIRD DAY.

Purse of $250—Mile Heats—Three in Five—For Running Horses.

☞ Entries to be made at the Magnolia Hotel for First Day's Race on MONDAY, 13th—three or more to make a Race, and two to start.

Liberal Purses will be given during the Meeting if a sufficient number of Horses attend to compete for them.

Entrance, 10 per cent.

The Races to be governed by the Rules of the Magnolia Jockey Club Association.

J. McLEANE, Proprietor.

The Purses, Mobile Daily RegisterVolume 1, Number 135, page 20July 4, 1868

Horses and jockeys at Magnolia Race Course Stables. 1880s. Image is from a sterio-opticon picture.
Image courtesy of the History Museum of Mobile.

Gamblers could place bets here at the Magnolia Hotel which could be reached by horse and carriage on Bay Shell Road, or the Hotel's dock on Mobile Bay.
Image courtesy of the History Museum of Mobile.

The Magnolia Race Track

Chapter 6
Dog River Factory

Mobile's First Cotton Mill on Dog River
1850 - 1861

For many years Civil War collectors have heard of the "Dog River sword factory".But the only large factory during the Civil War period on Dog River was the Dog River Cotton Factory, Mobile's first cotton mill located five miles southwest from Mobile along the banks of Dog River, where Dog River Park is now.

Before the Civil War, cotton was the largest crop and export in the commercial life of Mobile. But until 1850, all cotton exported from Mobile was in raw form, and all woven cotton goods were imported. In the late ante-bellum period tensions increased to build a cotton factory in Mobile. In 1849 the Mobile Manufacturing Company was formed and sold stock to raise the $80,000 that was needed. It took a year, but finally the company raised the capital and built the factory on Dog River, four and a half miles from Mobile. The factory, made of brick at a cost of $27,000 was 182 feet long, fifty-four feet wide and three stories high. It contained 176 looms on the first floor, 40 carding machines on the second, and 5,040 spindles on the third. A motor driven conveyer system transferred the work from one room to another. The factory hired two hundred mostly local people, three-quarters of whom were female, who could produce 6,000 yards of yard-wide Osnaberg cotton sheeting per day. Yarns and fabric were sold in Mobile. A large boarding house was built on the grounds to accommodate forty workers. The owner, Garland Goode also built twenty five-room cottages with kitchens attached to attract workers with families. Keeping the workforce was difficult. The 1850 census reveals that all but two of the skilled positions were occupied by weavers from England, France or Northern States. The workforce continued to dwindle. In 1850, Goode filled positions with his own slaves. Other difficulties included an outbreak of yellow fever in 1852 in the village. Even though it was showered with many difficulties, this "factory-community" was nonetheless an extremely valuable addition to the economic life of Mobile.[1]

1 Report on the epidemic yellow fever of 1853.
New Orleans SanitaryCommission 1854.

Life Inside the Factory

Children worked as doffers, removing the spindles that held spun fiber and replacing them with empty ones. Spinning and sweeping were other tasks required in the manufacture of spun textiles. "The doffer machines had to be started at the same time, taking some time to fill the bobbin. The periodic breaks gave doffer boys plenty of cigarette breaks. Children laborers wanted to mock their parents in every way: labor, and bad habits. Even though the doffers were able to spend up to half of their twelve-hour shift on a break, many would get diseases such as brown lung from the cotton dust."

"Along with the noxious debris in the air the machines threatened serious injuries. Many of the fast-moving machine engines would burn the incautious. The machines fast moving parts were exposed ready to snag a piece of clothing, or even worse, a finger. Broken bones and even death occurred from these unsafe machines. There was no worker insurance to cover any injuries sustained on the job. If a worker had hurt themselves they went home without pay until they were again able to work."[2]

The Burning of Dog River Factory in September, 1861

"We have learned from a reliable source the particulars of the loss by fire of the Dog River Cotton Factory. It appears that the fire was purely accidental having caught in the dressing room just over the boilers in such a place as to render suppression difficult. When discovered the headway was too great to be stayed and the work of destruction proceeded with great rapidity until the entire building with its valuable contents of stock and machinery was in ruins. No blame or charge of negligence lies against any person for this destruction."

"The establishment was valued between $100,000 to $125,000 only $42,000 of which was covered by insurance. It belonged exclusively to Col. Garland Goode and the estate of William Jones Jr. The loss at this time is heavy to the owners, but even more severe to the public and the operatives, some 250-300 in number who are thus in an instant thrown out of employment. Their case appeals strongly to the sympathies of our citizens and we hope will not be overlooked. The worst of it is that the machinery cannot now be replaced, and the work ceases at a time when the Factory was of particular service and value."[3]

---

2 Encyclopedia of Alabama Miller, Randall M. The Cotton Mill Movement in Antebellum Alabama. New York: Arno Press, 1978

3 Mobile Register and Advertiser, Sept 20, 1861, p. 2

Above: Boys who worked as doffers at the Barker Cotton Mill, built in 1898, on South Craft Highway across from Maudine Avenue in Mobile. It is similar in size to Garland Goode's Dog River Factory. These images are included to illustrate the lives of cottom mill workes similar to the Dog River Factory, since there are no known images of the factory on Dog River. 1914. Photograph by Lewis Hine. Library of Congress.

Quitting time for workers at Barker Cotton Mill in Mobile. 1914. Photograph by Lewis Hine, Library of Congress. The image illustrates a Mobile cotton mill similar in size to Goode's Cotton Factory on Dog River.

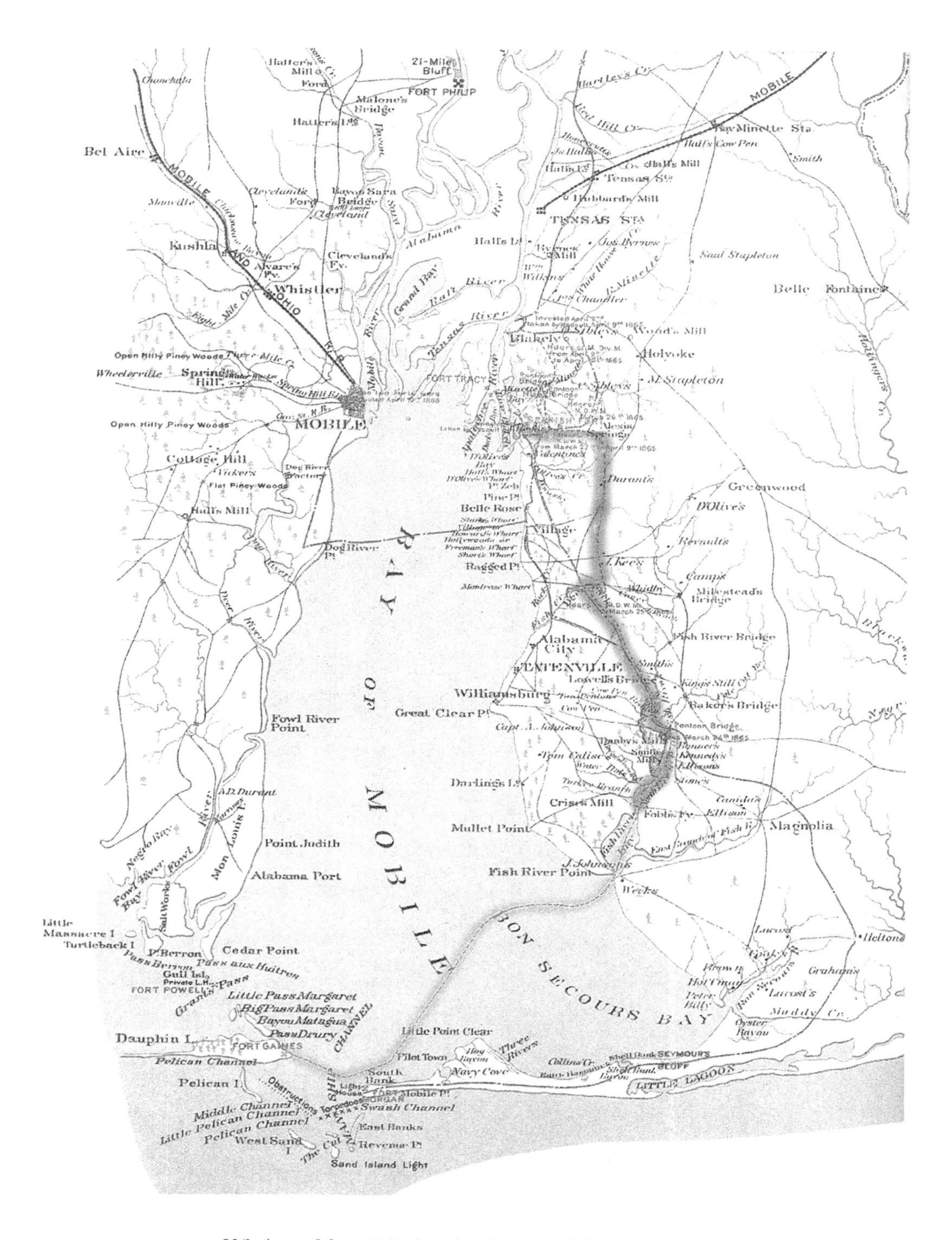

U.S. Army Map, 1865 showing the site of the Dog River Factory

Page 95, No. 194.—Major Garland Goode d. Jan. 7, 1887. The Mobile papers speak of him as follows: Major Goode had been an invalid for many years, but at one time he was a power in this community. For many years he was the head of the cotton factorage firm of Garland, Goode & Co., was one of the company that built the Dog River Cotton Factory, was interested in various lumber mills and an enterprising citizen in those days when Mobile was the third exporting city in the Union. In politics Major Goode was a democrat of the old school. He espoused the cause of Stephen A. Douglas, and presided when that great statesman spoke in Mobile.

Excerpt on Garland Goode's life by his Virginia Cousin, G. Brown Goode.

THE STATE OF ALABAMA.
MOBILE COUNTY.

To the Judge of Probate of said County:

I Hereby Certify, *That I this day solemnized the rites of Matrimony between* William Lamphere *and* Bridget A. [illegible] *who are within named, at* the Dog River Factory *in said County.*

Witness my hand, this the 9th *day of* January 1859.

Robert D. Kelley S. J.
Priest

Marriage record of William Lamphere at the Dog River Factory, 1859

CHAPTER 7
Civil War Recruitment Camp

At the Dog River Cotton Factory
1861

Although the Dog River Cotton Factory burned in September of 1861, the factory's village consisting of twenty-five houses built in a hollow square was spared. It was sold to the Confederacy, and the remaining buildings were used as a recruitment camp for fresh Southern volunteers who flocked to the Confederate cause from all parts of Alabama. There is a long-held erroneous belief that there was a place known as the "Dog River Sword Factory". Perhaps the conversion of the cotton factory into the Confederate recruitment camp known as Camp Goode created this lore. On the following pages are two letters that reveal interesting slices of life at the camp.

I ordered him to close the bar and told him if he sold another drop to anyone on the boat, I would throw his liquor into the river and him with it.
—HENRY C. SEMPLE

The author of the first letter from the Dog River encampment, Henry Churchill Semple (1822-1894) of Montgomery, Ala., was a captain and then a major in the Confederate Army. Semple's Battery was organized at Montgomery in March 1862, with officers and men almost all from Montgomery County. Ordered to Mobile, it then joined the Army of Tennessee. It marched into Kentucky, was engaged at Perryville, and later fought in Tennessee at Murfreesboro, Dug Gap, Chicamauga, Mission Ridge, Ringgold Gap, Resaca, Jonesboro, Franklin, and Nashville. Ordered to North Carolina, the battery reached Augusta, and there surrendered.

I look very much like a tall spare man who about the 20th Oct, 1852 surprised his wife by a sudden return after 3 years absence.
—EDMUND W. PETTUS

The second letter was written by Edmund Pettus. In 1847–49, Pettus served as a lieutenant with the Alabama Volunteers. In 1861, Pettus, an enthusiastic champion of the Confederate cause, was a Democratic Party delegate to the secession convention in Mississippi, where his brother John was serving as governor. Pettus helped organize the 20th Alabama Infantry. Pettus served in the Western Theater of the American Civil War. During the Stones River Campaign, he was captured by Union soldiers on December 29, 1862 and then exchanged a short time later for Union soldiers. Pettus was promoted to colonel on May 28, and given command of the 20th Alabama Regiment. His regiment participated in the Vickburg Campaign, the Chattanooga Campaign and he was promoted to brigadier general. Pettus and his command took part in the 1864 Atlanta Campaign and the Carolinas Campaign. He was hit in his right leg on the first day of the Battle of Bentonville. After the Confederacy surrendered at Appomattox, Pettus was pardoned by the U.S. Government. He went on to serve as a senator of Alabama. The Edmond Pettus Bridge in Selma is named after him.

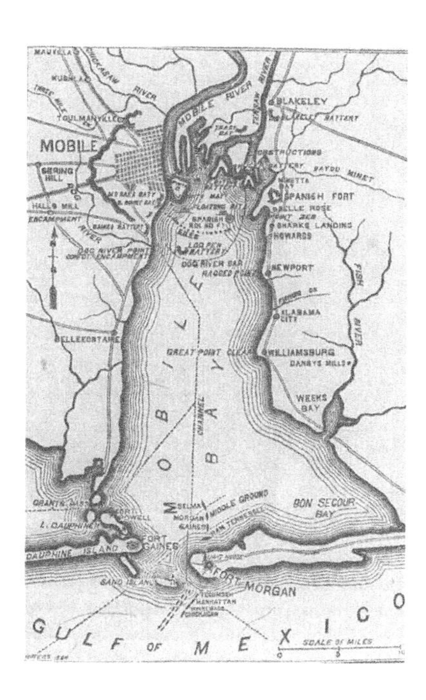

1865 Map showing two Civil War Encampment sites in South Mobile : the Halls Mill Civil War Encampment, and the Dog River Point Encampment. The recruitment Camp Goode located at the Cotton Mill Site is not shown on this map. Courtesy of Mobile Municipal Archives

Letter from Henry C. Semple

Dog River Factory
Cantonment Walker (near) Mobile

My darling; We are here now about 5 miles from Mobile. We have pleasant quarters, as the place is the site of the Dog River Factory, and we occupy the cottages erected for the operatives. The officers have the house which was occupied by the Supt. and I am to-day fitting up the rooms upstairs for a sort of Hospital, into which I intend to put every man, who is so unwell as to lay up. I shall make it so much more comfortable than their own quarters, that the men will readily go into it, when sick, & I can then control their diet & treatment – Several of them are now sick. Neil Taylor threatened with pneumonia, Brown [illegible] badly off with dysentery & several other men more or less unwell with colds & bowel complaints. They are all doing better this morning. I hope to have you down to Mobile, to pay me a visit before very long, but I shall let you know beforehand when it will be most conv't for me to go into town occasionally to see you –

I wrote a short letter to dear little Harry a few days ago: did he get it?

Write to me how you are all getting along, and all the [illegible] news. Has Smith got off yet, & if not what is he going to do?

I have been called off to attend to the arrangement of the men, among a greater number of houses, so as to give them more room. This must have been a very pretty place when the Factory was going. It has been destroyed by fire & no one

satisfied then I have kept the officers as well as men from having liquor & I am [illegible] [illegible] we have been here –

has occupied the house, but the soldiers who have been stationed here, and of course the fences have been burned, the house much abused &c.

Yesterday we had service here in the little Chapel near the parade ground – Father McEnery comes out every Sunday from Spring Hill every Sunday. Another Artillery Co. is stationed here so we are about 254 men. I have 112. & the other Co about 135. Several joined us yesterday & I learn there are 4 others now in Mobile from Montg'y to join us, we would get 200 if we wanted them. I only want about 15 more at present. I saw Father Gautrelet from Spring Hill in town on Saturday & he said he would send Lindsay out to see me on Thursday next. He says Lindsay is well & studying well considering the interest he takes in the war.

I am pretty well satisfied that we shall be kept here for a month or two at least for purposes of instruction, after tho' I fear there is no telling where we may be sent or whether we shall be kept here.

Elmore is the head of our mess, and we live very well. We have fresh beef, Charles is cook & catches a mess of fish every day, Enoch is valet & chamber maid, dining room servt. &c, & Dick takes care of our horses. If you have a chance I wish you would send Mc & Henry down to Mobile & I will take them out here for a few days, or you may bring them all to Mobile when you come –

I had a nice time on the boat. The bar keeper was selling liquor to the men & I was about a day [illegible] who were beginning to [illegible] for having [illegible] by drinking – I ordered him to close the bar & told him if he sold another drink to anyone on the boat, I would throw his liquor into the river & him with it – I reported to Col. Villipigue at Mobile who ordered the Capt. to shut up the bar in his boat for the future – Paper is very scarce. So I will say good bye to my dear wife with all love to the children & family – Your affectionate husband – Henry C. Semple

Transcription of Letter from Henry C. Semple

Dog River Factory
Cantonment Walter (near) Mobile

My darling; We are now about 5 miles from Mobile. We have pleasant quarters, as the place is the site of the Dog River Factory, and we occupy the cottages erected for the operations. The officers have the house which was occupied by the Supt. And I am to-day fitting up the rooms upstairs for a sort of Hospital, into which I intend to put every man, who is so unwell as to laynup. I shall make it so much more comfortable than their own quarters, that the men will readily go into it, when sick; and I can then control their diet and treatments – several of them are now sick. Ned Taylor threatened with pneumonia, Brown Jannay badly off with dysentery and several others more or less unwell with colds and bowell complaints. They are all doing better this morning. I hope to have you down to Mobile to pay me a visit before very long, but shall let you know beforehand when it will be most conv't for me to go into town occasionally to see you.

I wrote a short letter to dear little Henry a few days ago; did he get it! Write to me how you are all getting along, and all the Clarke news. Has Jewett got off yet? And if not what is he going to do!

I have been called off to attend to the arrangement of the men, among a greater number of houses, so as to give them more room. This must have been a pretty place when the Factory was going. It has been destroyed by fire and no one has occupied the houses, but the soldiers who have been stationed here, and of course the fences have been burned, the houses much abused etc.,

Yesterday we had a service here in the little chapel near the parade ground – Father McHenry comes out every Sunday from Spring Hill. Another Artillery Co. is stationed here so we are about 250 men. I have 112 and the other Co. about 135. Several joined us yesterday and I hear there are 6 others now in Mobile from Montgy to join us, we could get 200 if we wanted them. I only want about 15 more at present. I saw Father Gantrolit! From Spring Hill in Town on Saturday and he said he would send Lindsay out to see me on Thursday next. He says Lindsay is well and studying well considering the interest he takes in the war.

I am pretty well satisfied that we shall be kept here for a month or two at least for purposes of instruction, after the 1 June there is no telling where we may be sent or whether we shall be kept here.

Elmore is the head of our mess, and we live very well. We have good beef, cook Charley is cook and catches a mess of fish every day, Enoch is valet and chamber maid, dining room servt.etc., and Dick takes care of our horses. If you have a chance I wish you would send McK and Henry down to Mobile and I will take them out here for a few days, or you may bring them all to Mobile when you come.
I had a nice time on the boat. The bar keeper was selling liquor to the men and I had about a doz who were beginning to console themselves for leaving home by drinking. I ordered him to close the bar and told him if he sold another drop to anyone on the boat, I would throw his liquor into the river and him with it – I reported to Col Villipigue at Mobile, who ordered the Capt. To shut up the bar on his boat for the future.
Paper is very scarce so I will say god bye to my dear wife with all love to the children and family —

Your affectionate husband –
Henry C. Semple

I have forbid the officers as well as men from having liquor and I am satisfied there has not been a drop here while we have been here. H.S.

Letter from Edmund W. Pettus

Camp Goode, near Mobile,
Dec. 12th, 1861.

My dear Wife,—

I have had a right sharp attack of neuralgia in the left eye. I was taken sick last Sunday morning; and from the way I suffered, I am inclined to think that I had almost as soon have sick-headache.

Dr Moore put me through a regular Calomel course, in broken doses. The remedy was almost as severe as the ailment. I am not yet well; though entirely free from pain. The left eye was closed and much inflamed and I now wear a bandage over it and do not allow the light to visit it. I am walking about Camp and I think that I am free from the complaint. I am, however, more reduced than I ever was in so short a time. In appearance, I look very much like a tall spare man who about the 20th Oct. 1852 surprised his wife by a sudden return after 3 years absence. But I do not feel so much reduced in vital energy. I think that in three or four days, I will as well as ever.

There is nothing of special interest occurred here since I wrote; only our regiment is now under the Command of Brig. Genl. L. P. Walker. Brig. Genl. Withers is acting as Maj. Genl., commanding two Brigades.

Letter from Edmund W. Pettus, page 2

I rec'd. your letter day before yesterday
and as soon as I get so as to write
conveniently I will answer it in full

In reference to the Fambro matter—
At the time I collected money from Diggs
Col. Fambro owed the firm more than
that amount, and I applied the money
to pay what he owed the firm. Afterwards I loaned him $200, and did other
work for him which added together
will make him owe the firm
between $400 & $500. This is entirely indepen-
dent of his account for board. All of
these transactions are fully stated on
our books, and on Col. Fambro's book.

Give my kindest regards to
my friend & my best love to the dear
ones at home.

I am your loving husband,
Edmd. W. Pettus

Mrs. M. L. Pettus.
Cahaba,
Ala.

Transcription of Letter from Edmund W. Pettus

Camp Goode, near Mobile
Dec 12th, 1861

My dear Wife,

I have had a right sharp attack of neuralgia in the left eye. I was taken sick last Sunday morning and from the way I suffered, I am inclined to think that I had almost as soon have sick headaches.

Dr. Moore put us through a regular calormet course, in broken doses. The remedy was almost as severe as the ailment. I am not yet well; though entirely free from pain. The left eye was closed and much inflamed and I now wear a bandage over it and do not allow the light to visit it. I am walking about camp now and I think that I am free from the complaint. I am however, more reduced than I ever was in so short a time. In appearance, I look very much like a tall spare man who about the 20th Oct, 1852 surprised his wife by a sudden return after 3 years absence. But I do not feel so much reduced in vital energy. I think that in three or four days I will be as well as ever.

Uine is nothing of special interest, occurred here since I write; only our regiment is now under the Command of Brig Genl G.P. Walker[1]. Brig Genl Walker is acting as Maj. Genl, commanding two Brigades. I received your letter day before yesterday and as soon as I get so as to write conveniently I will answer it in full.

In reference to the Fambro matter – at the time I collected money from Duggs. Col. Fambro owed the firm more than that amount, and I applied the money to pay what he owed the firm. Afterwards I loaned him $200, and did other work for him which added together will make him owe the firm between $400 and $500. This is entirely independent of his account for board. All of these transactions are fully stated on our books, and on Col. Fambro' books.

Give my kindest regards to my friends and my best love to the dear ones at home.

I am your loving husband,
Edmund W. Pettus.

Mrs. Mr. S. Pettus
Cahaba,
Ala.

---

1 John George Walker (July 22, 1821 – July 20, 1893) was a Confederate general in the American Civil War. He served as a brigadier general under Stonewall Jackson and James Longstreet

Chapter 8
The Cedar Point Railroad

The Train from Mobile to Dog River
1837

Because it was almost impossible for large ships to reach the wharves in Mobile, most of them anchored at Mobile Point in the lower bay. There they received and discharged cargoes. Lightering involved transferring cargoes from oceangoing ships with deep draughts anchored at Mobile Point to smaller vessels with shallow draughts. There lighters, as the small vessels were called, carried cargoes thirty miles through Mobile Bay to the city wharves. In the late 1850s nearly one hundred local tug steamers or bay boats lightered cotton to what was called the Lower Fleet and imports from the Lower Fleet to city docks.

To avoid the expense of lightering, progressive businessmen in 1835 projected a railway to connect the city with the lower bay. They proposed a route to proceed from Mobile to Cedar Point with an extension to Mon Louis Island on the west side of Mobile Bay, twenty miles south of the city. Thus shippers might send cotton by rail to deep water at a cost lower than lightering. Among the organizers of the Mobile and Cedar Point Railroad Company were William R. Hallett, a banker; Philip McLoskey and James Innerarity, both merchants, and Will R. Robertson, M.D. Eslava and Joseph Krebs, real estate developers. Promoters estimated the cost at $134,405. By opening subscription books for 100 shares of stock at $100 each, they sold enough shares to finance construction of the rail line running parallel to the bay five miles from the city to Dog River. Service began on the first section of the route in 1837 with one locomotive. Much of the route was graded south of Dog River, but a bridge that was needed to cross Dog River was not built before the economic depression called the "Panic of 1837" disrupted work on the line. Bankrupted, the company never completed the railroad. Shippers continued to use lightering, a procedure that added both inconvenience and expense to commerce. Lightering charges for shipping in and out of Mobile harbor in 1846 were estimated to be $200,000.

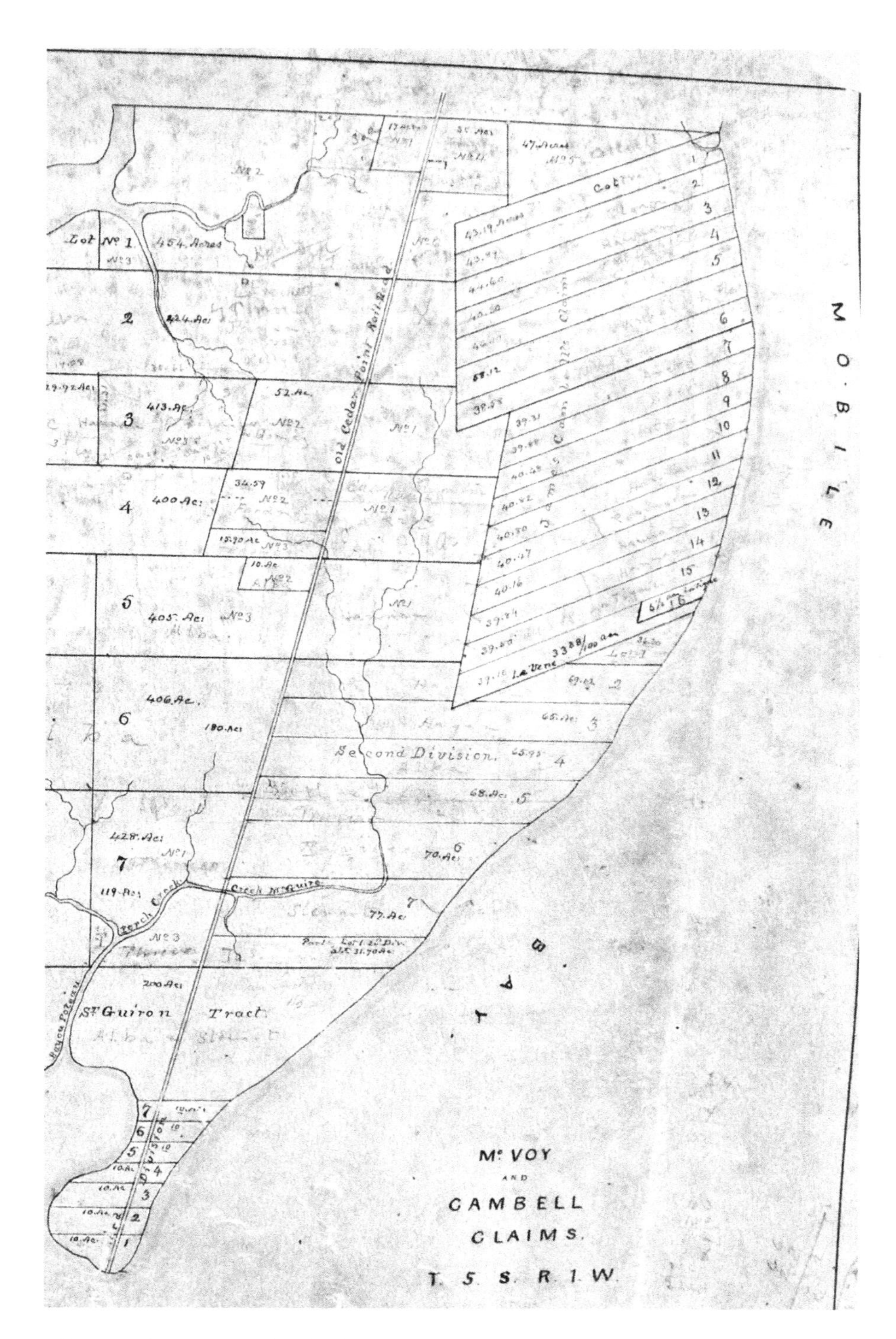

Created to ease the lightering problem, the Cedar Point Railroad, (diagonal line on map) ran from Mobile to Dog River beginning in the 1830s.

PART III

Places and Events

- Bay Shell Road
- Oldest Homes
- Shore Acres
- Satsuma Groves
- Dog River Bridges
- Alba Club
- Gulf Hunting Club
- Grand View Park
- Buccaneer Yacht Club
- Mobile Yacht Club
- Navco
- Brookley
- Night Clubs
- Early Aviation
- Businesses
- Schools
- Churches
- Cemeteries
- Fishing
- Oystering

CHAPTER 9

Bay Shell Road

"On That Beaming Streaming Gleaming Mobile Bay"

Bay Shell Road was built in the 1830s by private citizens as a "for profit" venture. It was a scenic toll road hugging the shoreline from Mobile to near today's Terrell Road. Until Brookley Air Force Base was built more than a hundred years later, the scenery included farms, open fields, the Magnolia Race Course, the first Mobile Country Club, Frascati beachfront rentals, restaurants and family homes, some with wharfs. Fort Sidney Johnson was built along the road in 1862 as a fortress to protect the city during the Civil War. The road was intermittently destroyed by hurricanes and was not rebuilt after the 1926 hurricane. A two mile stretch of Bay Shell Road, now called Bay Front Road, remains today on the south side of the Brookley Complex. Seven homes along this stretch are more than 75 years old.

Bay Shell Road. Cows roamed freely until the 1930s when they were required to be confined by fences. Courtesy of the Library of Congress.

54
Bay Shell Road

Facing Page: The Bay Shell Road Toll booth, top, and a carriage on the shells, bottom.
This Page: Two views of the first Mobile Country Club On Bay Shell Road.

Elizabeth McBride, above, who lived on Bay Front Road, poses on the sandy beach in front of her home at the corner of Bay Front and Cedar Crescent Roads in 1944. At right, Mrs. Edilea Bullen, her mother, in a wooden rowboat commonly used in the 1940s. Photos courtesy of the Bullen Family.

William H. Bullen poses with his sister, Lotte, on Bay Front Road. 1924.

Facing page top: William H. Bullen, sister Lottie and friend on Bay Shell Road, 1924. From the Bullen Family.

Facing page bottom: Friends enjoying the day on the shore of Bay Shell Road around 1900 in their bathing costumes with stockings. Courtesy of Harriet Dykes.

Above: A wooden boat with a happy couple on Bay Front Road around 1900. Courtesy of Harriet Dykes.

The Shaw family in front of Bay Front Road in the late 1940s. Image courtsey of Harry Shaw.

This secluded restaurant offered a quiet spot for dining on Bay Shell Road in the late 1800s. Courtesy of the Museum of Mobile.

CHAPTER 10

Oldest Homes

Martin Lindsey – Tate House - 1915
3112 Bay Front Rd.

"This is a wharf that even Jesus Christ himself couldn't knock down."
Martin Lindsey

Soaring above the other homes on Bay Front Road with a roof like heron wings curving skyward, the historic house, built five miles from Mobile in 1915 by Martin Lindsey, owner of the Lindsey Lumber and Export Company, was first intended to be a home to enjoy duck hunting, fishing and beautiful views of Mobile Bay. In 1915, there were no easy roads to reach the property, so wood for the structure was transferred by barge and offloaded onto a long pier equipped with a rail car to ferry the wood to land.

The style of the one-story wood-frame structure known locally as a Bay House, combines bungalow features with those of much older French Colonial buildings found along the Gulf Coast such as French doors instead of windows opening onto a wrap-around gallery porch and a roof with flared eaves. The home was built on what was then, Bay Shell Road and was added to the National Register of Historic Places on January 24, 1991. Retired Fire Captain David Pitt, a resident of Bay Front Road, told the story that when Mr. Lindsey finished building the 600-foot pier out into the Mobile Bay he said, "This is a wharf that even Jesus Christ himself couldn't knock down." Very shortly after the pier was completed in 1916, a hurricane did exactly that, but you can still see remnants of the stubs of the poles of the pier in front of the house, over a hundred years later.

During prohibition, several older residents report that the house served as a night club where people could freely gamble and drink. Rosa Boone, lived in the home in the 1950s and brought each of her ten babies back to this home after their birth at a hospital. She recalls talking to an Aunt who had visited the night club inside the house in the 1930s who remarked, "*Oh if these walls could talk*!" Today the home is owned by the Tim and Desire Tate Family who take great pride in maintaining it.

The Martin Lindsey - Tate House. 2018. Below: Martin Lindsey. 1915.

The Martin Lindsey house showing the 600-foot pier where lumber was off-loaded from boats and transferred onto carts on rails for building the home. 1916. Notice the cows on the beach. Photo courtesy of the Tate Family.

Above: The Lindsey children on the steps of their Bay Front Road home, 1915.

Left: One of the Lindsey daughters who rescued the home's old images from a safe inside the Lindsey house. Both photos courtesy of the Tate Family.

The Oldest Home – 1860-1880

"I never thought it would still be here"

Fred Lorge

Mr. Fred Lorge, a neighbor born in 1925, said that his family lived on a dairy farm near Rosedale Road when he was a boy in the 1920s. "*It was old then,*" he said. Later, while interviewing a resident with a large piece of property near Rosedale Road, I asked about the old house on her property. The owner said that this had been a dairy long ago and that the family had maintained the old house but only used it for storage now. When Mr. Lorge was told about the house he was eager to look for himself since it had been eighty-five years since he had last seen it. When we drove the long road up the gently sloping hill, the house, surrounded by moss draped oaks came into view. "*I never thought it would still be here*", he said when he saw it. Devereaux Bemis, local architectural historian dated the home from 1860 to 1880, making it the oldest home still standing in this South Mobile. The owner wishes for its location to remain private.

CHAPTER 11

Shore Acres

The First Subdivision in Mobile County - 1914

Shore Acres is a New Development in Mobile County (Article from the Mobile Register, December 8, 1914)

There is no more interesting section in the country than that lying along the western shore of Mobile bay, beginning at Monroe Park and extending south to Cedar Point. Although rich in history, commerce and opportunities, yet it is practically unknown to Mobilians.

The eastern or Baldwin shore is known to everyone because of the excellent transportation facilities to and from the city, but when the western shore is built up as it promises to be during the next few years it will offer a more varied opportunity for Mobile people to spend their summer vacations than can now be found from Daphne to Bon Secour.

The automobile is to play an important part in the rehabilitation of the western shore, which in the early days of Mobile was the home of many people. Practically everyone with a country home has an automobile, and Mobile is but half an hour's drive by machine from this interesting locality. Winter tourists will find it more convenient as a result of the good roads that are nearby to erect a winter home at one of the communities on the Mobile county shore than across the bay with a long wait for the boats to bring them to the city.

Probably the most elaborate of the communities that are springing up is the Shore Acres, located just six miles south of the court house on either the Old Shell or Cedar Point roads. It extends from the bay front back to Dog river, a distance of three miles. There are almost 700 acres in the project, which is being developed along modern lines.

The Shore Acres Company was organized just nineteen months ago by Mr. Richard Lee Fearn, an old Mobile boy, now of Washington, D.C.

A visit to Shores Acres is not complete without an inspection of the work that Mr. Martin Lindsey is doing in the development of the tract which he purchased this summer.

Three new homes are being built on this tract. He is clearing out a large acreage of pine and preparing it for orange trees this winter. There is 160 acres in the tract that is located in the very center of Shore Acres. He has arranged for the planting of 10,000 Satsuma orange trees and 2,600 pecan trees, all supplied by the Glen St. Mary Nursery Company. They are the very best trees that can be found on the coast.

He is also beautifying the bay front. He is bulkheading and sloping the bank, curbing the road and paving the sidewalk for a distance of half a mile. A 1500-foot wharf with railroad track has been built into the bay to a 6-foot channel allowing barges and light draft boat to reach it without difficulty. The barges bring lumber and other building material. Later he will dredge a foot channel to within 500 feet of the bulkhead.

The Shore Acres Company is also planning extensive improvements on its portion of the shore. It will dredge in and make a 6-foot channel. A breakwater will be constructed, thus affording a small landlocked harbor. A pavilion will be erected on the front and there will be an artificial bathing pool supplied from an artesian well.

Although the development work on Shore Acres has really only begun, it is being done on such an elaborate scale that it is well worth a visit. It shows that Mobile people are not concerned about the war abroad when they are going ahead and improving the land that lies close to their front yard and not going into another country to build up a community whose interests are diametrically opposite to those of Mobile."

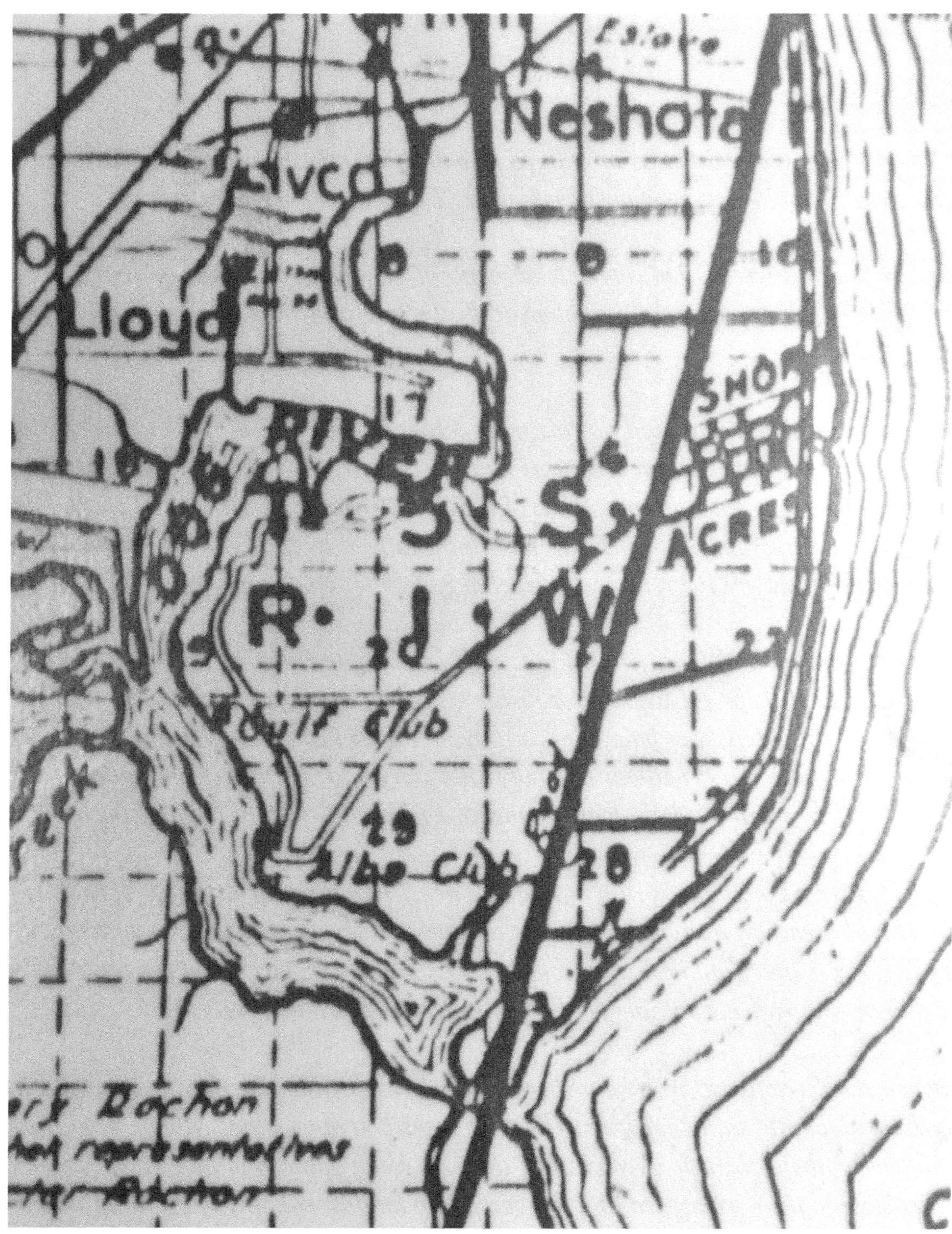

Map showing Shore Acres, and Clubhouse Road that took people to the Alba Club and the Gulf Hunting and Fishing Club. 1920s.

MOBILE REGISTER

E, ALABAMA, TUESDAY MORNING, DECEMBER 8, 1914.

SHORE ACRES IS A NEW DEVELOPMENT IN MOBILE COUNTY

Company Was Organized Nineteen Months Ago by Mr. Richard Lee Fearn.

PLANS LATER ALTERED TO TAKE IN SOME OTHERS

Mr. Martin Lindsey Is Making Extensive Improvements on His Holdings.

There is no more interesting section in the country than that lying along the western shore of Mobile bay, beginning at Monroe Park and extending south to Cedar Point. Although rich in history, romance and opportunities, yet it is practically unknown to Mobilians.

The eastern, or Baldwin shore, is known to every one because of the excellent transportation facilities to and from the city, but when the western shore is built up as it promises to be during the next few years, it will offer a more varied opportunity for Mobile people to spend their summer vacations than can now be found from Daphne to Bon Secour.

The automobile is to play an important part in the rehabilitation of the western shore, which in the early days of Mobile was the home of many people. Practically every one with a country home has an automobile, and Mobile is but half an hour's ride by machine from this interesting locality.

Winter tourists will find it more convenient as a result of the good roads that are nearby to erect a winter home at one of the communities on the Mobile county shore, than across the bay with a long wait for the boats to bring them to the city.

Probably the most elaborate of the communities that are springing up is Shore Acres, located just six miles south of the court house on either the Old Shell or Cedar Point roads. It extends from the bay front back to Dog river, a distance of three miles. There are about 700 acres in the project, which is being developed along modern lines.

What Development Cost.

The development on the tract, which includes clearing of lands, planting of citrus fruit trees and construction of residences and cottages at the present time represents an outlay of $50,000, which shows that the war abroad is not bothering the men who have already bought homes in Shore Acres.

The Shore Acres Company was organized just nineteen months ago by Mr. Richard Lee Fearn, an old Mobile boy, now of Washington, D. C. Associated with him was Mr. John G.

A visit to Shore Acres is not complete without an inspection of the work that Mr. Martin Lindsey is doing in the development of the tract which he purchased this summer.

Three new homes are being built on this tract. He is clearing out a large acreage of pine and preparing it for orange trees this winter. There is 160 acres in the tract, and is located in the very center of Shore Acres. He has arranged for the planting of 10,000 Satsuma orange trees and 2,600 pecan trees, all supplied by the Glen St. Mary Nursery Company. They are the very best trees that can be found on the coast.

Mr. Lindsey is also beautifying the bay front. He is bulkheading and sloping the bank, curbing the road and paving the sidewalk for a distance of half a mile. A 1,500 foot wharf with railroad track has been built into the bay to a 6 foot channel allowing barges and light draft boats to reach it without difficulty. The barges bring lumber and other building material. Later he will dredge a foot channel to within 600 feet of the bulkhead.

The Shore Acres Company is also planning extensive improvements on its portion of the shore. It will dredge in and make a 6 foot channel. A breakwater will be constructed, thus affording a small landlocked harbor. A pavilion will be erected on the front and there will be an artificial bathing pool supplied from an artesian well.

Although the development work at Shore Acres has really only begun it is being done on such an elaborate scale that it is well worth a visit. It shows that Mobile people are not concerned about the war abroad when they are going ahead and improving the land that lies close to their front yard and not going into another country to build up a community whose interests are diametrically opposite to those of Mobile.

Virgin pine trees stood upon the property when they assumed charge, except in a few places where some old residents of the bay country had small developed tracts. Where thousands of tall pine trees stood one can find today more than 15,000 Satsuma oranges, 5,000 paper-shell pecan, besides other fruit trees.

A year ago the plans of the company were altered to include Messrs. W. K. Syson, George Fearn and George Fearn, Jr. The plan included the intensive improvement of the bay front and along Dog river with relatively small units. In the rear of this frontal development the units were to be five acre tracts. A number of units are planted to orange and pecan trees, the planting being under the direction of an expert from the Salbara Nursery Company, which is located on Shore Acres.

Orange Trees The Best.

The orange trees are among the very best that the Salbara Nursery had in stock when planted. At least 10,000 additional orange trees will be planted the winter upon land that is now being cleared and broken.

Mr. Goodwin, one of the original purchasers, is making considerable improvements to a portion of the tract. He is having a modern cottage built and will occupy it this winter.

Another handsome building on Shore Acres is the bungalow of Mr. George A. Maloney, government demonstration agent, on Dog River. Mr. Robert Windom, the architect, is erecting an attractive residence that faces the bay. It is modern and will cost approximately $8,000 to $10,000. It is structures like Mr. Windom's that proves that the development of Shore Acres is not just for today, but for the future.

The landscape work that is planned for the continuation of Old Shell road

(Continued on Page Three.)

SHORE ACRES IS A NEW DEVELOPMENT IN MOBILE COUNTY

Company Was Organized Nineteen Months Ago by Mr. Richard Lee Fearn.

(Continued from Page One.)

in front of Shore Acres property is most elaborate. The roads will be widened and made perfectly level. On the west side will be planted camphor trees for shading and in front oleanders for color effect.

The main bay road also connects with thoroughfares that have been built to connect with Cedar Point Road. These are all of ample width and will also be decorated with camphor and oleander trees.

few trees as an experiment. They showed up well and a few more were secured and planted, and as they were planted the confidence of the people grew, so that now I venture to say that there are 30,000 acres planted between Ocean Springs and Mobile and in the vicinity of Pascagoula, and the next twelve months will increase the acreage to 30,000 or more. It is believed the Satsuma orange tree will stand 10 degrees above zero, and as it seldom gets as cold as 25 degrees here there appears to be no danger from cold along the coast.

A World Market.

The fruit has thus far readily sold for $3.50 to $4 per box (standard orange box), a very much better price than the California or Florida orange, and like the pecan it has the world for a market. It is little known, but is being introduced in Northern cities, where it is extravagantly praised as being the best orange that was ever put on the market. It is a winner and no mistake. Many trees in this territory have been known to bear from 500 to 1,000 oranges, two to five boxes.

There is a tide of immigration from the North and West to the Gulf Coast and the lands are being bought rapidly, many of the purchasers developing and other far-seeing people buying for investment. Lands here have advanced from $2 to $20 and $40 in the past ten years, and a $100 per acre increase is a conservative estimate in the next five years.

I have noted with much interest the sturdy development of the lands in this territory and I say with all confidence that in less than ten years the territory from Mobile to New Orleans will be producing as many oranges as the same amount of territory in any part of California.

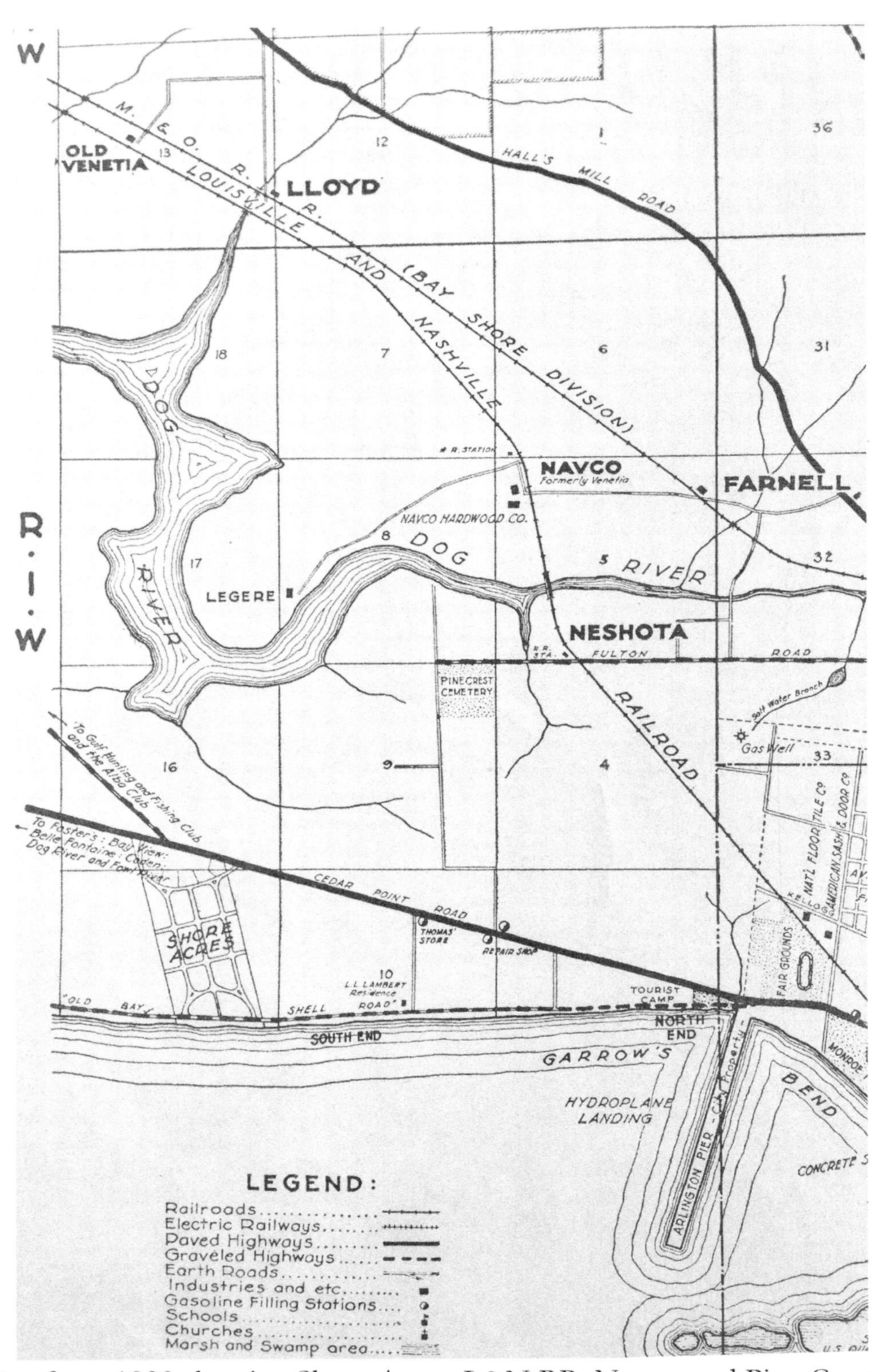

Map from 1930 showing Shore Acres, L&N RR, Navco, and Pine Crest.

CHAPTER 12
Satsuma Orange Groves

I say with all confidence that in less than ten years the territory from Mobile to New Orleans will be producing as many oranges as the wine amount of territory in any part of California.
Mobile Register, 1914.

In 1897, Mr. E. Legere planted the first satsuma orange grove on Dog River on a point which still bears his name. He also started an annual Satsuma Parade in downtown Mobile. Mrs. Rosa Boone, a resident since 1921, said that when her family moved to South Mobile, "*groves of satsumas could be seen as far as the eye could see in the areas north and south of Dog River*". The following account from the Mobile Register in 1914 shows the excitement over this new crop.

The fruit has thus far readily sold for $3.50 to $4.00 per box (standard orange box), a very much better price than the California or Florida orange, and like the pecan it has the world for a market. It is little known, but is being introduced in Northern cities, where it is extravagantly praised as being the best orange that was ever put on the market. Many trees in this territory have been known to bear from 500 to 1000 oranges, two to five boxes.

There is a tide of immigration from the North and West to the Gulf Coast and the lands are being bought rapidly, many of the purchasers developing and other far-seeing people looking for investment. Lands here have advanced from $2 to $20 and $40 in the past ten years, and a $100 per acre increase is a conservative estimate in the next five years.

I have noted with much interest the sturdy development of the lands in this territory and I say with all confidence that in less than ten years the territory from Mobile to New Orleans will be producing as many oranges as the wine amount of territory in any part of California

Crops were shipped out of South Mobile by train, and for a time the fulfillment of the prediction was met, but back to back freezes in the winters of 1926 and 1927 decimated the satsuma trees and orchards, and they were never replanted in mass again.

Ellen DeBretton with her father Bernard DeBretton in 1917 at Herman and Louise Lartique Legere's cow farm on Legere's Point. Both photos courtesy of Ellen's daughter, Sharon Carter Cain.

Mr. Legere's winning car inz the Satsuma Parade in Mobile. 1910.

CHAPTER 13

Dog River Bridges

The First Bridge

Before the first wooden bridge was built a quarter of a mile north of the mouth of Dog River around the turn of the twentieth century, the only way to cross Dog River was by ferry. There is only one known photograph of the wooden bridge and one person, Rosa Boone remembed it in her poem below, *A Bouquet of Dried Flowers.*

Dog River Bridge, made of wood,

Gee, crabbing under it was good!

I'd set the line with stringy meat,

A driftwood log made a good seat.

And thus I'd spend a summer day;

For hours I would stalk my prey,

When Mr. crab would bite and jerk

I patiently began my work.

Slowly I would pull that line

Then --- SCOOP --- that blue-shelled prize was mine

End of story I'll unfold:

A pot of gumbo was my goal.

The first Dog River bridge was wooden and built at the turn of the century about a quarter of a mile from the mouth of Dog River. Image courtesy of the Mobile Historical Commission.

The Second Bridge - 1939

Land was being subdivided and sold to an influx of people causing a need for a new bridge over Dog River. The Dog River drawbridge, a double leaf bascule bridge (from the French word for "seesaw" or "rocker", operating from counterweights under the deck) was built in 1939 at the mouth of Dog River. It had the advantage of opening and closing quickly. It served both maritime and land-bound traffic for more than 60 years.

The Construction of the second Dog River Bridge in 1939, looking north. Notice that there are no buildings looking north. Image coursesy of Dog River Marina.

A popular Dog River Bridge painting, by the late Brian Haithcock, 1993.

The Third Bridge - 1990s

A modern fixed-span bridge replaced the charming drawbridge in the late 1990s. Its construction damaged portions of a three-hundred-year-old important archaeological site which resulted in a more than two-year archaeological dig by archaeologists and students from the University of South Alabama. (see Part1, Chapter 2 in this book) A report of the dig revealed a wealth of data on the culture of Native Americans, French colonists, the Rochon family, and African slaves who lived on Dog River during the French (1702-1763) and British (1763-1781) colonial periods. The construction of the new bridge also required the demise of a long-term and popular gathering spot, the Beachcomber.

The Dog River Bridge today. 2017. Photo courtesy of Sonny Middleton.

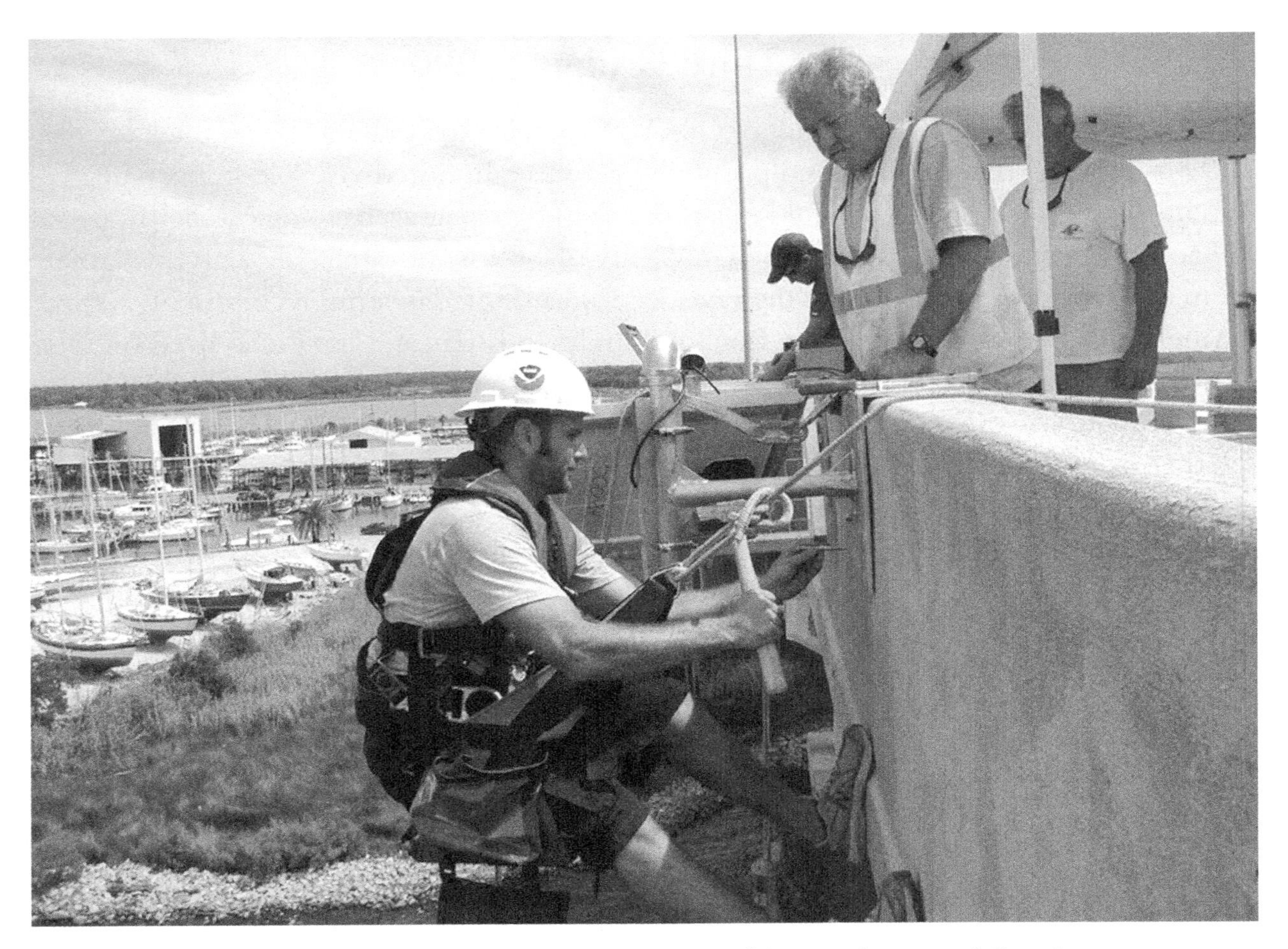

Staff from the Center for Operational Oceanographic Products and Services personnel install a microwave radar water level sensor on the third Dog River Bridge, one of five stations set up to monitor storm surges. 2011.

CHAPTER 14
The Alba Club

The Alba Club was founded in 1903

You feel as though you have stepped back in time as you drive through the entrance and along an extended driveway lined by moss draped oaks to enter the grounds. Located on nine beautifully landscapes acres, the Alba Club has provided recreation on Dog River for families since it was founded in 1903. There is a stately clubhouse with a fishing pier, a harbor for boats and a children's swimming pool on the eastern side of Dog River across from Rabbit and Hall's Mill Creek.

Alba Club was named in honor of Peter Frances Alba, an Indian fighter with Robert E. Lee, a Confederate cavalry captain, and founder of the Mobile Humane Society. Before there were telephones, a large bell was rung to signal that a ferry would be bringing people across Dog River to the club. The bell still sits on the property by the water on a post.

The Alba Club sustained major damage from hurricane Katrina in in 2005, but has rebuilt its structures and still retains the calm and tranquil feeling it always had on this graceful property.

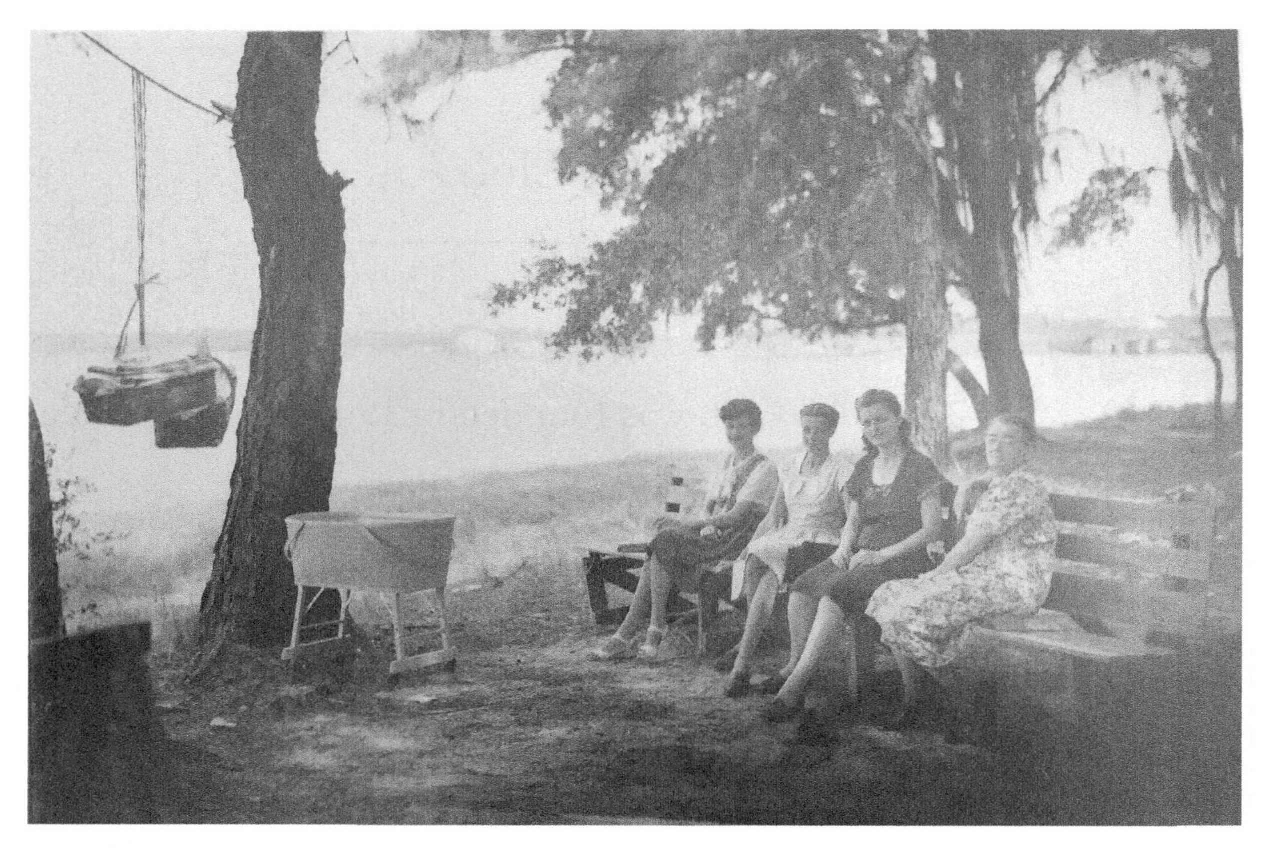

The Alba Club in the 1940s above, in the 1920s below and in the 1960s on facing page.
Images courtesy of Alba Club.

The Alba Club

Peter F. Alba, 1910.
Image courtesy of Library of Congress.

Captain Alba was born in Pensacola, Florida. His father, John F. De Alba, was of Spanish ancestry. His mother Eugenia Souchet, was of French heritage. His family settled in the Florida Panhandle during the 17th century. He moved with his mother, and three sisters to Mobile, Alabama at the age of eight. Peter attended an all-boys school in Springhill, where he rode horseback daily. This began his affection for animals, horses in particular. Even as a young boy he was very skilled as a horseman, a superior swimmer and an excellent marksman with firearms and a bow and arrow.

As a teenager, his yearning for adventure led him to quit school at the age of 15 and set out on his own, moving first to New Orleans and then to Saint Louis Missouri. At the age of 20 he joined the U.S. Army. He achieved the rank of Sergeant and worked as a Ranger on the Southwest Plains fighting Indians.

Peter Alba served in the Indian Wars prior to the outbreak of the Civil War and was severely wounded fighting Comanche Indians, on May 13th, 1858, while in Company B, of the 2nd U.S. Cavalry, in Texas. He was discharged from the U.S. Army due to his wounds, only to reenlist again in the Confederate Military to train cavalrymen. He joined company K of the 15th Alabama Cavalry and was promoted to Sergeant.

Captain Alba returned to Mobile following the war and evolved into a popular and prosperous business man. He ran a livery stable and "Alba's Pasture" for the care and boarding of horses near downtown Mobile. He traveled the world and shipped exotic horses from foreign lands home to Mobile. He was an undertaker, a cabinet maker and served as the City Sexton or gravedigger for Mobile in 1890 and 1891. He established Mobile Transfer Company (a baggage handling company). He was king of the Mobile Carnival festival in 1875 and instrumental in the forming of the Mobile Humane Society.

Captain Alba was well known for sharing his prosperity with local charities. He donated land in Grand Bay, Alabama for the building of a Rosenwald School for African American children in the early 20th century. Alba High School (Now Alba Middle School) in south Mobile County was named in his honor, as was the Alba Club, Alba Road, and Alba Beach. He owned a grand and beautiful villa in Coden, Alabama. Captain Alba was laid to rest in historic Magnolia Cemetery in 1915 in Mobile near his three children who preceded him in death.

The bell that signaled when ferries were arriving is still on the Alba Club property. Image courtesy of the Alba Club.

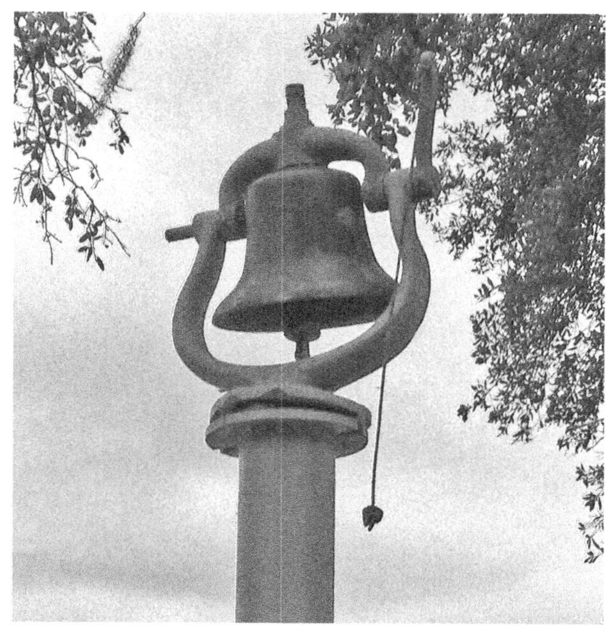

CHAPTER 15

Gulf Hunting and Fishing Club

1894-1983

One can only imagine the tales of adventure enjoyed at the Gulf Hunting and Fishing Club, a not-for-profit two-story lodge established by a group of Mobile businessmen in 1894. Located at the end of Clubhouse Road, (named for the club) in the woods on Dog River, the club was created for members and guests to enjoy hunting and fishing excursions. The name was changed to Gulf Fishing and Boating in the 1950s. After hurricane Frederick in 1979, twenty-two acres of land and thirteen hundred feet on Dog River was sold to Thomas and David Bender for 1.1 million dollars. Private homes now sit on the site.

The First Water Skis

Mrs. Katharine Phillips Singer, sister of Dr. Sidney Phillips Jr., recalled the first water skis on Dog River in front of the Gulf Hunting and Fishing Club in 1936:

> *"My friend Marie and I freely ran through the club and played off the wharf. We often swam across Dog River. One time, there came a motor boat right toward us with a young man on skis hanging onto a rope behind. I didn't want to drown so to save myself I dived down as deep as I could and the boat passed over me. I swam back to the pier and the young man circled around and jumped off onto the wharf and asked if I was ok. It was D. R. Dunlap of the Dunlaps of the Alabama Dry Dock and Shipbuilding. He was a very good looking young man, but he was killed in the war. Dunlap Street is named after him."*

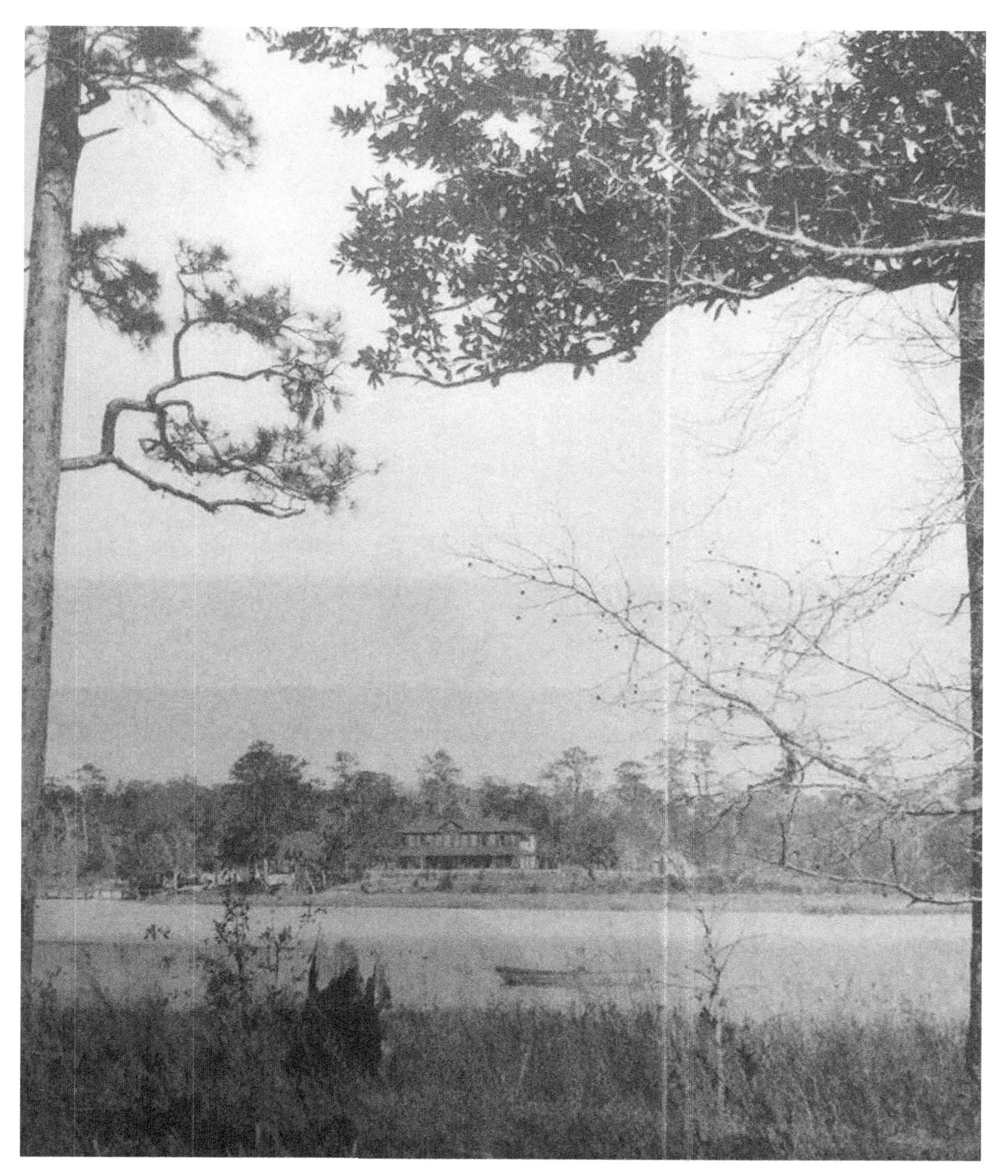

Gulf Hunting and Fishing Club. 1900. Image courtesy of Homer McClure.

Above: Gulf Hunting and Fishing Club. 1900. Image courtesy of archives of the Historic Mobile Preservation Society.

Facing page top: Gulf Hunting and Fishing Club. 1920. Image courtesy of John Word.

Facing page bottom: Certificate of Membership, Gulf Fishing and Boating Club, 1962. Image courtesy of archives of the Historic Mobile Preservation Society.

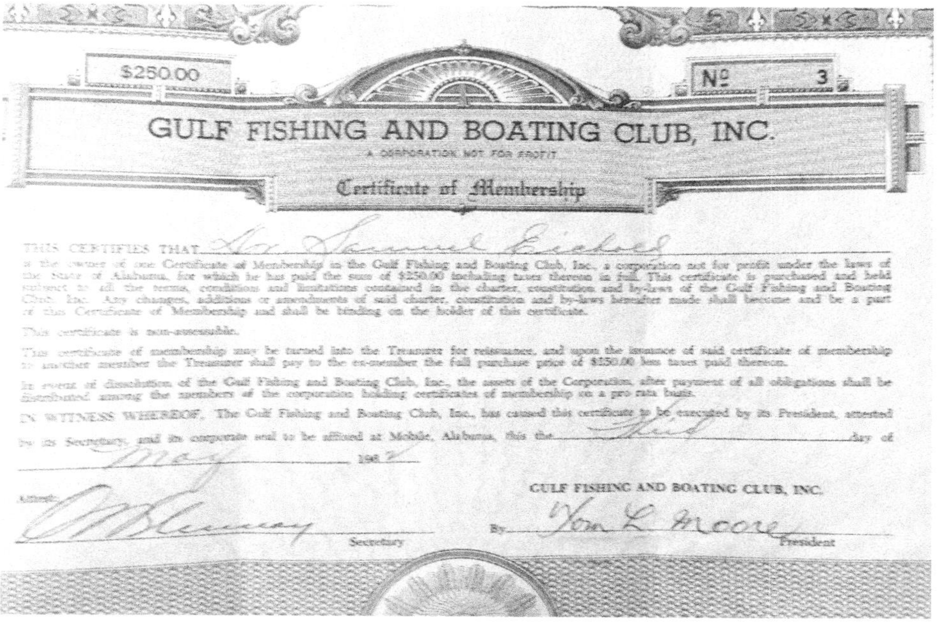

$250.00

No 3

GULF FISHING AND BOATING CLUB, INC.

A CORPORATION NOT FOR PROFIT

Certificate of Membership

THIS CERTIFIES THAT Dr. Samuel Eichold
is the owner of one Certificate of Membership in the Gulf Fishing and Boating Club, Inc., a corporation not for profit under the laws of the State of Alabama, for which he has paid the sum of $250.00 including taxes thereon in full. This certificate is purchased and held subject to all the terms, conditions and limitations contained in the charter, constitution and by-laws of the Gulf Fishing and Boating Club, Inc. Any changes, additions or amendments of said charter, constitution and by-laws hereafter made shall become and be a part of this Certificate of Membership and shall be binding on the holder of this certificate.

This certificate is non-assessable.

This certificate of membership may be turned into the Treasurer for reissuance, and upon the issuance of said certificate of membership to another member the Treasurer shall pay to the ex-member the full purchase price of $250.00 less taxes paid thereon.

In event of dissolution of the Gulf Fishing and Boating Club, Inc., the assets of the Corporation, after payment of all obligations shall be distributed among the members of the corporation holding certificates of membership on a pro rata basis.

IN WITNESS WHEREOF, The Gulf Fishing and Boating Club, Inc., has caused this certificate to be executed by its President, attested by its Secretary, and its corporate seal to be affixed at Mobile, Alabama, this the Third day of May 196[illegible]

Attest: [illegible] Secretary

GULF FISHING AND BOATING CLUB, INC.

By Tom L. Moore President

87
Gulf Hunting and Fishing Club

CHAPTER 16

Early Aviation in Mobile

John Fowler

Ten years before Kitty Hawk, Mobilian John Fowler, a clock and sewing machine repair shop owner in Mobile, began tinkering with building primitive flying machines in South Mobile near Arlington Park. He helped finance his work by allowing curious onlookers to view his work for a small admission. In 1902, he created a monoplane which was comprised of a Victorian cane chair, bicycle wheels, wide fabric covered wings and tail stretched over a light wooden frame. The Wright Brothers visited Fowler and modeled their airplane's wing structure on his. There is no concrete evidence that Fowler's plane ever flew, but some citizens and family members swore that they observed him flying across the bay.

John Fowler constructing his airplane. 1902.
Photo courtesy of USA Archives.

In 1917 Mobile leased a 100-acre tract of land at the foot of Ann Street as a municipal landing field. It had a 1700 foot grass runway and served as a landing and takeoff site for mail delivery for a decade. Mrs. Catharine Phillips Singer recalls that an entrepreneur had created large dirt piles over which thrill seekers could drive their cars for a small fee. "*It was such simple fun*". Mrs. Rosa Boone, a resident since 1922, wrote a poem about watching the mail deliveries there as a child.

And still the memory I retain. When we'd go watch for the mail plane.
It landed usually 'bout nine. Near Cedar Point Road, down the line.
Old Cedar Point Road is no more, But it lives on in Mobile's lore.

Bates Field

In 1929, the city of Mobile bought farmland south of the city from Cecil Bates, a former Mobile Mayor, to create Bates Field, the city's first municipal airport. Located on Cedar Point Road, four miles south of the city's downtown. Bates Field had two sod runways, an office building, restrooms and a telephone. According to Billy Singleton, author of "Mobile Aviation", night landings were tricky in the early days of aviation. "*Pilots had to depend on a row of oil drums that would be set aflame to illuminate the runway when landing after dark.*"

Mobile Mardi Gras Court in front of "The City of Mobile" plane on Bates Field. 1931. Photo courtesy of USA Archives.

CHAPTER 17
Buccaneer Yacht Club

1928 - present

"All for one and one for all" is not an empty motto for members of the Buccaneer Yacht Club because for over ninety years they have taken great pride in promoting and participating in the sport of yachting and sailing in Mobile, and educating the next generation of sailing enthusiasts. Reaching even further into the community, they sponsor an annual Leukemia Cup Regatta and benefit that has raised over half a million dollars for medical research and treatment for individuals with leukemia.

The Club's history is one of the most interesting in the world. For starters, their unusual name is due to the circumstances of the club's founding. In 1928, four friends, Leon Delaplaine, Foster Pfleger, John Mandeville, and Ben Mayfield joined forces to have a thirty-foot foot gaff-rigged cabin sloop built. The boat was christened the "Buccaneer", and the four men soon caught yachting fever, spending nearly all their spare time on the boat. They were so enthusiastic about sailing on the Bay, they decided to form their own yacht club. By July of 1928 they accomplished their goal. Officers were elected: the first Commodore was Leon Delaplaine. A constitution was drawn, and a name for the club was selected from the boat that brought them all together - the sloop "Buccaneer".

The original sloop, "Buccaneer" in 1928

Next, a clubhouse was needed because the club had progressed rapidly. Races were held off Arlington Pier with a small fleet. The club also built three "fish class" boats, 21-foot, gaff-rigged sloops which could compete for the magnificent silver trophy (the Lipton Cup) presented to the Gulf Yachting Association, by Sir Thomas Lipton, a British Tea magnate. In 1929, the club decided to purchase a site owned by Mr. W. J. Barrett, at Alba Beach, a quarter of a mile north of Dog River on Mobile Bay. The first clubhouse was a two-story structure with "every modern convenience" built by Mr. Barrett over the water about one thousand feet from the beach.

Above: The Buccaneer Yacht Club under construction in 1928 at Barrett's beach, near Dog River on the Bay. Below: Members enjoy the wharf and first Buccaneer clubhouse in the early 1930s.

Facing Page:
"Remember the Resolute" has special meaning for all club members, because the Resolute was a four-masted cargo schooner built in 1902 that became the Buccaneer's second clubhouse, one unlike any other in the world. The schooner was purchased by the Club in 1932 after it brought its final cargo of lumber to Mobile.

The four-masted cargo schooner, the Resolute, harbored in the Mobile River. 1932

Springer Tam, the Club's second Commodore, elected in 1929, said: "The Resolute was towed down river and tied up alongside of Arlington Pier. A dredge had dug a slip at the end of Arlington, and with her rock ballast removed, and at mean high tide, the ship was humped into the slip and made fast. Holes were bored in her hull to allow the water to flow in and out and create a suction to hold her fast in the sand." An oak dance floor was put down over the deck, and a roof garden and glassed-in enclosure finished the remodel of the ship which now had the appearance of Noah's Ark and officially became the Buccaneer Yacht Club in May, 1932, the only Yacht Club building of this type in the world. It served this purpose for many years until the Army Air Corps requested use of it. during World War II and eventually purchased it outright.

Fast in a final mooring
Life's evening watch she stands;
Yet all her beams are soaked with dreams -
And these she understands:
She knows the song of the vagabond waves,
And each one tells of the shore it laves;
So does she - dreaming - live once more
In many a port on some far-flung shore;
And the dancing throng on her deck would seem
The patter of workers' feet in her dream.
She hears the voice of the roving wind,
And if it comes with hurricane din -
Dreaming - she feels her timbers creak;
And dreaming she springs a phantom leak;
yet sturdy and proud, she knows her dream
tWill end where lights in her home port gleam.
Fast in a final mooring
Life's evening watch she stands;
Yet all her beams are soaked with dreams,
And the Seven Seas she spans.

Author unknown, in Buccaneer Breeze Magazine. 1935.

Above: Aerial view shows the clubship and other facilities on the "Pleasure Peninsula", at Arlington. 1932. Below: Remodeling the clubhouse on Arlington Point. 1932.

Above: Constructing the Clubhouse, 1939. Below: Clubhouse and pier.
Facing page top: Turtle Races on deck of the Resolute. 1940.
Facing page below: A dance on the clubship, Buccaneer Yacht Club, during WWII.

Above and next two pages: Cover artworks of Bucaneer Breeze Issues. 1930s.
Left: An early regatta on Mobile Bay.

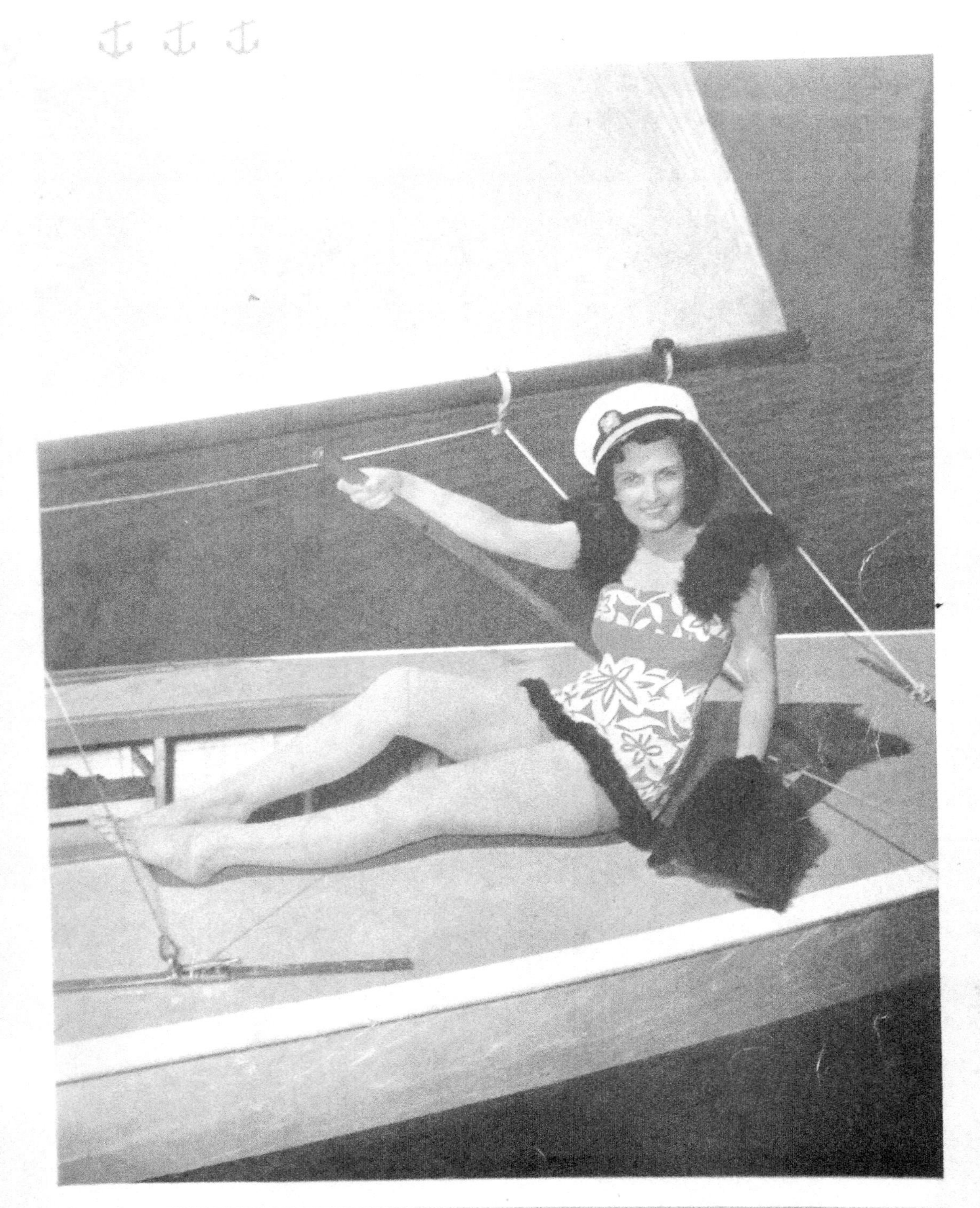
BUCCANEER BREEZE

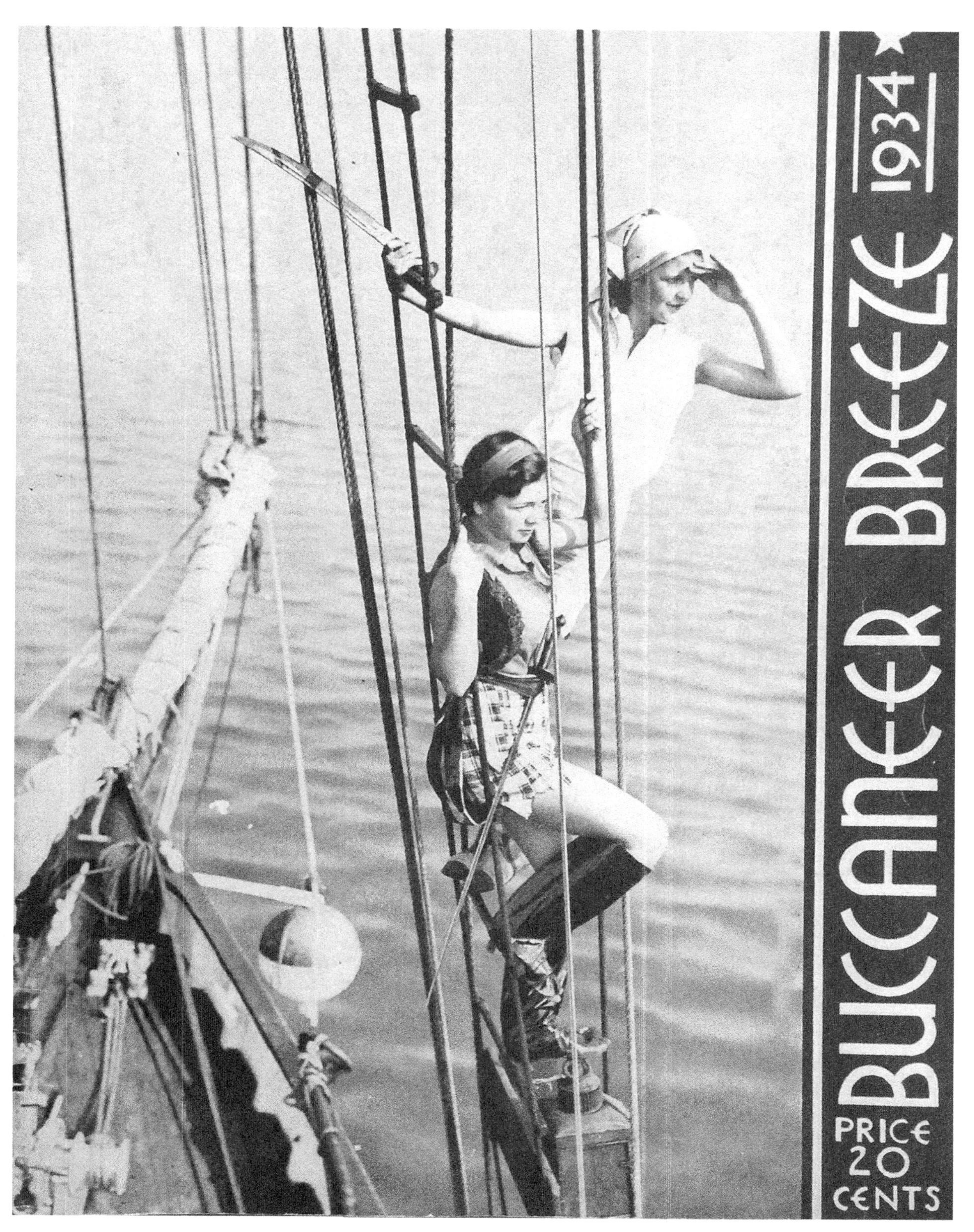

Buccaneer Yacht Club

Bucaneer Breeze Issue, 1939.

Another clubhouse was needed after World War II. The current clubhouse property adjacent to and including McNally Park was purchased in 1947, on land then known as Foster's Beach. With dedicated work from its members, the club has flourished and now has a clubhouse, harbor facilities, a bar, and a pool with cabana.

All images were shared by Kenny Kleinschrodt, Buccaneer Yacht Club Historian. Quotations, some images, and other information are from the Buccaneer Breeze Magazine, a publication of the Buccaneer Yacht Club.

Third clubhouse of the Bucaneer Yacht Club. 1950s.

CHAPTER 18

Mobile Yacht Club

1847- present
One Hundred and Seventy Years Old and Seven Clubhouses

Established in 1847 by Mobile sailors, Mobile Yacht Club is the second oldest private boating and sailing club in the United States and the oldest club on the Gulf Coast. It was called the Mobile Regatta Club in 1847 and members organized large competitions held on the Eastern Shore at Battles Wharf.

First Clubhouse 1882

The Civil War discouraged yacht racing but it began again in 1867 when members established regattas between Mobile and New Orleans that were held in Point Clear. In 1882 the Club raised funds through the sale of stock at $25 per share to build a new Clubhouse on the east bank of the Mobile River. The new Clubhouse was built over the water with a small pier to one side and was reached by a sail ferry which could be hailed with a whistle blown by a member waiting transportation from across the river.

Incorporation and Second Clubhouse 1894

Mobile Yacht Club was Incorporated in 1894 and in 1897, after fifteen years in the first clubhouse, growing membership required a larger one. Prominent yachtsman and architect, Thomas Sully designed an elaborate structure near the old location on Mobile River. But boating and social activities ended abruptly with the enormous hurricane of 1906. The clubhouse survived, but the river and site conditions were no longer workable for mooring and sailing. A new location was sought.

Gulf Coast Yachting Association formed 1901

Mobile Yacht Club joined Biloxi Yacht Club and Southern Yacht Club of New Orleans to organize the Southern Gulf Coast Yachting Association in 1901. Reorganized in 1920 the association was renamed the Gulf Yachting Association (GYA) and Mobile Yacht Club hosted its first meeting in Mobile.

Monroe Park Clubhouse 1907-1916

There was never a more beautiful structure built over the water in Mobile Bay than Mobile Yacht Club's third clubhouse in front of Monroe Park at the end of a 600-foot public wharf. It was a lavish two-storied structure with wide verandas, and balconies topped with a pair of towers offering grand views of the maritime activities on the Bay. It was decorated with pictures of famous yachts. The hurricane of July, 1916 completely demolished it. Rev. S. D. Monroe reported that "It was torn into splinters and part of the building was thrown onto Bay Avenue and the Shell Road". Only the pilings remained. When the United States declared war on Germany and its allies in 1917, little thought was given to sailing or rebuilding the clubhouse until 1919 when a committee composed of E. B. Overton, S. Blake McNeely, Joe L. Hermann, L. H. Gaynor and A. D. Spotswood met at the Cawthon Hotel and decided to build a clubhouse on the eastern shore. They purchased two lots at Magnolia Beach.

The Club on the Eastern Shore

Using their experience of the old Mobile Yacht Club which was washed away by the 1916 hurricane, this clubhouse was built on the bank of the bay, instead of over the water. It was a two-story building, fifty feet long and thirty-five feet wide, with a roomy porch with swings and chairs surrounding the west and south sides. The lower floor was a reception hall decorated flags and pennants of different yachts, while the upper floor was a dormitory fitted with cots. Every Sunday afternoon crowds gathered on the end of the pier to watch exciting races of the boats belonging to club members.

The Club moves to Barrett's Beach near Dog River 1934 - 1939

An interest developed in finding a new club location near a protected harbor. Barrett's Beach Clubhouse had been vacant since 1930 and with its nearness to Dog River and easy accessibility was an perfect choice and the Club moved there in 1934. The building at Barrett's beach was similar to the club in Magnolia Springs with a great hall downstairs and dormitories upstairs. The entrance to the building was on the north side facing the public pier and there were other outlets to a walkway that surrounded the building.

The Clubhouse on Dog River 1940

Raising the needed funds for a new clubhouse would not easy in the late 1930s during the depression. The beloved Commodore L. G. Beauvais led the group with untiring efforts and his ability to obtain financing. Each member bought a bond with five coupons attached. When dues came around each year, a coupon was clipped and remitted as part of the total dues due. The beauty of this plan was that when all the coupons had been rendered, the club had no obligation to these bonds. Commodore Tom Kroutter who succeeded Beauvais, was chairman of the building committee and was the city engineer. During the course of the city work at that time, granite curb stones were being removed during a construction project. When this building was demolished in 1980 after Hurricane Frederick, the granite stones were saved with its memorial markers and used to form a new fireplace in the new building.

The Dauphin Island Regatta - 1958

This popular race was conceived by Dr. Dixon Meyers and Victor Hudson who wanted to find a way to bring tourists to Mobile in April and May. They met with members from the Mobile, Buccaneer and Fairhope Yacht Clubs. At first the idea was to have both a sailboat and an outboard motor competitive event, but the outboard portion never culminated. During the first few years the competition included team races only among the yacht clubs, but over time involved boats from any recognized sailing organization located on inland or coastal waters. The race grew to 100 boats in 1963, up to 200 in the 1970s and in 1989 there were 383 vessels from twenty-four yacht clubs participating.

Mobile Yacht Club and pier. 1960s. Photos courtesy of Mobile Yacht Club.

The Clubhouse of 1980 - present

Hurricane Frederick struck Mobile on September 12, 1979. After the storm, the club building was a constructive total loss and the marina was left in shambles. Father Paul Tipton provided the club a meeting room at Spring Hill College and at this meeting, plans were presented for a new building to be located a few feet north of the old slab. The plans included a large kitchen with commercial cooking equipment for an expansive dining room with windows overlooking the bay. It would be built on pilings to withstand future storm tides, and the dormitory feature was eliminated. Since its building, the club has withstood five hurricanes causing the loss only of the knock-away part of the clubhouse, and the wharf. The wharf was rebuilt in 2000.

The Mobile Yacht Club sponsors and annually participates in several club regattas as well as races within the Gulf Yachting Association including the Dauphin Island Regatta, The Middle Bay Light Regatta, the Broken Triangle Race, the Around-the-Rig Regatta, and the MYC Anniversary Regatta. One of the most successful races sponsored by the club is the Thursday Night Fun Race, open to and participated in by other yacht clubs. The beautiful sight of many large white sails heading out into the bay can be seen at 6:30 every Thursday in the summer as sailors venture out to test their skills alongside other sailing enthusiasts.

CHAPTER 19

Navco

NAVCO - New Albany Veneer Company

1920 - 1930

Everyone knows Navco Park and has driven along Navco Road, but the origin of the name has become obscure. This area is named after the New Albany Veneer Company (NAVCO) in Indiana, which was the world's largest producer of high-grade plywood at the turn of the century.

In 1920 the Navco area was called Venetia by Milton Smith of the L and N Railroad to honor Venetia Neville Danner, of Mobile. Col. Eugene Knight purchased Henry Tacon's homesite on Dog river and 75 acres from his widow in 1920 for $15.000. Col Knight then opened a veneering plant on the site and changed the name from Venetia to Navco and moved his family to a Dog River home adjoining the plant site.

The area was especially suitable for a new veneer factory because it was near to both a railway line and the river. Gum trees from Clark County Alabama and mahogany trees from South America were stored on Dog River frontage where it was less susceptible to worm damage. Trains and boats then transported the lumber to the plant in Indiana where it was made into mahogany veneered cabinets for the RCA Victrola and the Columbia Phonograph Companies.

The financial downturn during the depression of the 1930s led to the closing of both veneer plants in Mobile and Indiana. In the 1950s, Knight's home was demolished to make way for Navco Park, later called Luscher Park and today called Dog River Park. Modern Homes and Equipment Company visible from I-65, now occupies the old plant site.

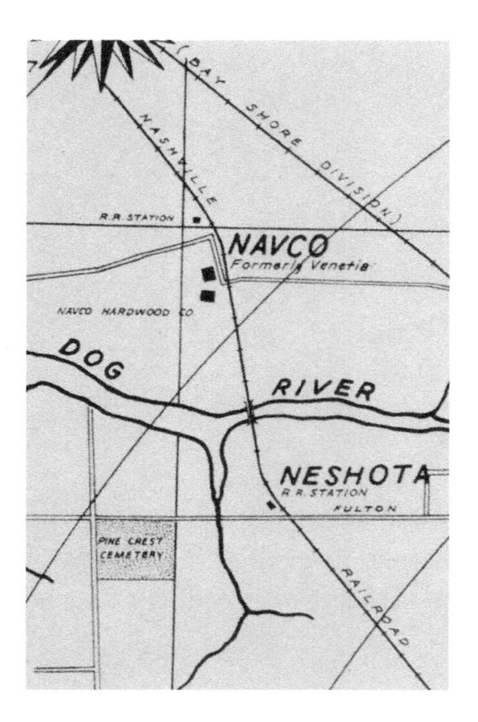

Left: Map showing the location of the Veneer Plant and its proximity to the railroad and river. Map courtesy of Mobile County Archives.

Below: Col. Eugene Knight who opened the Veneer plant.

The Danner Family at the turn of the Century: Paul Danner, his two sisters, and his father, Capt. Albert Danner, with Venetia, for whom the area near Dog River Park was first named. Images courtesy of Mobile Municipal Archives.

CHAPTER 20

Brookley Air Force Base

1939-1969

WWII brought the Hopper family to Mobile. *"We came from the country in Tennessee during hard times. We heard from a relative that there were jobs here. We left Jackson, Tennessee at midnight and rode The Rebel train that ran from Mobile to St. Louis. After riding all night, stopping in every little station on the way, we arrived in the most beautiful station. I saw palm trees for the first time, and I could even taste the salt."* Bond Hopper, former resident, Park Road

Effects of Brookley on South Mobile

Nothing has had a greater impact on south Mobile than the establishment of Brookley Army Air Field in 1939. (Renamed Brookley Air Force Base in 1949) To gain the needed space, neighborhoods were divided. Houses, streets and a Catholic Church were either moved or demolished. Bay Shell Road which previously extended along the bay all the way from downtown Mobile to Terrell Road was bisected to make way for the significant new runway. Graves of the Lartigue family were excavated and relocated to Perimeter Road to make way for the runway.

The Great Depression was still in full swing in 1939 with nearly twenty percent unemployment in the United States. When news of the base became known, people from surrounding states swarmed into Mobile seeking work at Brookley.
By March 1944, Mobile County's population would grow from 112,000 to 233,000, up sixty-four percent from 1940. Schools were over-filled, public services were strained and there was a huge housing shortage. In just a few years, in 1943, Brookley would reach its peak employment of 17,097.

Consequently, thousands of people moved into South Mobile because of its proximity to the Base. Citizens rented out rooms, converted porches, garages and even chicken coops into living space to alleviate the housing shortage. Just outside of Brookley, a federal housing project called "Thomas James Place", known as "Birdville" because the streets were named after birds, was quickly built to house Air Force workers. Some people lived in tents until they could build something better. Others built their homes from wood salvaged from warehouse crates from Brookley. Mrs. Lucy Leggett, age 98, remembered washing clothes for her husband and baby in a tributary of Dog River when she first came to live off Riverside Road in 1942. "There was no electricity, or running water", she recalled.

Above: Mrs. Lucy Leggett in 1942.

Right: Mrs. Doris Tippins sits in front of her home in Thomas James Place, "Birdville", 1950. Picture courtesy of Hal Tippins.

Left: In December of 1940, the War Department directed that the new base be named for Air Corps Capt. Wendell H. Brookley, left, who was killed while testing a wooden propeller on an airplane Feb. 28, 1934, at Bolling Field in Washington.

Below: The new amphibian airplane, inspected by a Congressional Committee at Bolling Field. Third from right is Lt. Wendell H. Brookley, who piloted the machine from New York to Washington. Both images are Courtesy of the Library of Congress.

Brookley's Purpose During the War

The Army chose the Bates Field area primarily because of its waterfront location and flying-suitable weather conditions. The Base was to serve two purposes: a fighter overhaul and maintenance base, and an Air Material Command supplying the Air Force bases around the world. To fulfill its mission, the Army built enormous hangars, large warehouses, its own cargo plane fleet, and took advantage of the existing Arlington Point dock. The dock's function was to allow ocean-going vessels to offload aircraft and transport them to the repair facilities within Brookley without using public roads. Repaired aircraft would then fly back into service. The base had amenities for all human needs: a commissary, a church, housing, a hospital, swimming pools, a movie theatre, a cafeteria, library, and even its own newspaper, The Brookley Bay Breeze.

"Might be first in a hearse", Sign at the entrance for the 17,000+ workers at Brookley where traffic lines were long. The Air Force Base exchange is behind the cars. 1950s. Courtesy of USA Archives.

Life and Work on Brookley Air Force Base

Mrs. Jean Hopper Turner, right, a resident in our area, worked at Brookley for a year during the WWII. "*I balanced rotors that went into flight indicators. Before that I assembled ball bearings for the flight indicators. The assembly room had to be dust free so there were no windows at all. One day the lights went out and we were completely in the dark. After the war ended we weren't needed anymore.*"

Above: The outside of the base commisary, 1950s. Courtesy USA Archives.
Below: The inside of the base commisary, 1950s.

118
Brookley

Above: Aerial View of the Construction of Brookley, looking toward the Bay. 1939
Facing page top and bottom: The outside and inside of the base chapel, 1950s.

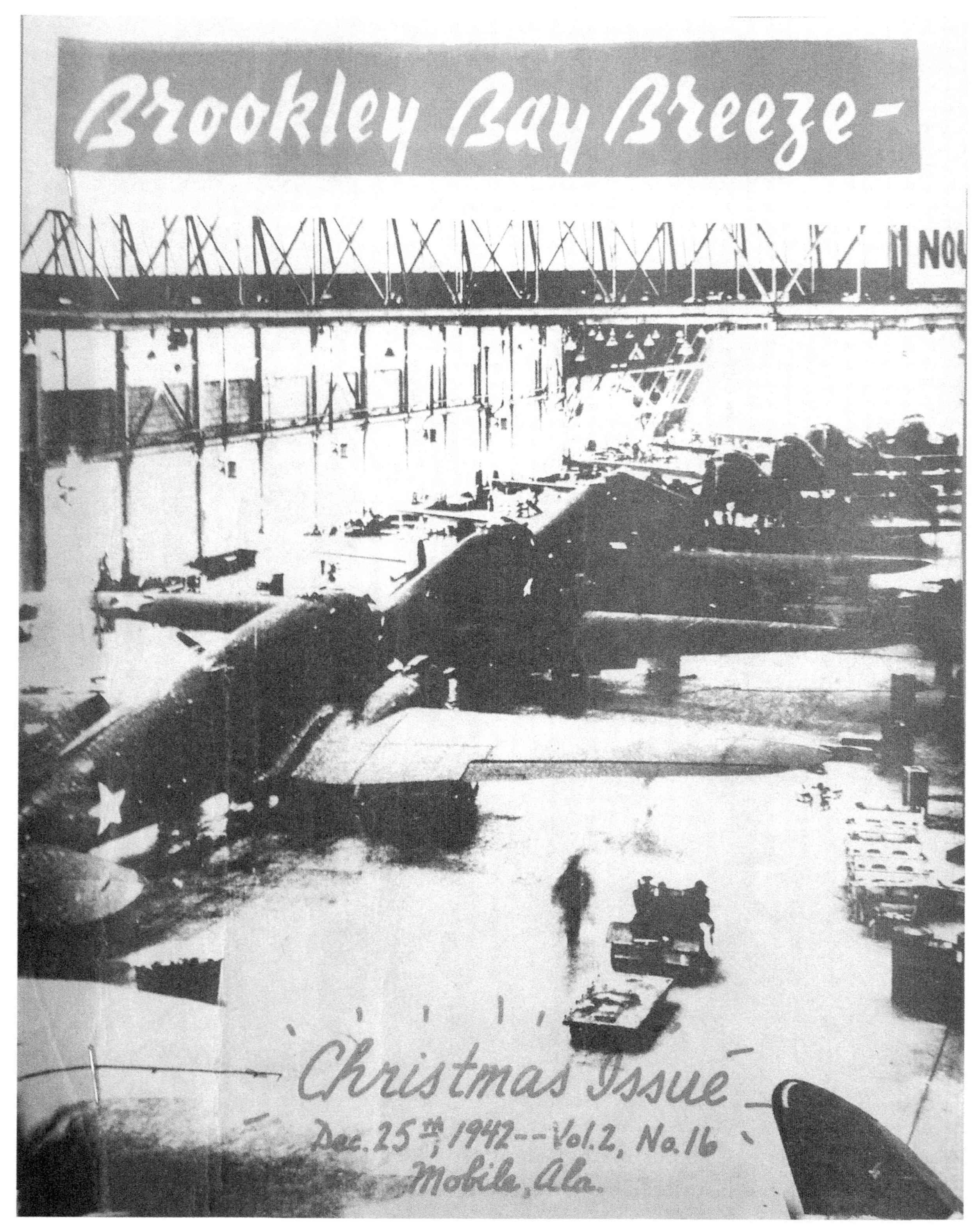
Brookley Bay Breeze -
NOU
Christmas Issue
Dec. 25th, 1942 -- Vol. 2, No. 16
Mobile, Ala.

Facing Page: Brookley Bay Breeze Magazine cover, 1942. From the Local History and Geneaology Library of Mobile Public Library.

This page: "Christmas Stocking Woman" in the Brookley Bay Breeze Magazine, before polital correctness in 1942. From the Local History and Genealogy Library of Mobile Public Library.

Next two pages: Private Perplexed questions and answers in the Brookley Bay Breeze Magazine from the 1942.

ter. Thru
sailors have
their own
he result of
Ostini, arts
y Archer,

rd of three
last Friday,
the Friday
variety pro-
ve unearthed
ost among the
t Jack Barrett
ohn Purser,
low, golden
ers are want-
so sign up to-

, the USO will
onor of its
r of Christ-
ir with a
eshments. All
d Hostesses
ance will be
ember 25th,
r's Eve.
the USO every

============

rom page 20)
of Swamp Root)
anta Claus
t "Skinny" Wil-

loch

============

ge 14)
at the Finance
life or death
earned that yet.
won't rest until
begging for

ris Singman

Life Insurance Officer. Extension 606.

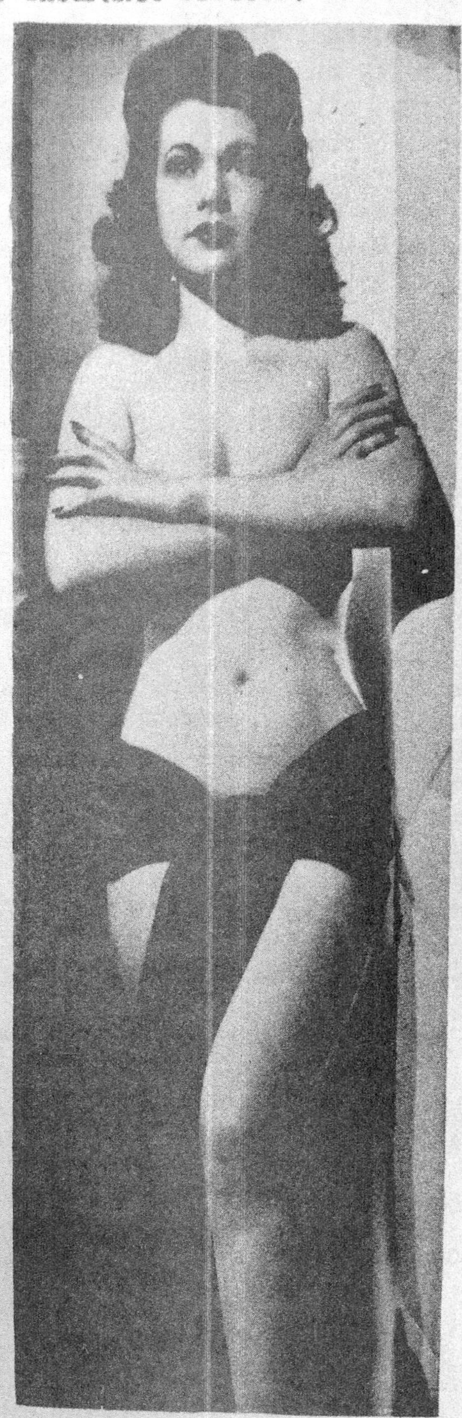

HOW WOULD YOU LIKE TO FIND THIS IN YOUR CHRISTMAS STOCKING?!!!

10

(alias Cpl R.L Dietrich)

BY PVT PERPLEXED

Amid the blare of trumpets - a mighty fanfare - the "Maestro" again appears before his children to answer their numerous interrogations. The Swami speaks!

Dear Pvt. Perplexed I have come across some pretty dumb mechanics in the past few days One couldn't tell a nut from a bolt Do you know of any similar examples?

T/Sgt. Noit All

Dear Sgt Yes, I have. I know one crew that thinks propwash is carried around in buckets

Dear Pvt Perplexed. I have a very dark problem I'm supposed to go out on a blind date. What shall I do?

Pvt. Twenty-twenty Vision

Dear Ten-ten (for short) Just feel your way around.

Dear Pvt. Perplexed: My girl friend is very ignorant -- just plain dumb and I don't know what to do with her. Are all girls that way?

Pvt. Wondering Why

Dear Pvt W W Most girls are, so don't worry I know one chic who is so dumb she thinks lettuce is a proposition!

Dear Pvt. Perplexed: My girl tells me I am the only man in her life, but I've seen her with three other fellows this week. Do you think she's lying?

Pvt. Justa Skeptic

Dear Pvt. J.S. Is your grammar always that bad?

Dear Pvt. Perplexed I have heard much discussion on the merits and demerits of the zipper on women's clothes. Some say it is the undoing of the modern girl. Could you put me right on the subject?

Pvt. Zipper Lipper

Dear Pvt. Zip Lip: The zipper may be the undoing of the modern girl, but on the other hand it opens up great opportunities!

Dear Pvt. Perplexed: I always hear a lot of talk about old maids. Exactly what is an old maid?

Cpl. Got Me Guessin

Dear Cpl. Not Me: An old maid is a girl who knows all the answers, but who has never been asked the questions.

Court Martial of Human Relations...

by Private Perplexed

HAVE YOU A PROBLEM? DOES IT HURT WHEN YOU STEP ON BROKEN BOTTLES IN YOUR BARE FEET? ARE YOU MAD BECAUSE WOMEN DON'T MAKE PASSES AT YOU OR BECAUSE THEY IGNORE YOUR PASSES? SEND YOUR TROUBLES IN A KIT-BAG TO PVT. PERPLEXED AND YOU'LL RECEIVE QUICKER RESULTS THAN THE GOOD WILL COURT.

Dear Pvt. Perplexed: Since I've been in the Army I've met some pretty dumb rookies. What is the dopiest case you've run across?
Sgt. Studious

Dear Sargy: The dumbest soldier I've seen is the draftee who thinks fallen women are the ones you see on a slippery street.

Dear Pvt Perplexed: A friend of mine told me he received a broken arm fighting for a woman's honor. I don't understand. Can you explain?
Pvt. M.T. Head

Dear M.T.: Maybe she wanted to keep it.

Dear Pvt. Perplexed: Enclosed is a picture of my girl in the sweater I sent her for her birthday last month. I think she's quite a honey. What do you think?
Pvt Pete Pullover

Dear Pete: She has her good points.

Dear Pvt Perplexed: My girl and I are planning on entering into a companionate marriage where we can live together a while and then if we find we've made a mistake, we can separate. Do you think this will work out O.K.?
Cpl. You Know Best

Dear I Sure Do: Yes, but... what'll you do with the mistake?

Dear Pvt. Perplexed: You know my First Sergeant pretty well. His name is Smelldovich. What ever caused him and his girl to have a fight? We thought they were madly in love.
Pvt I Smell A Rat

Dear Pvt. It's Not Me: At first he fascinated her and she kissed him. Then he tried to unfascinate her and she slapped him!

Some Highlights of Brookley's Past

Norden Bomb Sight

One of the keys to Allied victory in Europe was the Norden Bomb Sight, which enabled bomber squadrons to target Germany's war-making industry and infrastructure much more accurately. The military repaired and calibrated the bombsights at Brookley in a secret facility, still standing and in use today. After the war, Brookley continued to operate as an Air Material Command.

A pilot sits behind a Norden bomb sight during WWII. Image courtesy of the Library of Congress.

Ivory Soap Project

In 1944, the Army decided to take advantage of Brookley's large, skilled workforce for its top-secret "Ivory Soap" project to hasten victory in the Pacific. The project required twenty-four large vessels to be re-modeled into Aircraft Repair and Maintenance Units that had to be able to accommodate B-29 bombers, P-51 bombers' protectors, two big R-4B Sikorsky helicopters, and amphibious vehicles, DUKWs or Ducks. The Air Force delivered all 24 vessels to Mobile, Alabama in spring 1944 to start the remodeling process. Some 5,000 personnel underwent a complex training process that prepared them to rebuild the vessels and operate them once on the water. By the end of the year, the vessels departed Mobile.

Space Shuttle

In 1984, NASA wanted to display the revolutionary Space Shuttle at the New Orleans World's Fair. NASA needed a runway long enough to land a specially modified 747 carrying the Space Shuttle on its back. Once on land, the Shuttle was too big to transport by road or rail, so the runway had to have immediate access to a deep-water port where the craft could be loaded onto a barge and carried to the World's Fair site. Once again, Brookley's unique combination of long runway and deep-water port at Arlington Point saved the day, and it was the only facility able to handle the transfer.

Right: Catherine Hain in front of the Space Shuttle, when it landed in Brookley Field in 1984.

LT. FRANCIS CLARK
. . . jumps to safety.

Pilot Survives Jet Crash Here

A Brookley test [illegible] ed yesterday afternoon from an F84F jet fighter-bomber and landed in an open field on Clubhouse

1950's Jets

In the 1950s Brookley became a center to perfect jet planes. To protect civilians, jets launched and flew over the bay. Sergeant Thomas Robert Willis, USAF, was positioned in a hut outside Ft. Gaines, and it was his job to rescue pilots who might crash into the waters. Only one pilot crashed into Dog River in 1957, but he ejected and survived. The image on the left is from the Mobile Register.

Brookley's Closing

The Secretary of Defense, Robert S. McNamara announced its closure in 1964, widely believed to be President Lyndon Johnson's retaliation for Alabama voting for his opponent Barry Goldwater in the 1964 presidential election. At the time of the decision to phase out this enormous base, its resources included roughly 2,000 acres of land at Brookley and 94 on Dauphin Island. Its overall replacement value was estimated at $253,700,000. There were 29 miles of roads, eight miles of railroad track, two major runways: one 9600 feet long and the other 8852 feet, more than a million and a half square feet of covered maintenance space and covered warehouse space of 2,600,000 square feet. When Brookley officially closed in June 1969, nearly 10% of the local workforce lost their jobs, greatly affecting the local economy. This was the largest base closure in history. Since the closing of Brookley Air Force Base, it has been reinvented by the Mobile Airport Authority as the Brookley Complex and has become the home to industries, many related to the aerospace and technology fields including Teledyne Continental Motors, (now Continental Motors) Mobile Aerospace Engineering, Star Aviation, and EADS.

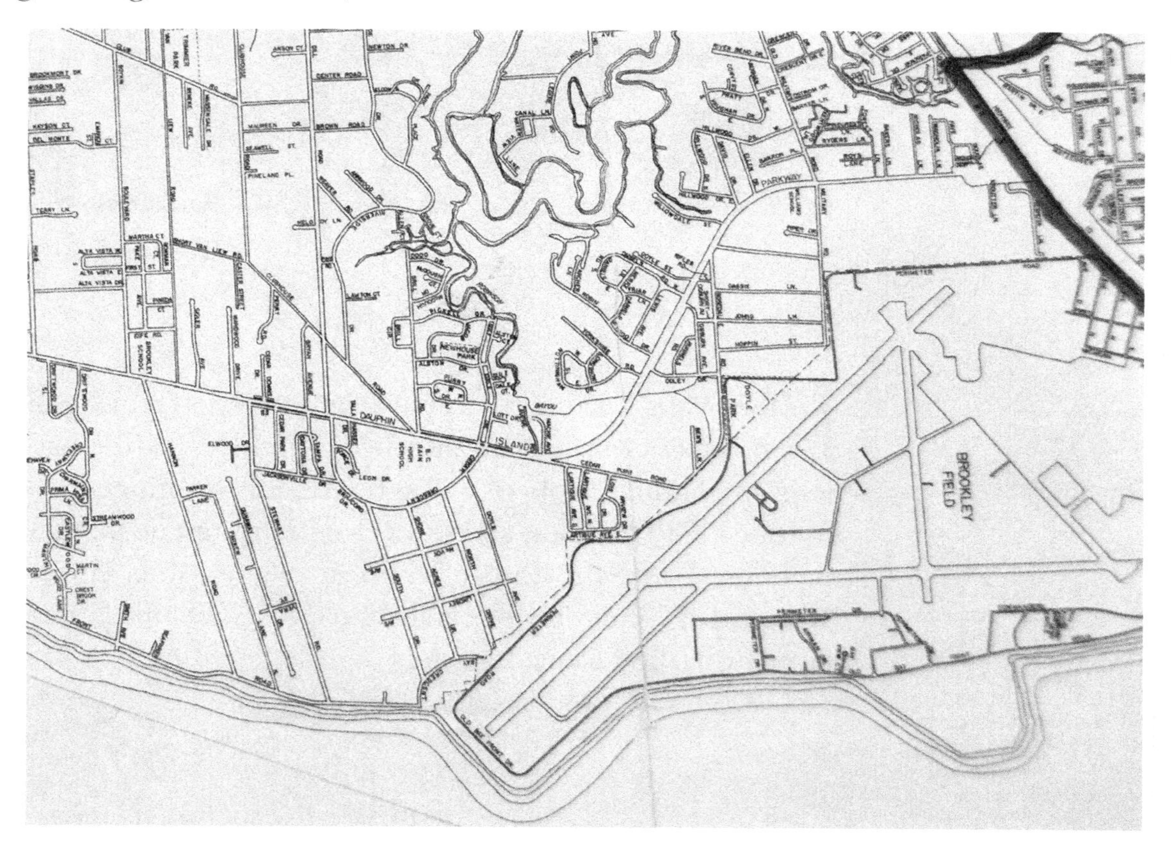

Above: Aerial view of Brookley Air Force Base in 1960. Courtesy of Mobile Municipal Archives.

Facing page: Map showing the runway that cut through Cedar Crescent neighborhood, and bisected Bay Shell Road. 1960. Courtesy of Mobile Municipal Archives.

Surviving the Closing of Brookley - One Story

"Crickets" by Eugene Moseley

Mr. Eugene Moseley, who sold crickets to survive after the closing of Brookey, went on to become a well known and successful insurance agent and investment counselor with Prudential. He described his cricket business below.

"My father taught me how to raise crickets. He sold them to neighbors for fishing, but I made a real business out of it after Brookley closed when I had to support three children. I built the cages and painted the upper part with enamel paint so that the crickets wouldn't be able to crawl out. I had to use Australian crickets because the local wild ones would not multiply. The way to raise them was to take peat moss and wet it, let the water soak in, and put it in the bottom of the cage. Then I put the crickets on top and fed them with a little chicken mash. When the crickets laid their eggs, I sold the adults because they wouldn't be able to lay eggs anymore. I'd sell them by the thousands. I shook them through a funnel into a quart jar which would hold about a thousand give or take a few. The crickets were perfect for catching brim because they had a little hood on their back where a hook could slide through. I had the sole dealership with Hoppe's Fish Camp and Don Q and others where people would buy crickets from my cages."

CHAPTER 21

Grand View Park

Many Mobilians have treasured memories of time spent at Grand View Park enjoying fishing off the 600-foot pier from a covered pavilion, swimming in the sandy shores of Mobile Bay, riding the colorful horses on the carousel, picnicking under the trees, or seeing exotic animals in the zoo. The park was located on the south side of Dog River, the site of the present-day Harbor Landing Apartments.

Mrs. Jean Hopper Turner and her brother, Mr. Bond Hopper's father was one of the managers of Grand View Park. "*The Government owned the park during World War II and used it as a recreation area for military people. The pavilion had a dance floor and a PX for beer and cigarettes. MPs stood at the gate and there were a few slot machines for servicemen, but not for civilians. There was a big walk-in safe where slot machines were kept on Sundays. Mr. Hopper ran the park for two years until the war ended. Joe Paluchi bought Grand View from the Government and added the famous carousel. There was also a house, an artesian well, civil war cannons for display, a small lake, horses to ride and a zoo. Men's bathing suits were made of wool and could be rented from the store.*"

Barbara McCafferty relates that "*some of my happiest childhood memories are of family visits to Grand View Park. I recall a beautifully wooded large area with all sorts of interesting, fun, and fascinating experiences awaiting us. A long pier extended out over beautiful Mobile Bay with a sandy beach to walk on. Warm summer days would find many families enjoying this unique area. Grand View Park boasted a small zoo with monkeys as one of the main attractions. On one of our many visits to the park, someone had handed a small mirror to one of the caged monkeys. It was beyond hilarious to watch the monkeys grimacing and laughing at their reflections in the mirrors. Another vivid memory is of the magnificent merry-go-round with beautiful prancing horses. The music lent to the enchantment as my brother and I rode around and around waving to our parents. In my memory, this was a carefree world, filled with the security of love, although these events happened during the great depression which profoundly affected my parents and most of our relatives and friends. To my knowledge, there was no charge attached to attendance at the park. Some time later, it was dismantled and now is home to beautiful, modern (and expensive) condominiums and apartments. I am forever thankful for these treasured memories.*"

The beach in front of Grand View Park. The old Dog River drawbridge can be seen in the distance.

Left: For years there was a Fourth of July swimming race from Fairhope to Grand View Park. This image shows the 1933 winners of the race in their woolen swim trunks with girl friends who cheered them on sitting on the Grand View Pier.

Above: A dance inside the Grand View Park Pavilion in the 1950s.

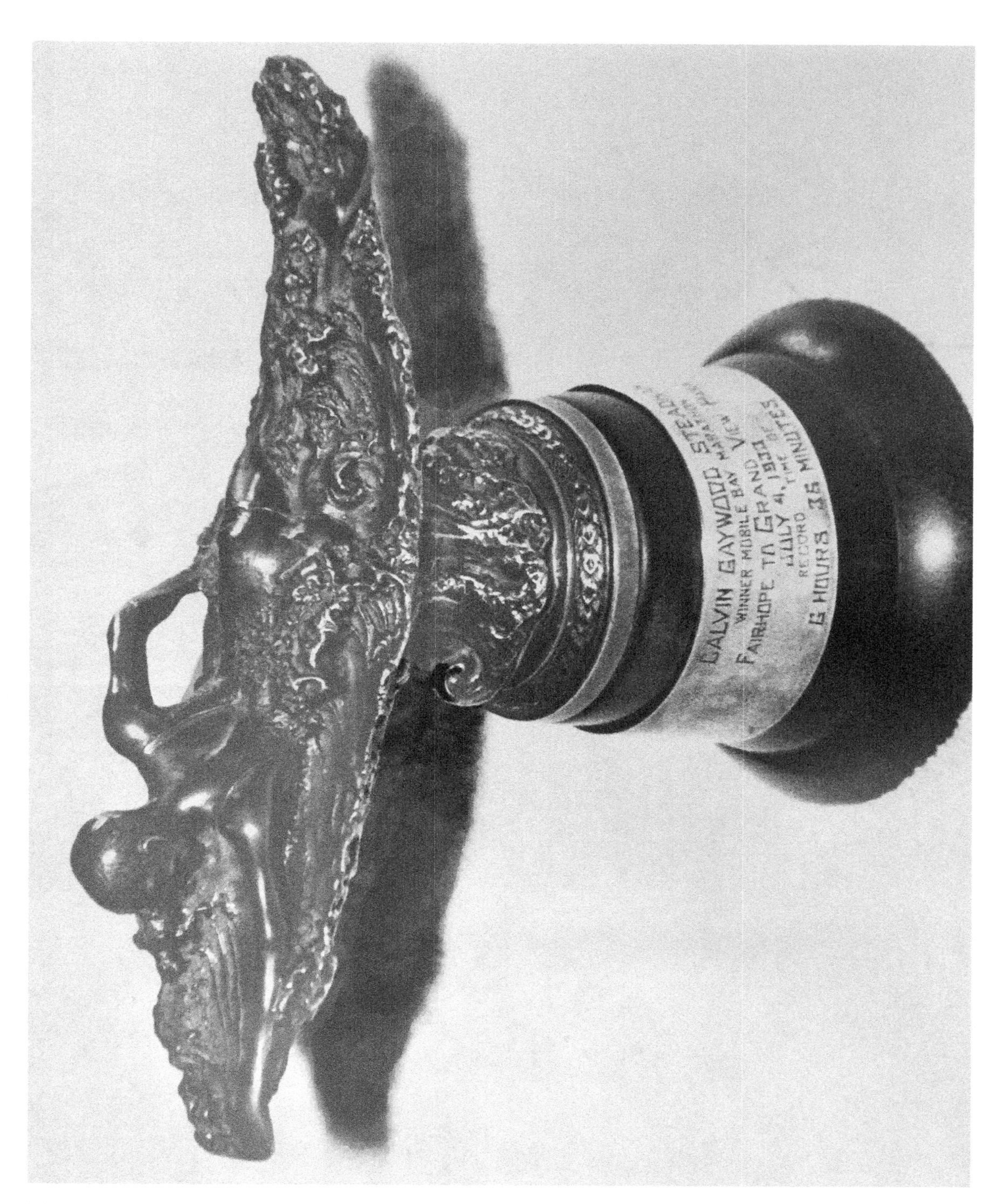

Trophy for winner of the Fairhope to Grand View Park Swimming race. Inscription: Calvin Gaywood Steadham, winner Mobile Bay Marathon, Fairhope to Grand View Park, July 4, 1933, record time of 6 hours 33 minutes.

CHAPTER 22
Night Clubs

Before it was annexed into the city of Mobile in 1956, South Mobile entertained a history of being more colorful and unrestricted than the original city of Mobile. In the 1940s and 1950s there were nineteen churches and almost as many night clubs. Some of the club names were The Vogue, The Brown Derby, Curtis Gordon's Radio Ranch, Don Q, Frazier's, Rio Vista, The Plaza, The Curve, The Zebra Club, Club Rendesvous, Rio Vista Night Club, The Beachcomber, and Allie Levene's Carosel and Happy Landing, all located on or near Cedar Point Road. (now Dauphin Island Parkway)

Curtis Gordon's Radio Ranch Night Club

Between 1952 - 1954, Curtis Gordon, originally from Georgia, released a number of 45s on RCA Victor, all of which sold solidly including three classics, "Draggin", "Mobile Alabama", and "Rock Roll Jump and Jive". Curtis opened the biggest Night Club in Mobile, called "Radio Ranch" where his style of western swing provided some of the best music around. People came from all parts of the South to experience that "Gordon Sound".

Facing Page Top: The Bay side of the Grand View Park Clubhouse.

Facing Page Bottom: The ponies at the park for children to ride.

Sharon Tharp Lindsay with Curtis Gordon at the Radio Ranch in the early 1950s. Photos courtesy of Sharon Tharp Lindsay.

A show inside the Radio Ranch, 1950s.

Elvis made several appearances at shows at the Radio Ranch Club, at the beginning of his career in 1955, sharing the bill with Gordon and his "Radio Ranch Boys" on at least three occasions. A Mobile Register ad reads, "Wed and Thurs, June 29 and 30, (1955) a subsid. Of Do Drive In, 8:30 p.m.-1:00 a.m., 4 1/2 hours of fun and dancing, In Person, Elvis Presley, Scotty and Bill, "That's All Right Mama", "Blue Moon of Kentucky", "Good Rockin' Tonite","Heartbreaker", plus Curtis Gordon's Radio Ranch Boys." Some local churches were not so enamored with Elvis because of his "gyrations", and even had a "music burning" of his records, Ivan Boatwright, former resident recalled.

"Elvis thought he was tough, but he found out the river boys were tougher"
Sonny Hall

Elvis returned on October 28th, performing shows at the Greater Gulf State Fair and Vigor High School. Sylvia Osborne remembers "*a swarm of teenage girls chasing the heartbreakingly gorgeous rebel musician across the Ladd Stadium football field.*" Sonny Hall, the owner of the Beachcomber recalls riding horses and fishing with Elvis along Dog River on mounts from Grand View Park on the south shore of Dog River. He recalled that "*Elvis thought he was tough, but he found out the river boys were tougher.*"

Other famous performers, like Jerry Lee Lewis came to the Radio Ranch. On November 6, 1958, the Mobile Register advertised "The Jerry Lee Lewis Show. See the blond-headed ball of fire tonite at Beautiful Radio Ranch, Mobile's largest nite spot! Located on Cedar Point Road. Dance after the show to the music of Don Davis & the Dixie All Stars. Don't Miss It!"

Happy Landing

Another well known night club of the 1940s on Cedar Pt Road was Happy Landing. Both this club and the Carosel were owned by the Levene family. There you could dance to such classics as "Night and Day", "Sentimental Journey", "Paper Doll", and "I'll be Seeing You". Ed Berger Sr., father of Edward Berger Jr., former Fire Chief of Mobile, was a pianist at Happy Landing in the 1940s.

Happy Landing Night Club. Belle Brown, Singer, Ed Berger Sr. on the keyboards, and Hugh Coleman on saxophone. 1944. Photo courtesy of Ed Berger Jr.

Happy Landing Night Club. 1944. Photo courtesy of Ed Berger Jr.

The Beachcomber 1930-1988

The Beachcomber is a colorful icon etched into the memories of thousands of people. George Hall, the son of Mary Pearson Hall who owned the Beachcomber said, "*Bailey's is where you went to eat and the Beachcomber is where you went to get drunk*". Most of the images of the club were lost in Hurricane Katrina but the Hall's have salvaged a cast made in 1988 of the old Beachcomber showing Mary Pearson's white Cadillac and club's location relative to the old Dog River Bridge, and an original drawing of the Beachcomber logo drawn on a paper napkin. A modern fixed-span bridge replaced the charming old Dog River drawbridge in the late 1990s. Its construction damaged portions of a three-hundred-year-old important archaeological site which resulted in a three-year archaeological dig by archaeologists and students from the University of South Alabama. The construction of the new bridge forced the demise of this long-popular gathering spot.

Beachcomber (continued)

Excerpts from an article in the Mobile Register by Earl Sweatt on Nov 15, 1988, detail the final days of the Beachcomber with an interview with the owner, Mary Hall. "The Beachcomber was named after a friend, a guy we knew as Shorty who worked on the rainroad. He could often be found walking down the beach picking up bottles to be sold for what he called his "mad money". Ms. Hall said they started calling him Beachcomber and decided to name the club after him.

"We've had weddings under that giant oak tree, and at one time we had fish fries on Friday nights, and people would be lined up outside. People really liked those mullet fillets. If you kept your paper plate, it was $1.50 for all the fish you could eat, If you got another paper plate, it cost another $1.50."

"The Beachcomber wasn't always a club. When it first opened in about 1930, it was a kind of corner grocery store and the only one on Hollingers island with a telephone", she recalled. "Uncle Bob Pearson would sit around the pot belly stove and if a customer came in and wanted to buy something, but didn't have the correct change, he might as well go on down the road. Uncle Bob didn't want to be disturbed."

Mary lamented the closing. "There won't be any crowds of people at the club during the Christmas on Dog River boat parade, or times like the old Dog River Fishing Rodeo when the place was packed to the rafters. Those days will be gone along with lots of memories."

Ms. Hall did not believe there was a need for a multi-million dollar bridge. "They could put it on the other side just as well", she said. Although Ms. Hall and her sons, George and Leslie "Caboose", fought against the state and the bridge construction, in the end they knew they would be out of business because the construction of the bridge would take two years and required the frontage of the Beachcomber. The Beachcomber became history on Wednesday, November 16, 1988 when it was boarded closed. "My sons and myself really appreciate everything the people have done for us over the years. The club has been good to the Hall family and the people have been the best. I'm really going to miss them and the club."

Right: The Beach-comber in the 1970s.

Below: The original drawing of the Beachcomber logo. Courtesy of Sonny Hall.

BEACHCOMBER

CLUB AND EATERY INC

Downtown Dog River, Ala.

ORIGINALLY ESTABLISHED APRIL 17, 1955, BY THE HALL FAMILY
CURRENTLY OPERATED BY GEORGE L. HALL AND BEVERLY B. HALL

APPETIZERS

SEAFOOD GUMBO - A Bounty of the Gulf Coast's Finest
Cup.......2.75
Bowl.......3.75

NACHOS -
A Tijuana Temptation-Dog River Style.......4.50

FRIED MUSHROOMS -
Served with Our Chef's Special Horseradish Sauce.......3.95

CRAB CLAWS - A House Favorite
Fried - Golden Brown and Served with Our Own Cocktail Sauce
Marinated - Laced with Our Special Herb Vinegarette Dressing
1/2 Pound.......7.25
1 Pound.......11.95

ENTREES

RIBEYE STEAK - 10 Ounces USDA Choice
Cooked to Perfection and Served with Grilled Onions.......11.95

GOLDEN FRIED SHRIMP -
Lightly Breaded with a Hint of Cajun Flair.......8.25

FRIED OYSTERS -
Delicately Fried to a Golden Brown.......8.95

FRESH SEAFOOD PLATTER -
An Ample Array of Shrimp, Oysters, Crab Claws, Fish Filet and Stuffed Crab Served with Twin Sauces.......10.25

THE BEACHCOMBER CATCH OF THE DAY -
Please Consult Your Server.......Market Price

CAJUN CHICKEN BREAST - Boneless
Flavorfully Grilled with a Hint of Pepper.......5.95

HAWAIIAN CHICKEN BREAST - Boneless
Glazed with a Tropical Flair.......5.95

COMBER COMBINATION - The Best of Both Waters
Fried Shrimp and Fried Oysters.......9.20

All Entrees are Served with Tossed Salad, and a Choice of Combination Brown and White Rice Pilaf or French Fries.

SIDE ORDERS

TOSSED SALAD.......1.25
FRENCH FRIES.......1.50
ONION RINGS.......1.75
HUSHPUPPIES.......1.25

PLEASE CONSULT YOUR SERVER FOR CHEF'S DAILY SPECIALS

ALL TO GO ITEMS
.50 EXTRA

SANDWICHES

GRILLED CHEESE.......2.75
With Bacon.......3.50

REUBEN GRILL -
Thinly Sliced Corned Beef, Baby Swiss Cheese, Sauerkraut, and Russian Dressing on Grilled Rye.......4.50

B.L.T. -
Crisp Bacon, Lettuce and Thinly Sliced Tomato on Toasted White Bread.......3.20

CLUB SANDWICH -
A Double Decker with Thinly Sliced Turkey, Ham, Crisp Bacon, Baby Swiss Cheese, Lettuce and Tomato.......4.95

SHRIMP PO BOY -
Served on a Crisp Captain's Roll.......3.95

OYSTER PO BOY -
Served on a Crisp Captain's Roll.......4.10

BURGERS

HAMBURGER - 1/4 Pound 100% Freshly Ground Chuck.......3.10
With Bacon.......3.85

CHEESEBURGER - 1/4 Pound 100% Freshly Ground Chuck.......3.40
With Bacon.......4.15

SEASONAL SEAFOOD
(When Available, Please Consult Your Server)

BOILED SHRIMP.......Market Price
OYSTERS ON THE HALF SHELL.......Market Price
CRAWFISH.......Market Price

BEVERAGES

TEA.......60
Sanka or MAXWELL HOUSE COFFEE.......60

Consult Your Server For Bar Favorites

Before the Beachcomber was torn down, Mary Hall had this model made of the Beachcomber showing its relationship to Dog River Bridge. 1988.

Club Rendezvous

We felt it was our duty to entertain the boys.

Katharine Phillips Singer

Katharine Phillips Singer recalled an evening at Club Rendezvous: "*Everything started at Frascatti beach and went all the way to Dog River. Night clubs had sprung up all along Cedar Point Road. The most famous night club was called the Airport Restaurant – real important dates were taken there – the other clubs were considered "joints" on Cedar Point Road.*"

"*One night three of my girlfriends and four marines went to Club Rendezvous. The marines had not been too long from Guadalcanal. We settled in and danced. A sailor bumped into one of the ladies on the dance floor, and my date asked him to apologize to the lady. He refused, so they escorted us back to the table and said excuse us, we'll be right back. They took the sailor outside. He returned kind of swaggering. The sailor then had some of his friends join him to challenge the marines. They went outside again, only to return to challenge the marines once more. Then a Navy Chief came over, grabbed the sailor by his collar and said, "Haven't you learned your lesson? Leave those damn Marines alone!" We felt it was our duty to entertain the boys.*"

Left: Mrs. Katharine Phillips Singer

Facing page top: From left to right, Mr. Mrs William McCants, Mr and Mrs. W.H. Bullen, and Mr. and Mrs. R. L. Rouillier enjoy an evening at the Plaza on Cedar Pt. Road. 1944. Photo courtesy of the Bullen Family.

Facing page bottom: A Plaza Souvenir Photo Cover, 1944.

SOUVENIR PHOTO

The New

PLAZA

Alabama's Largest
and Most Luxurious Night Club

AIR CONDITIONED

ON CEDAR POINT ROAD -:- MOBILE, ALABAMA

CHAPTER 23
Businesses

Corrine's Kitchen
Owner: Corrine Williams

Before many women had their own businesses, Corrine Williams created, owned and operated a very successful restaurant on Dauphin Island Parkway in the 1940s. The restaurant was in business for over forty years. It was located in front of the current Galliard Elementary School. Hal Tippins frequented the restaurant and enjoyed talking with Ms. Williams. He remembered that "*You could bring her wild game and swap it out for meals. She would feed you and you could pay her later. There would sometimes be a high stakes gambling game on Saturday nights. She kept her oven door shut with a well-worn two by four. It was a friendly place. Sometimes she would get a customer to check the oven.*" Ms. Williams also worked for Congressman Frank Boykin in the 1940s, caring for his chidren.

Mobile Press Register image from an article about Corrine Williams and her restaurant. 1970s.

Facing Page: Hal Tippins and Corrine Willams inside her restaurant in 1983. Image courtesy of Mr. Tippins.

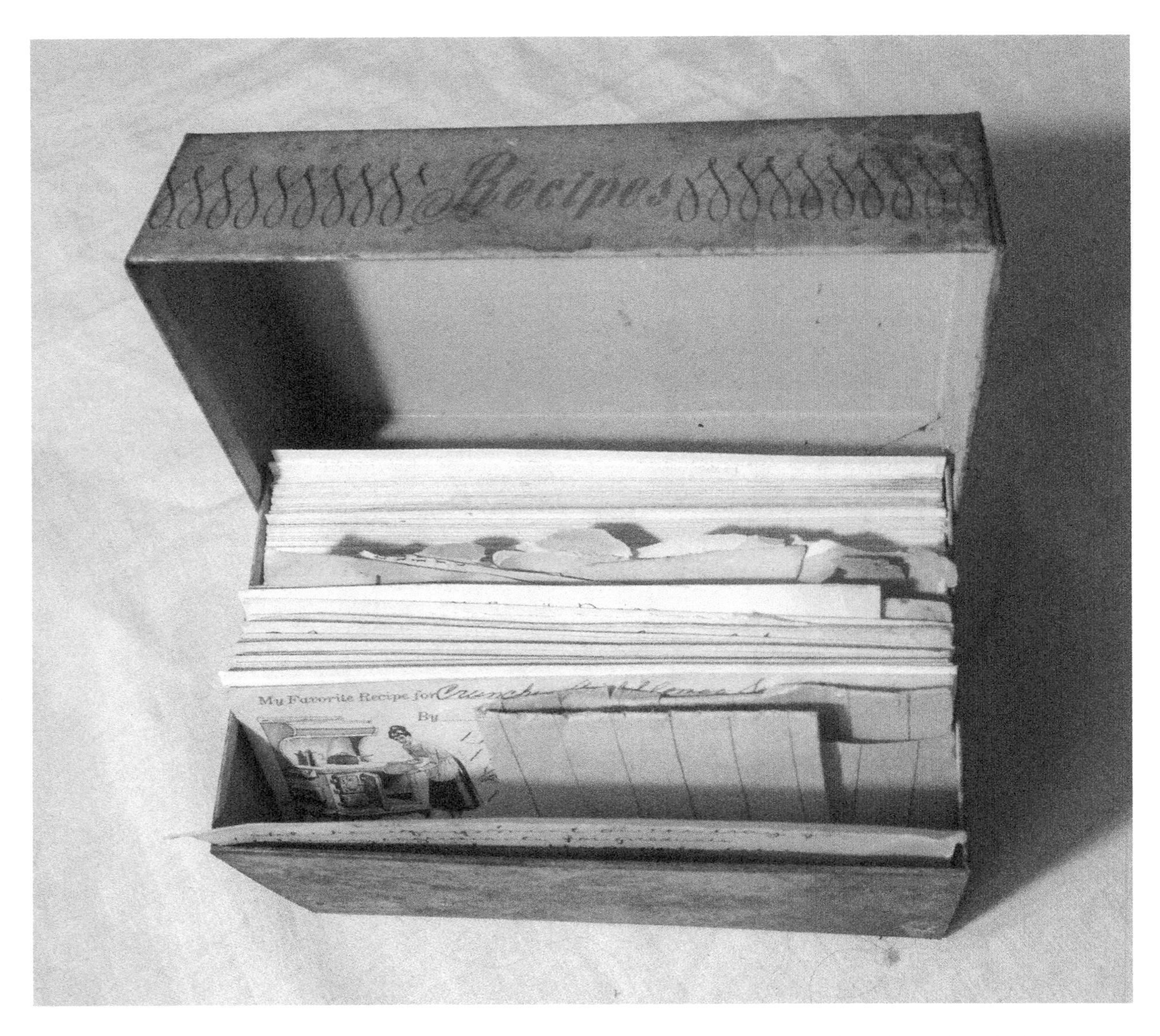

One of Corrrine William's relatives, Mrs. Martha Pringle Kidd, shared this image of Corrine's recipe box, (above) and on the facing page, Corrine's recipe for Crab Cakes in Corrine's handwriting.

Crab Cakes

1. LB Crab meat
1. tsp old Bay seasoning
1/4 tsp. Salt

1. tabelspoon of mayonaise
1. tablespoon Worchestershere
1. tea. chopper parsley

1 teas. Baking powder

1 Egg 2. Slices of Breed.

mix like you do when

making hambergers. Frey
in tee Brown crisp

Crystal Pool 1933-1939

In February of 1933, it was announced that "Mobile's Most Beautiful Swimming Place" would be completed. It was created from an artesian spring located across from present day Fort Whiting. The price to swim was ten cents in this large pool with a sandy bottom surrounded by boardwalks. Near the pool were dressing rooms, a concession stand, and "ample seating under beautiful moss-covered trees for non-swimmers". The construction of Brookley Field and World War II led to its destruction.

Above and on facing page: Views of the swimming fun at the Crystal Pool that was located on property later replaced by Brookley Field. Images courtesy of the Mobile Municipal Archives.

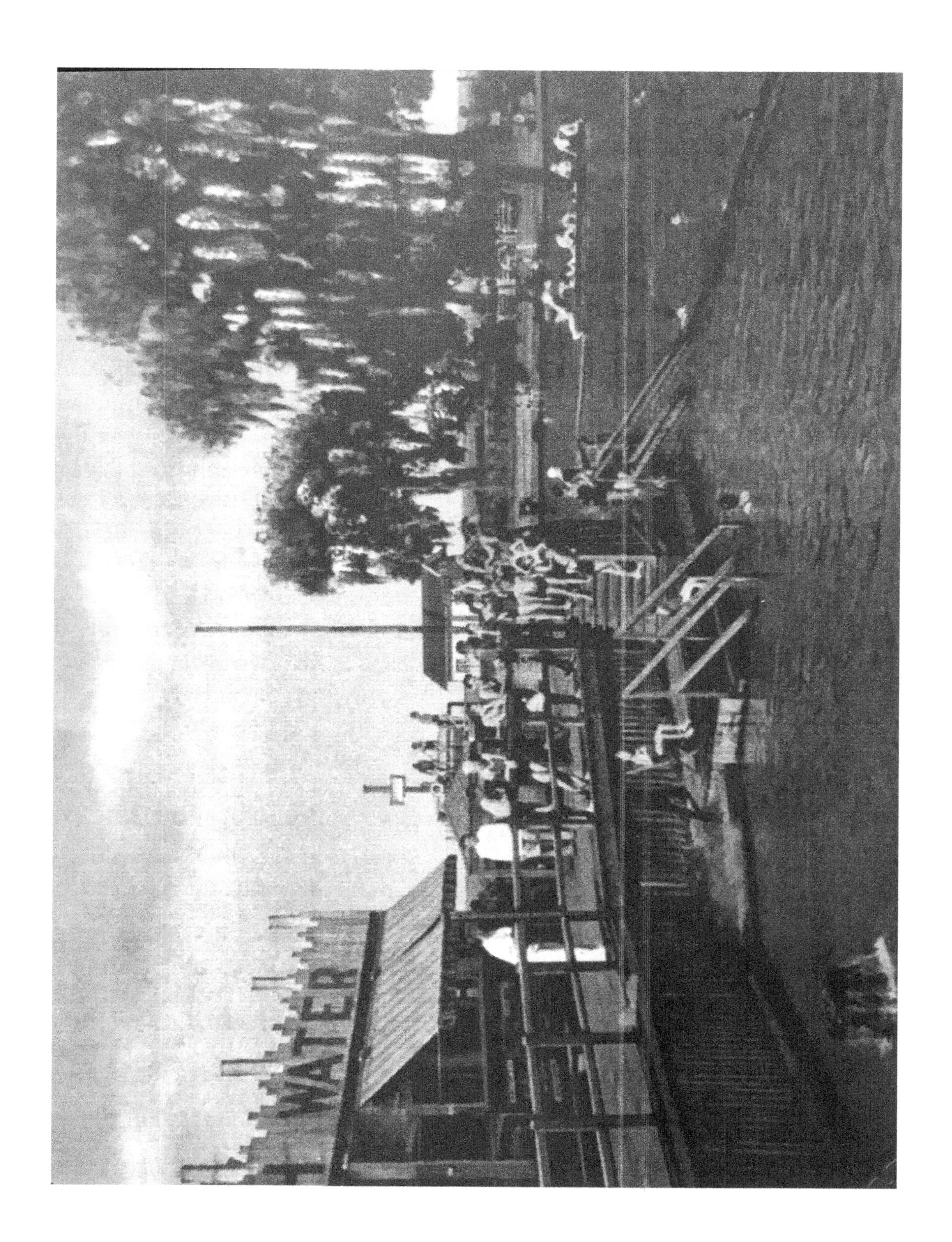

149
Businesses - Crystal Pool

Dog River Marina

"I never worked a day in my life"
Sonny Middleton.

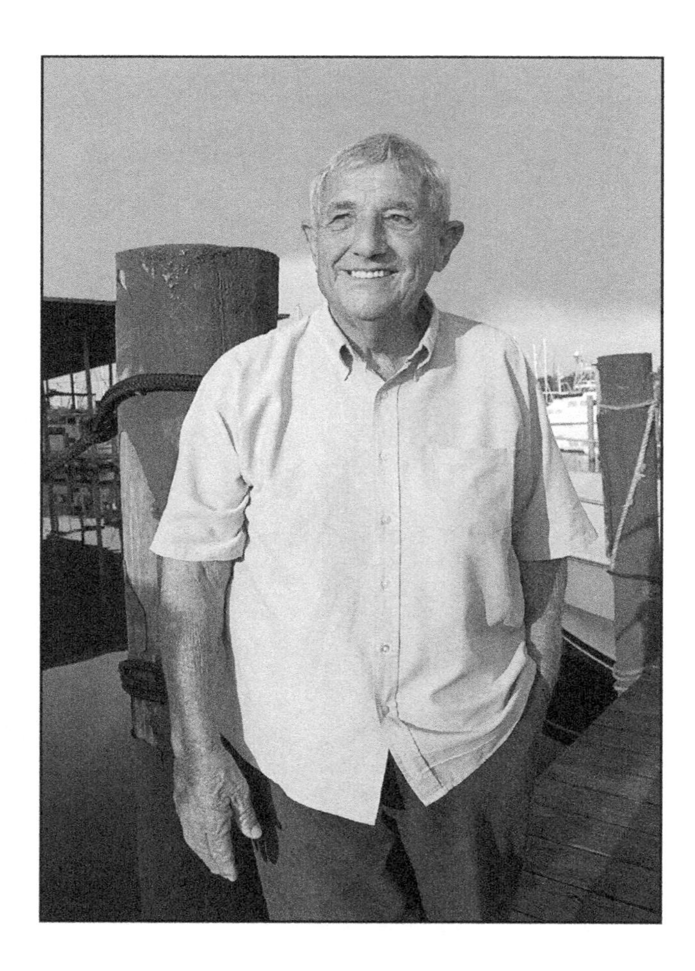

Dog River Marina is forever linked to its founder, Sonny Middleton. Although he was only nineteen when his father, John Middleton, passed away in 1957, Sonny took charge and formed Middleton Marine Engine Service. Over the next sixty years he grew the business to include Dog River Marina, A&M Yacht Sales, Dog River Fuel and Supply, and Middleton Marine. He said it was a team effort and that he did not have employees but family and friends. He loved what he did and always said "he never worked a day in his life".

Dog River Marina was named Marina of the Year in 2000, and was the first to receive the Clean Marina designation in the state of Alabama.

Above: Sonny Middleton, owner and founder of Dog River Marina. photo courtesy of Dog River Marina

Facing Page: Dog River Marina, 1967. Photo courtesy of Sonny Middleton.

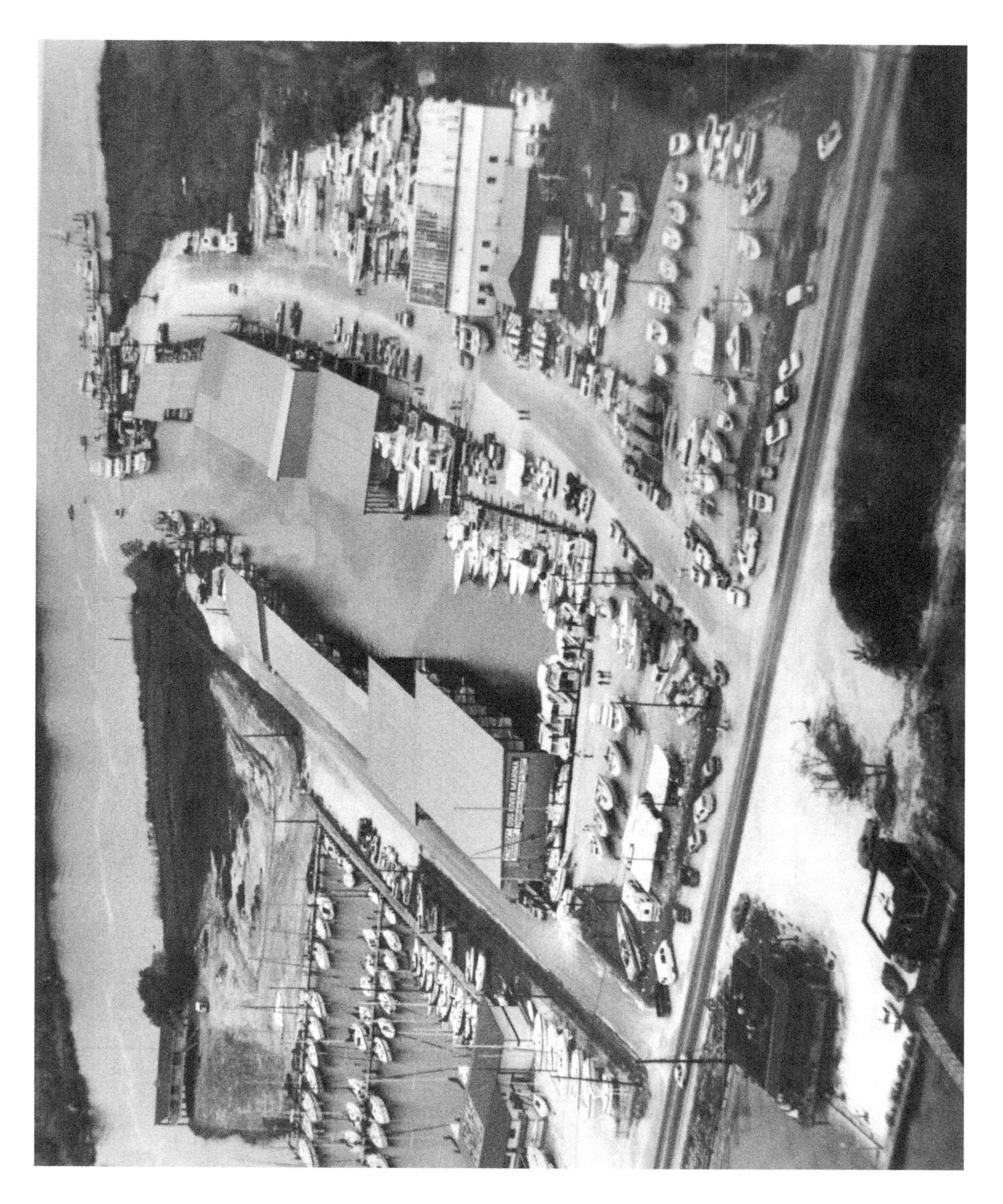

Businesses - Dog River Marina

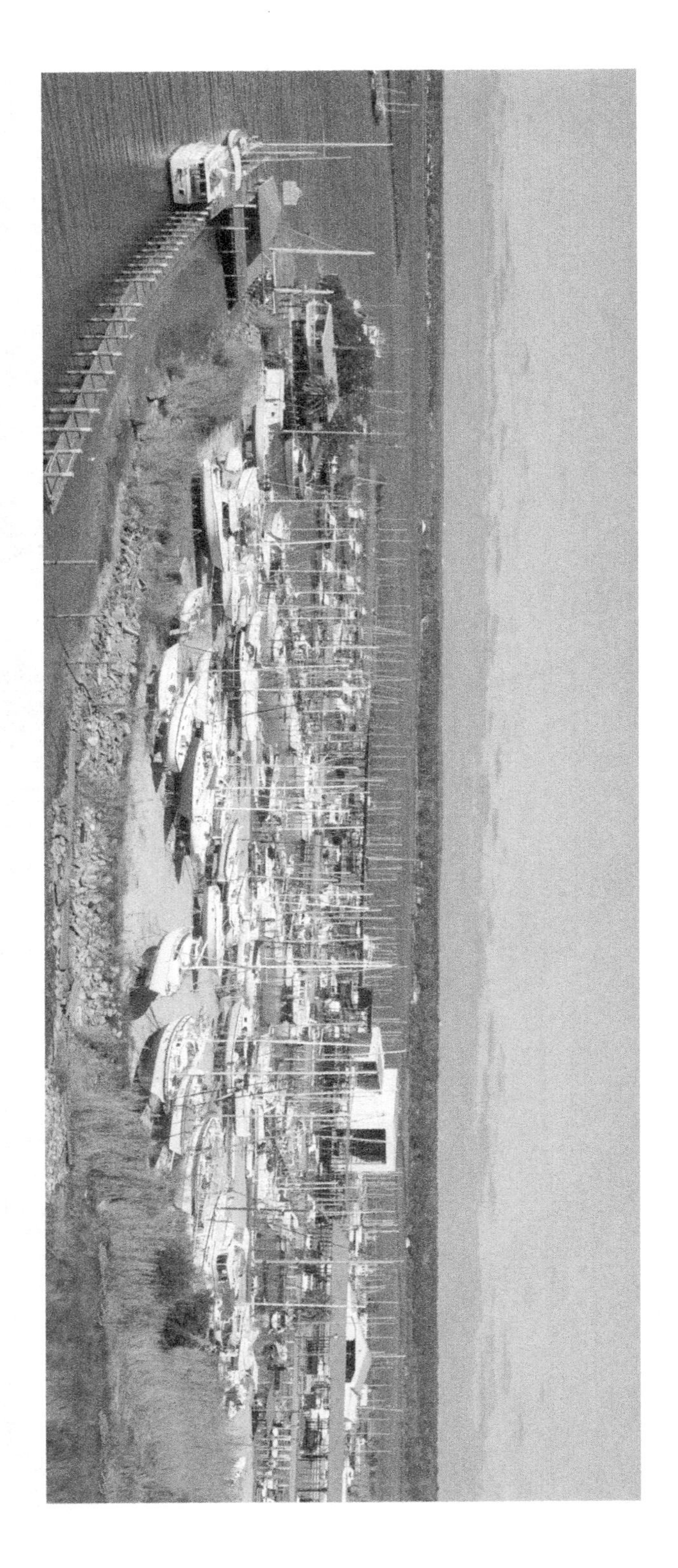

Dog River Marina, 2018.
Photo by Susan Rouillier

The Grand Mariner Restaurant and Marina

An iconic landmark on Dog River, The Mariner was established in the 1940s by Herb Frost. He kept a boat at the marina until the 1980s and would often fuel up and visit with friends. Sonny Middleton who later owned and operated Dog River Marina, Middleton Marine and A&M Yacht Sales was one of his employees. Mr. Frost died in the 1990s when he accidently drove into Dog River. The Blue Jay Restaurant, originally at Springdale Mall, rented the restaurant prior to Mr. Frost's death.

Dorothy, Bill and Mary Moore purchased the property in the late 1970s. The Restaurant was turned over to Hollis Gray who changed the name to the S.S. Mariner and ran it until 1992 when he gave up the lease to run a restaurant on Cody Road.

Capt. Eddie Carlson and his wife, Louise bought the Restaurant and Marina in 1982. The Carlson family saw the "for sale" sign on the property, asked Bill Moore the price, and shook hands to seal the deal. Captain Carlson captained John B. Waterman, Lyman Hall, as well as the Robert E. Lee, one of three sister-ships built for Waterman in the mid 1970s: Stonewall Jackson, Robert E. Lee and Sam Houston, commercial cargo vessels traveling between the U.S. East and Gulf Coasts and ports in the Indian Ocean via the Suez Canal.

The Carlson's had four children who still own and run the facilities today. The community looks forward to the first Saturday of December for the annual Christmas on the River Boat Parade organized by the Grand Mariner every year since they accepted running it in the 1980s from the Mobile Yacht Club.

Next Page: The Grand Mariner Restaurant, 2018. Photo by Susan Rouillier

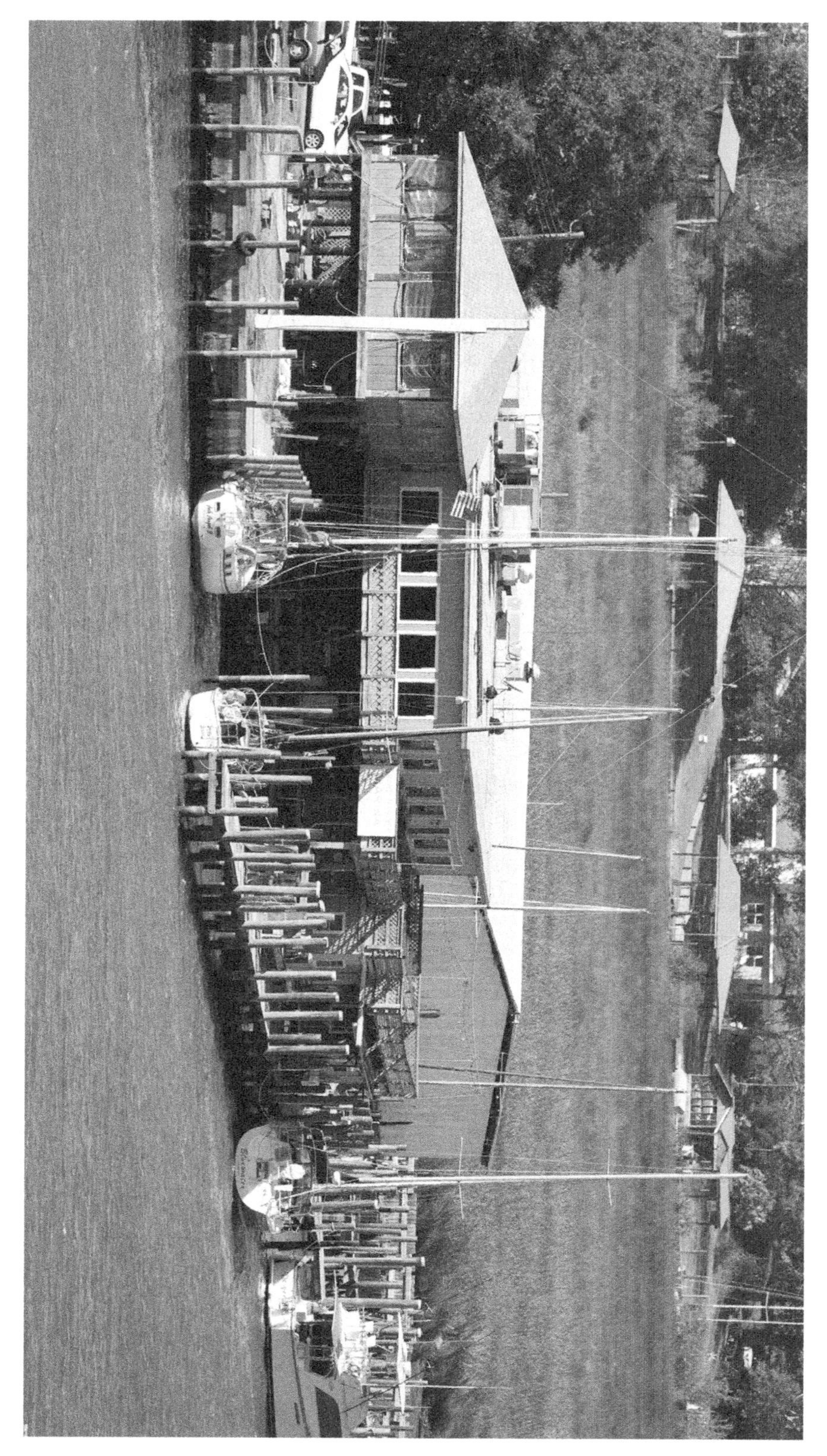

154
Businesses - Grand Mariner Restaurant

Jackson Store

Jackson store, built in the 1920s was a landmark at the corner of Cedar Point and Hannon Roads. Inside was an inviting and warm community gathering place where customers could purchase candy, snacks, bread, and cut meats. Several small tables were on one side for workmen to stop by after work to unwind and talk before heading home. The front entrance had a covered roof sheltering glass-topped pumps for gas and kerosene. Three steps up brought customers through screen doors that remained open during the summer months.

Closest: Lillian Jackson (Dutie), Mrs. Mamie Larsen Jackson, Mrs. Thelma Wilhelmina Jackson Reimer, and unidentified. (Picture courtesy of Dr. and Mrs. Dan Reimer)

Mamie Larsen was born in 1897 and married Dan Jackson in 1913. They moved to the corner of Cedar Point and Hannon Roads and built the Jackson Store in the 1920s. Dan and his friends built a thirty-foot sailboat on this property and in order to launch it, used logs to roll the boat down Hannon Road, a distance of one mile, into the bay. Widowed at a young age, Mrs. Mamie Jackson put her efforts into raising her four children and running the store. Their children were Thelma, Lillian, Gaillard, and Aaron.

She is remembered as a benevolent and caring person who would help those in need of food. Years after the store was gone, people would stop by Mrs. Jackson's home to pay a little on their bills. She would take out the old paper register, record their payment, and continue to encourage them. Today an apartment complex sits on the site of the old Jackson Store.

Peter Dais III, who lived on Hannon Road, related that as a little black child in the 1950s, he and his friends would go in the Jackson store and buy bubble gum or candy while grown white men sat at tables eating. "*No one ever messed with us. We did not live in fear here.*" He attributed their good behavior to the civilized and honorable standards set by Mrs. Jackson. "*We had to go downtown to experience Jim Crow at places like Kress's and Woolworth's.*"

Mrs. Joan Lorge remembers that even though someone else offered Mrs. Jackson a much higher price for land that she and her husband had only verbally offered, Mrs. Jackson honored her agreement with the Lorge family.

Mrs. Jackson's daughter, Lillian Jackson, became an outspoken community watchdog of Mobile City's Government. For years, she bravely criticized their decisions and methods both at their meetings, and through the newspaper, radio and television. For example, before its construction, Lillian foresaw the problems of the modern Mobile Government Plaza Building, dubbing it "Gump Tower" because of its seventy-three million-dollar price tag and large open, unusable space. She kept local government on its toes, and later they honored her by designating a "Lillian Jackson Day" in the city of Mobile. A true trailblazer, Lillian also was the first female assistant bank trust manager in Mobile in 1971.

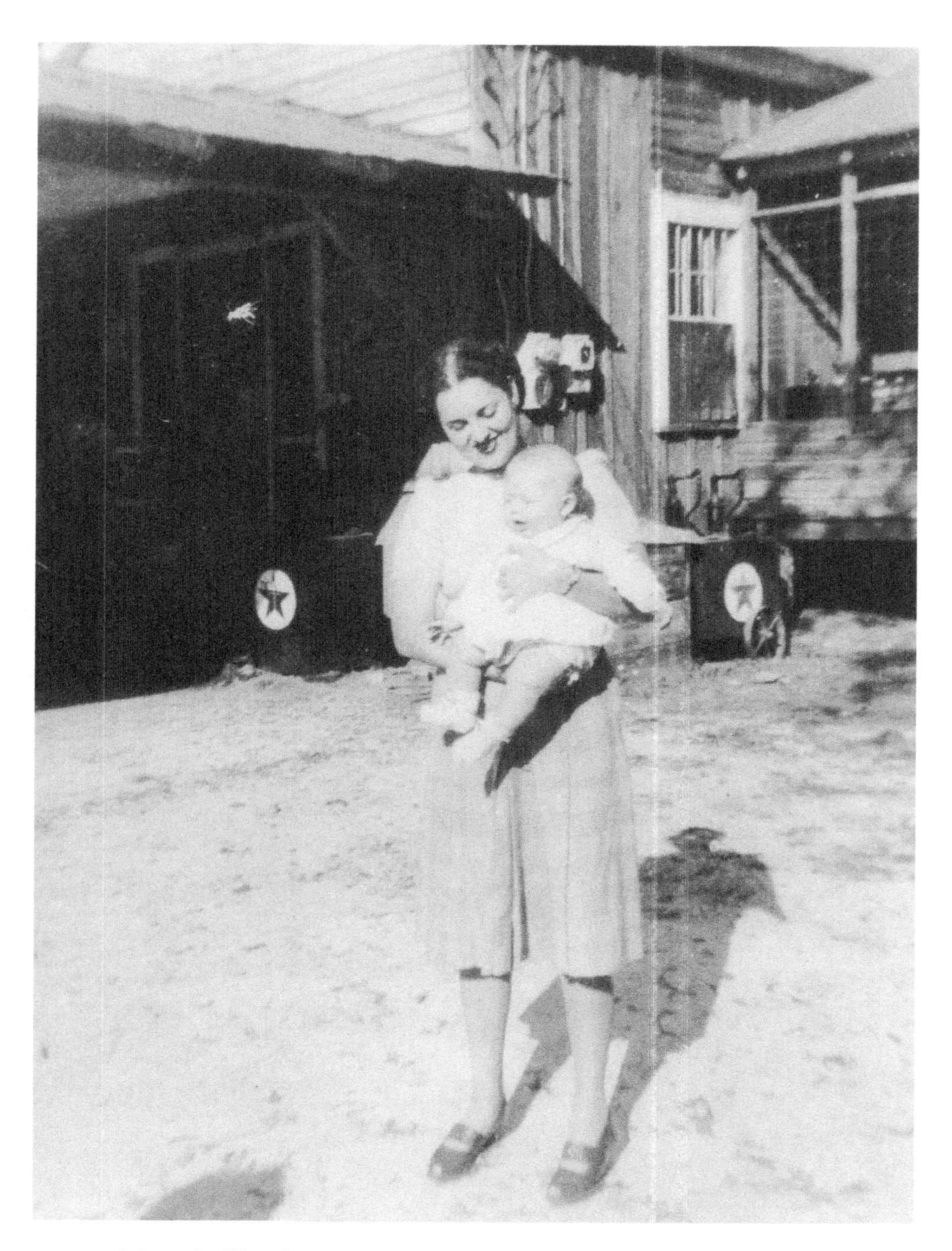

Mrs. Gaillard Jackson in front of Jackson Store. 1940s.
Picture courtesy of Dr. and Mrs. Dan Reimer.

Miss Lillian Jackson with Jeff Sessions. 1970s. Pictures are courtesy of Dr. and Mrs. Dan Reimer.

Above: Miss Lillian Jackson, Mobile's first Assistant Trust Officer in 1971.

Below: Gaillard Jackson during WWII.

Shore Acres Nursery

1945-present

Why would a large nursery in Theodore be called Shore Acres Nursery, if there are no shores within miles of it? The answer is that the man who founded Shore Acres Nursery, Oliver Washington, Sr. began selling azaleas in 1945 at his home on Hannon Road, near the oldest neighborhood in South Mobile named Shore Acres because the streets ended at the shores of the Bayfront.

Shore Acres Plant Farm is still family owned, but it has grown tremendously from its simple beginning. It is now a huge greenhouse nursery located on a 50-acre facility in Theodore, Alabama. Shore Acres specializes in growing blooming seasonal annuals for the Gulf Coast Region. Clients consist of large retailers, landscape contractors, garden centers and local municipalities and the general public.

There are many notable Washington decendants South Mobile. One gandson, Melvin Washington, returned to Mobile after many years in New York. He holds an undergraduate degree in Electrical Engineering from Howard University, an MBA from New York University and completed the Administration Executive Education Program at Wharton School of Business. He held executive level positions in the financial services and telecommunications sectors at top tier firms including AT&T, Salomon Brothers, Morgan Stanley, JP Morgan Chase, and Citibank. In Mobile he has served on the boards of Prichard Preparatory School, Mobile Baykeeper and the Melton Center for Entrepreneurship and Innovation. Mr. Washington is currently the Regional Director of the Small Business Development Center at the University of South Alabama

Facing page: Mr. Oliver Washington, Sr., in 1945 with azaleas that he grew and sold on Hannon Road. Image courtesy of Shore Acres Nursery.

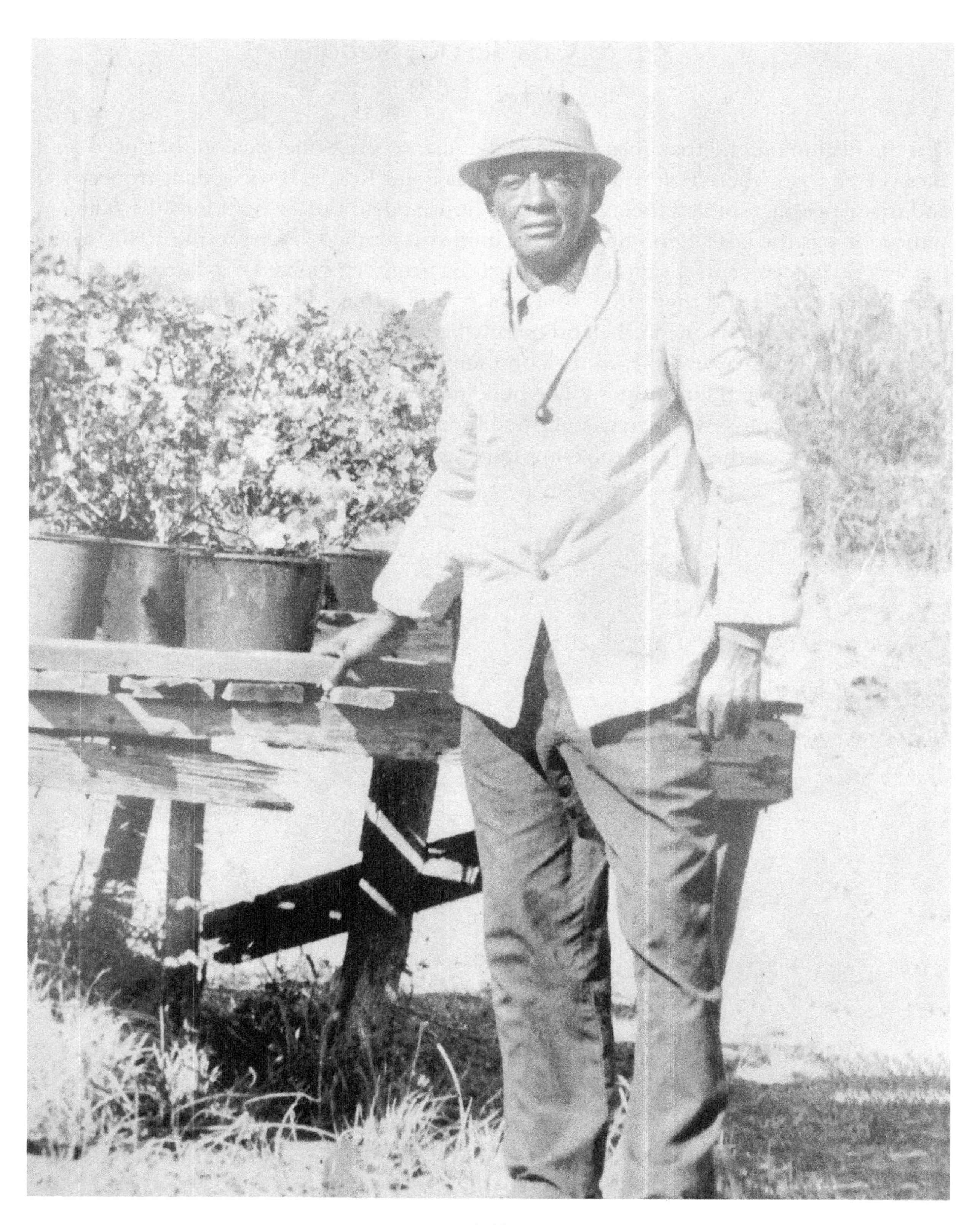

Businesses - Shore Acres Nurs-

Zip & Vic's Service Station
1945 - 1990

In the beginning, the triangular building, familiar to everyone, was on the curve on a two-lane road where Fulton Road met Cedar Point Roads. It was a dangerous spot and many people tumbled their car into the house next door or right into the filling station. It was the last station on the road until you reached Coden in the 1940s when gas was seventeen cents a gallon. It was built by brothers Zip and Vic Lartigue, right after World War II and they ran it until they retired in the 1990s. They were loved and respected by everyone in the community because they were generous, trusting, and helped virtually everybody in the community at one time or another during their decades of running their business. The building is still there and used as a tire store now, but the people who drive past it by still remember the generosity of the Lartigue brothers who kept the cars of the community running for so long.

This image shows Francis "Tutt" Singleton who worked with the Lartigues for twenty-six years, Zip Lartigue, Arthur Lartigue, and Victor Lartigue, in the early 1940s in front of their new Pan Am filling station. Image courtesy of the Lartigue family.

Zepra (Zip) Lartigue was a blacksmith who co-authored an ironwork book that was used by Southwest State Technical School, now Bishop State Community College. Victor (Vic) Ben Lartigue was an accomplished mechanic, served in the Army Air Corps, and when he returned from the war, he and Zip went into business to open the Pan-Am filling station. Pan-Am was considered a premium gas without lead and could be used in Coleman stoves. It was also used as a fuel for floundering lights. Many people stopped there to fill their lanterns before an evening of walking the bay looking for the tasty flat fish. Their father, Authur Lartigue retired from the shipyard, and helped in their business. Tutt Singleton worked with the Lartigues for twenty-six years until he retired. Over the years many people found their start into the work world at Zip and Vic's and each was given a nick-name. Some were Bill Wynn, Freddie Large, Chris Fairley, and Bill "bougar-red" Young.

The Lartigue brothers built, sold and repaired lawnmowers, copying the dimensions from the Lawnboy lawnmower design. They were not too concerned with patents, but had to stop making lawn mowers when the Lawnboy Company complained. People would bring their cars and lawnmowers from all over the city for repair because the brothers could repair almost anything. Vic used a stethoscope (an oak broom handle) to listen to sounds of the engine for diagnosing engine and other car ailments. The Air Force on Brookley Field came to him on several occasions to get advice on maintaining old aircraft. Once, the brothers even repaired a prosthetic leg for a customer.

Vic Lartigue built the first airboat in South Mobile. The brothers and father saw one in Florida, took measurements from it, came home and built one. They used the airboat for duck-hunting. When an airplane from Brookley crashed into the Mobile Delta in 1959, the Lartigues were asked to search for it in the airboat.

They did a lot of pro-bono work for people. One boy, Edward Detiege, lived on Hollinger's Island and rode his bicycle over six miles each way to go to school at Pure Heart of Mary. One day his bike broke on his way home, and the Lartigues repaired it. Edward said he had no money to pay, but the Lartigues repaired it anyway.

Bartering was a way of life. The Fraziers owned a large farm adjacent to the filling station. When the Frazier's crops would come in, they would bring the Lartigues corn, tomatoes, and other vegetables, in exchange for repair of some of their farm instruments when broken. The Fraziers also had an ice-crusher, ice house, and sold block ice, also used as barter. The only other place that sold ice was the Loop Ice house.

(Zip and Vic's Service Station, continued)

The Lartigues made their own acetylene gas, and when the area was annexed into the city, in 1956, the city fire inspector came to inspect the business. "What is this?" he asked. "It's a boiler full of acetylene gas used to fire the torches for blacksmithing." The inspector said appologetically, "You're in the city now and I have to shut this down. If it exploded, half the city would blow up". Vic also used coke and had a fire pit to make wrought iron pieces. He even made some of the altar pieces for Our Lady of Lourdes Catholic Church. They also sold propane to fill benzomatic bottles.

Vic was determined. One day a customer came in with a rattle in a Mercedes convertible. The customer was so frustrated that Vic agreed to ride down the road sitting in the trunk to find the rattle. Vic rode down the road but was unable to find the rattle. The man left the car with Vic who finally found the source of the rattle after a lot of searching and dismantling of the trunk. It was a golf ball rolling around in the tire well.

The business offered credit to customers. When a customer would buy gas, they could sign for it on a multi-layered paper card that was stored in a vertical metal filing box with slots for each customer. Once a month, the top copy of the paper bill would be mailed. As more and more stations came to Dauphin Island Parkway, gas wars began. "They went kicking and screaming to credit cards", Lou Lartigue related. Zip and Vic are gone, but the sweetness of the way they lived and treated people is remembered by thousands. There is a large boat on Dauphin Island named "The Zip and Vic" and they are also immortalized in Eric Erdman's "The DIP Song". (Information was provided by Zip Lartigue's son, Lou Lartigue)

Zip and Vics Service Station with their hand-built lawnmowers in front. 1960s.

Coulson's Boat Building
1940s

Charles Coulson, a university graduate in design engineering, was the head of a machine shop in Brookley during the war, and afterwards decided to start a boat building business. His first shop was on Bay Front Road across from Joe McGovern's Restaurant, where he built boats in his backyard. Later he opened a shop on Dauphin Island Parkway, south of Perch Creek near Dog River.

He taught his son Chilton the business. Chilton remembers helping his father pull boats out of the water when he was nine years old. One of Chilton's favorite boats that he built and still owns is a Baby Blue design out of Popular Mechanics Magazine. One of the Coulson's boats appeared in a documentary about "Alabama from North to South". The following photos are of boats built for Robert Stewart's father in the 1940s.

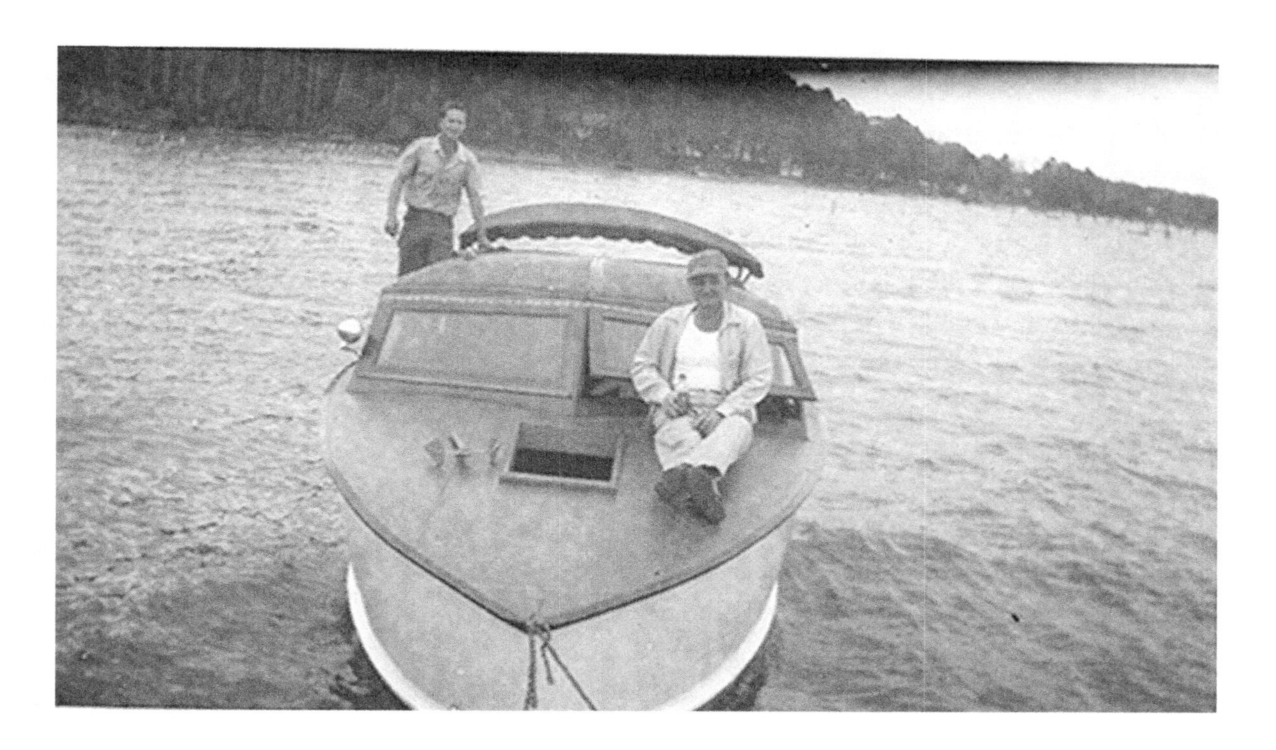

After the builder, Charles Coulson completed the boat, he enjoyed a launching party. He is standing in the back with a friend of the boat owner, Robert Stewart. 1940s. Photo courtesy of Robert Stewart.

CHAPTER 24
Schools

Congress Corner School - Race Track School
Circa 1890-1950s

Race Track School was the first school in South Mobile. The Gaines-Frazier family donated land for the school located near Cedar Point and Cedar Crescent Roads, close to New Hope Baptist Church, and volunteers from his large family and others actually built it themselves. It was called "Congress Corner School" and nicknamed "Race Track", because it was located very near the old Magnolia Race Course. A signature on the back of an image contributed by Mrs. Martha Pringle Kidd, reads, "Congress Corner School, May 6th, 1923, Mrs. L.D. Harris, In(structor)" The school appears to be in full operation in the image on the facing page in 1923. The school had a single teacher and one room for all grades. Mrs. Kidd (pictured above) was a student at Race Track in the late 1940s.

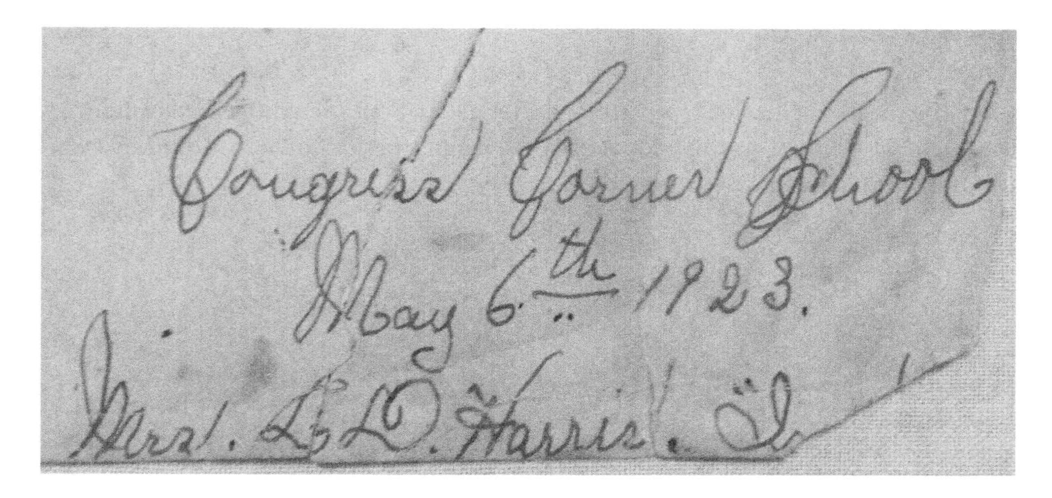

Congress Corner School
May 6th 1923.
Mrs. L. D. Harris. I.

Schools - Congress Corner School

South Brookley Elementary School
1942 - 2006

Students rode a school bus sitting on wooden benches to South Brookley when it opened in September of 1942. Because little money was available due to WWII efforts, the school had minimal facilities, so students brought their lunches. Students worked in wooden desks with inkwells in a building housing eight classrooms for grades first through eighth. Boys carried wood inside for the stoves to heat the building and volunteered to be on safety-patrol. If students misbehaved, they were "taken to the woodshed".

With no intercom, many local people recall that the principal, Mrs. Becton, rang a hand-held bell to call students inside for the start of the school day and for all other events during the daytime. Mrs. Jean Hopper Turner who taught second grade at South Brookley sewed dresses for children who needed them. She also said, "*Mrs. Becton was tough, but she made a good teacher out of me.*"

Mrs. Linda Jones recalled transoms to cool the rooms on hot days, and a coal heater in each room. "*When the weather was cold, we had to have coal put in each heater. Someone would get the janitor, and he would bring a gig bucket of coal. This would happen a couple of times a day. The teacher would allow us to take our shoes off and put our feet on the heaters. They were just warm enough to heat our feet a little bit. This old fashioned classroom is always on my mind.*"

Harriet Sue Shaw Pitts remembered a Mardi-Gras parade down the hallway. "*The students made little floats and walked down the hallway and turned around and came back.*"

Everyone worked together. The Parent-Teachers-Association and the community furnished labor and funding to build the first cafeteria in 1946. The school's library was created by parent volunteer hours in 1951-52. Another building housing six classrooms was completed in 1952. South Brookley was air-conditioned in 1988, but because of the transoms, former students said that it was not intolerably hot without air-conditioning. South Brookley school combined with Adelia Williams Elementary School to form the Dr. Robert Gilliard Elementary School in 2006. Today the old school building is still in use for children's education housing a Head-Start Program.

Facing page top: South Brookley Elementary School as it appeared in the 1940s, and bottom: South Brookley Cafeteria built by parents, 1946.

It was an honor to be on the student safety patrol at South Brookley.

Mrs. Becton, left, Principal, rang this handbell each morning. Note that the wooden handle has been replaced with a WWII artillery shell casing. Today, the bell is in Gilliard Elementary School.

Teachers at South Brookley, in the early 1940s.

Harriet, Harry, and James Shaw, students at South Brookley, have lived in South Mobile for decades. Harriet Shaw Pitt lived on Bay Front Road for over seventy years.

Above: Students at South Brookley gather to receive good citizenship awards in the 1940s.

Left: Mrs. Bron Dixon, a teacher at South Brookley, went on to found the Mobile Chapter of the Sweet Adelines, a worldwide organization of women singers. Under her leadership, the Mobile chapter won competitions both nationally and internationally.

Our Lady of Lourdes School
1949

In the 1940s when Father Paro began working at Our Lady of Lourdes, he noticed that there was an urgent need for a school. Of the fifty-five children of school age in the parish, only thirty-seven attended Catholic schools. He resolved to help provide them with the means to get a Catholic education. He bought busses to transport them to Catholic schools in the city. By 1946, there were eighty-three children transported by bus to nine schools. The next year there were one-hundred and eighteen. Father Paro wanted to have his own parochial school and set about raising funds to accomplish this. He and his parishioners had bazaars, lawn parties, raffles, bingos, and accumulated $2500 in the first year toward the building fund. The next year another $3977 was added as well as the acquisition of two and a quarter acres west of the Church property as a site for the school.

In the spring of 1949, Father Paro started building the four-room modern school of brick and tile. It faced Boykin Boulevard and had playgrounds behind the building. But finding teaching sisters was difficult. Father Paro traveled through a large part of the United States, interviewing religious superiors and provincials. He successfully hired three School Sisters of Notre Dame from St. Louis to begin the school year in September of 1949. They taught all eight grades in four rooms. The first three Sisters hired were Sister Suzanne, Sister Anselm, and Sister Bertille. Mrs. Tomlinson, a lay teacher, was the fourth teacher. During the first year there were one hundred and forty-four students in the school which cost $65,000. The School Sisters of Notre Dame turned over the school to lay leadership in 1985.

Father Paro was very active within the school organizing Easter egg hunts, Halloween parties, the drum corps, and athletic teams for the school. He also organized an annual May Day celebration and crowning, that were popular in the 1940s and 1950s.

Oprah Winfrey visited South Brookley School in the early 1990s because of a pilot program there called "Pay it Forward" organized by Carol Dupre. The school was closed in 2004 because of dwindling enrollment.

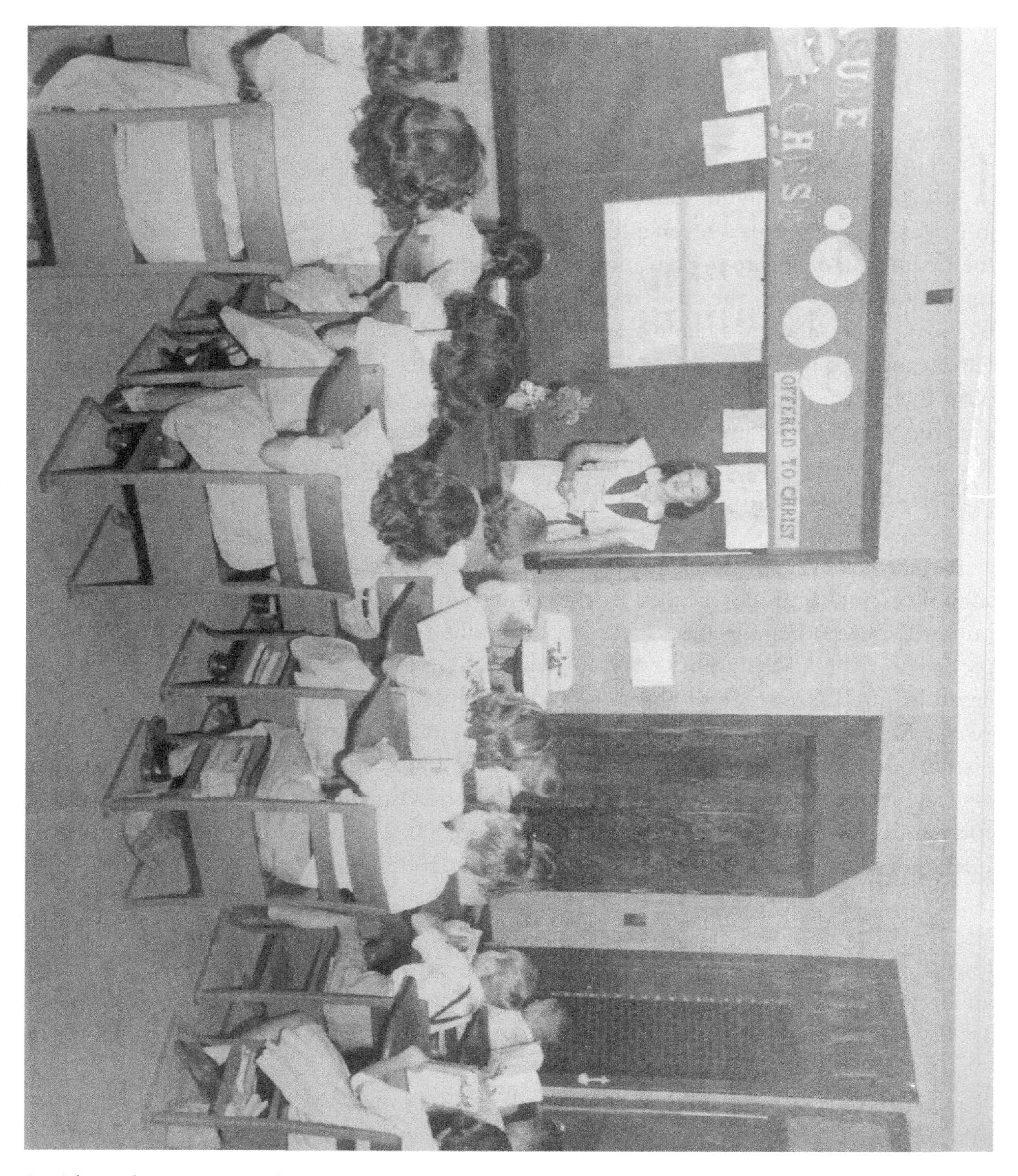

Inside a classroom in Our Lady of Lourdes School. 1949. Photo courtesy of Father Sophie, Priest at Our Lady of Lourdes Catholic Church.

Adelia Williams Elementary School
1987 - 2006

Adelia Williams School located just south of Pine Crest Cemetery was in operation from 1987 until it combined with South Brookley to form the Dr. Robert Gilliard Elementary School in 2006. It served 450 students from grades kindergarten to fifth grade and was named for Miss Adelia Williams, shown below, who lived most of her life with her two unmarried sisters in a house on St. Francis Street. Adelia's father, James M. Williams was in the Confederate Army and the subject of a book called *From That Terrible Field* by John Folmar. He commanded a small fort called Fort Powell near Dauphin Island on Grant's Pass during the Battle of Mobile Bay. Miss Williams is buried in Magnolia Cemetery.

Ben C. Rain High School
1959-present

To meet the needs of a fast-growing community of South Mobile, B. C. Rain High School was organized in 1959, the students housed temporarily in the old Robert E. Lee School on Madison Street until September of 1963 when the doors to the New High School were opened to admit 1,200 students. Mr. W. S. Van Landingham (pictured right) was the first principal. The school was named for Ben Cato Rain, secretary to the Board of School Commissioners from 1923-1945, who was admired by citizens and associates during a period of great challenges during the depression and between wars.

Mr. Ben Glover, (pictured left) was a graduate of Leroy High School and Mississippi State. The beloved Principal, accepted the head football coaching assignment at B. C. Rain High School in 1965 and became the Principal four years later, remaining in this role until his retirement in 1990. He understood the importance of teamwork, and built a faculty that worked happily together for the betterment of the students for decades. "He knew every student by name and was the best principal I ever had," a former teacher at Rain commented. "He really put his heart into the school."

Facing Page: Groundbreaking for construction of B. C. Rain High School. 1964.

Schools - B. C. Rain High School

Coach William "Billy" Howard, (pictured left) coached for thirty-four years at B.C. Rain High School. He was the head baseball coach for twenty-six years and also was an assistant football coach for all thirty-four years. After his retirement, the City of Mobile named the baseball field at Trimmier Park "Billy Howard Field." His jersey was retired in 2004 in honor of Howard's years of dedication and service to the school and community. Feb. 14, 2004 was proclaimed "Coach William G. Howard Day" by Mobile City Councilman Ben Brooks.

In the 1980s enrollment began to decline at the school, as the population in local neighborhoods waned due to the closing of Brookley Field and as people moved to west Mobile and Baldwin Counties. By 2007 the number of students was just over 300. Principal Marion Firle, (pictured right, and on facing page), oversaw the one million dollar renovation of B. C. Rain into a Signature Academy where students could focus on career fields: Aviation and Aerospace, Information Technology, or Video and Music Production. The enrollment has now reached it former levels and the school is again thriving.

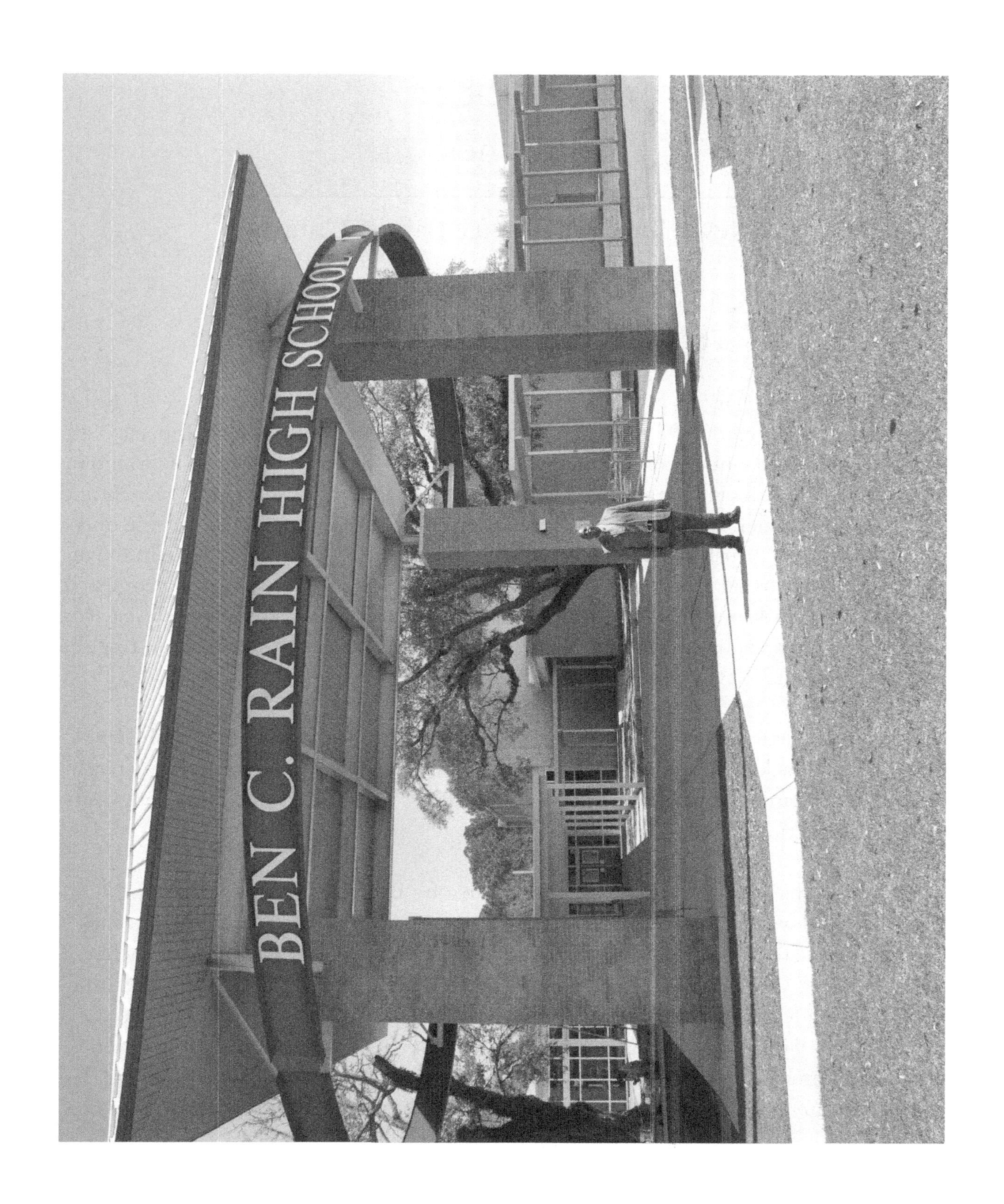

Schools - B. C. Rain High School

CHAPTER 25
Churches

New Hope Missionary Baptist Church

1897 - present
The oldest church in South Mobile

New Hope Missionary Baptist Church was set up as a mission by the Stone Street Baptist Church around 1897 making it the oldest church in South Mobile. It began with only five members who lived in the rural farmlands of Cedar Point Road. The founding members were Robert Hagan, Gaines Frazier, Dan Price, Sister Evaline Hagan and Sister Carrie Frazier. Before there was a building, members worshipped outside under an arbor made of brushwood. Land for the church was purchased from William Frazier for $50.00 and a small wooden building was erected which had a steeple and a large bell. The bell was used to inform the community of special events such as church services, deaths, and funerals by ringing it with a specific frequency. The janitor would ring the bell on New Year's Eve for ten minutes at midnight.

Some parishioners were buried in the Casher Cemetery located on Club House Road. Many black settlers who made their living farming are buried in this cemetery. Some of the names of early black settlers were Rice, Bonner, Frazier, Singleton, Caster, Crockett, Pringle, and Hagan.

Baptisms were held in the river in Robinson's Bayou, and members of the church would walk across Cedar Crescent Road and straight down Brill Road to the river for the ceremony. The Church also served as a school-house and had a teacher. Peter Dais, Sr. was a student at the school called "Race Track" because it was near the old Magnolia Race Track. He recalled that his teacher's name was Miss Erma Lee. In the early 1940s the church and school burned. Services were held in a rented tent until the church could be rebuilt in 1962. New Hope was remodeled in 1989-1992. It still resides in the same place where it began over a hundred and twenty years ago near the corner of Cedar Crescent Drive and Dauphin Island Parkway. The image on the facing page was taken in 2018.

Churches - New Hope Missionary Baptist Church

Our Lady of Lourdes Catholic Church
1907 - present

Our Lady of Lourdes began as a mission church for St. Matthew's Catholic Church in 1907. At that time it was called St. Margaret's and was located on property now occupied by the Brookley Complex. In 1940 the property on which St. Margaret's stood was purchased by the U.S. War Department. The little chapel had to come down and the land annexed to Brookley Field. The Most Reverend Bishop Thomas J. Toolen, Bishop of Mobile, asked the Edmundite fathers on Mon Louis Island to find a new location for the church and to run the mission. They agreed to take over and build a new and larger church. Mass continued to be celebrated at St. Margaret's until the spring of 1941 when the church was told it had to be dismantled.

Father Casey said in church's 1940 newsletter, "*Well! It's still hanging on. The local governmental officials are overlooking the fact that we haven't moved yet, even though work on the new army air base is going all around the poor old chapel. I just haven't been able to find funds to start a new chapel in this poor but rapidly growing mission and I can't start until do.*" The little old dilapidated St. Margaret's Chapel gradually emerged from the woods as the workmen cleared away around it and finally it was the last building left on the army air base. "*All one could think of in seeing it was that the last stump was sticking up on one end in the midst of barren desolation*".

Finally, Father Joseph P. Walsh, S.S.E. (Society of Saint Edmund), in charge of the mission, was notified that the old chapel must be out of the way by April 15, 1941. On Easter Monday, April 14, 1941, the members began tearing down the chapel, and on Easter Tuesday, there was nothing left of it. Arrangements were made to hire an abandoned dance hall which had been closed by police for various reasons, so that they might continue to keep this little congregation intact. Just as they were ready to rent it, it was leased to a dry cleaner.

Help came from Dr. H. Alphonse Zieman who presented both the pastor and congregation temporary sanctuary in the basement of his large summer cottage on Bay Front Road in 1941. Mass was offered in his large basement on an improvised altar, and after Mass, there were catechism classes.

Meanwhile, Father John Casey S.S.E., traveled to Boykin Boulevard and with the $850 he had left from the government from buying the land, started to frame the new chapel from plans he had drawn. He supervised W.P.A. workers in leveling the land and church, he arranged for the storage of salvaged lumber from the original St. Margaret's Chapel, and he started a frame house for Father Joseph. The chapel, rectory and equipment cost about $7,500 but less than a third of this was on hand when the work began.

Mass was said for the first time on May 25, 1941, in a partially completed church with open studs and a roof covered with building paper. The altar from the old St. Margaret's was salvaged and pews that were purchased or donated from here and there were put into service. Some iron alter pieces were made by Zip Lartigue. The parishioners rejoiced, but the work on the church and rectory came to an abrupt stop in June when funds ran out. Father Francis Casey went north seeking funds to finish the work. Finally, in September of 1941, the hammers, saws and other tools were put away, scaffolds dismantled, blueprints rolled up, and the church and rectory were completed.

Over the years, Our Lady of Lourdes Church was able to raise assets in many ways to fund construction for a school, a new church building, and other facilities. Besides raffles, dinners, and lawn parties, a May Day celebration as fancy as a Mardi Gras party was held each year in the 1950s complete with King and Queen, tableaux, floats and parades. The king and queen and court wore elaborate costumes and were chosen based on whose parents sold the most raffle tickets.

Twenty years after the first church was built, a new modern brick and glass church was constructed across the street from the old church in 1962. Father Francis Moriarity, S.S.E., was the pastor who conducted the first Mass there on Christmas Day, 1962. The church continues to thrive and serve the community, and in 1992, a modern gym and parish center were dedicated.

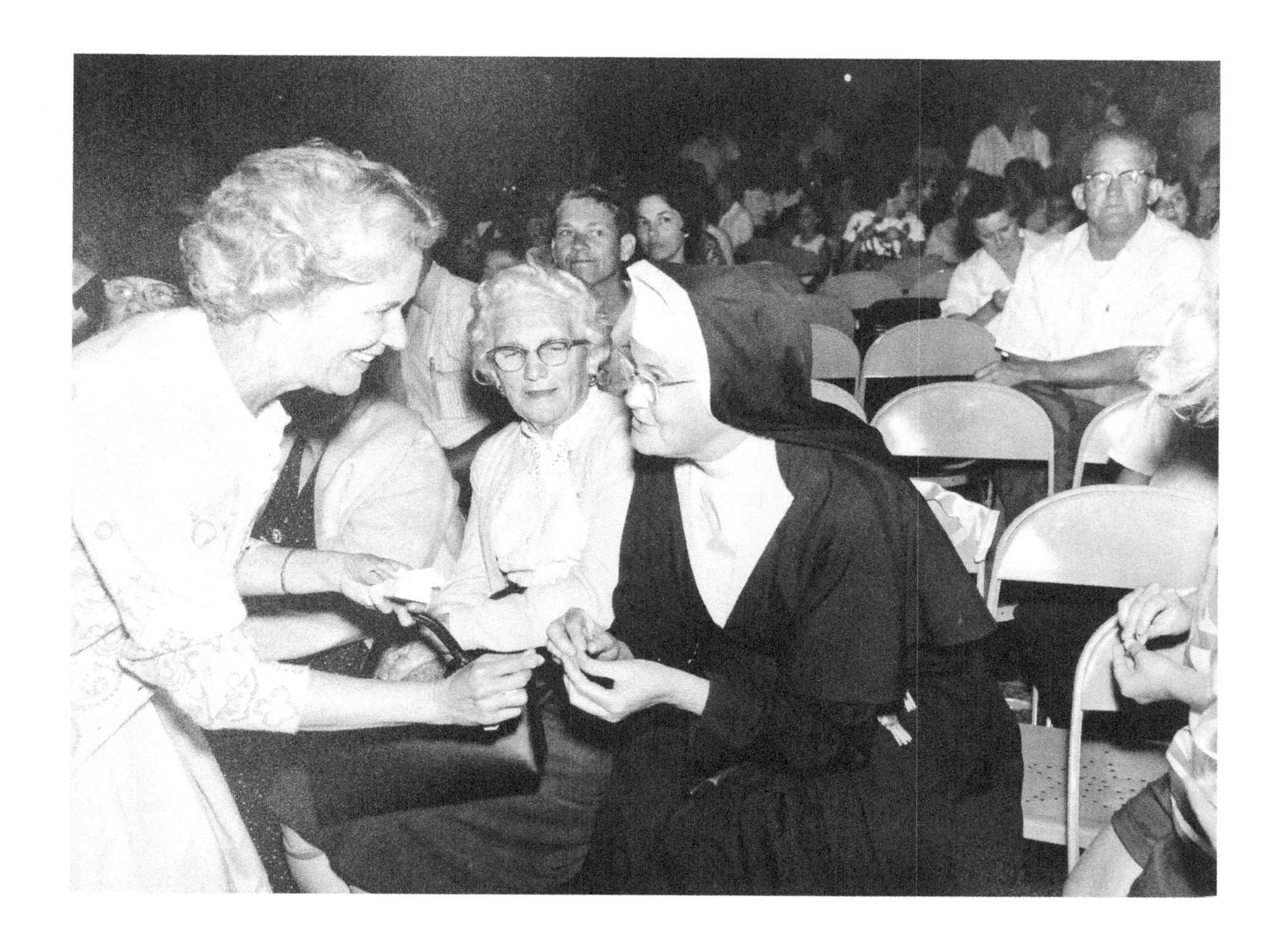

Above: Mrs. Toenes speaks with Sister Mary Ella, School Sister of Notre Dame before a May Day celebration. 1964.

Facing Page Top: Our Lady of Lourdes Catholic Church on Boykin Blvd in 1941, to the right of the convent for the School Sister of Notre Dame.

Facing Page Bottom: First Communion inside Our Lady of Lourdes in the 1950s.

Images courtesy of Father Sophie, and Our Lady of Lourdes Catholic Church.

May Day Celebrations at Our Lady of Lourdes were grand and festive. Above is a ten-gun archway for the coronation of the King and Queen at the May Day Celebration, King Darrell Ladnier, and Queen Billie Marie Voivedich, in Mardi Gras style attire. The children of the family selling the most tickets could become king and queen. 1964.

Facing Page: The stage and participants of the May Day Celebration. 1964.

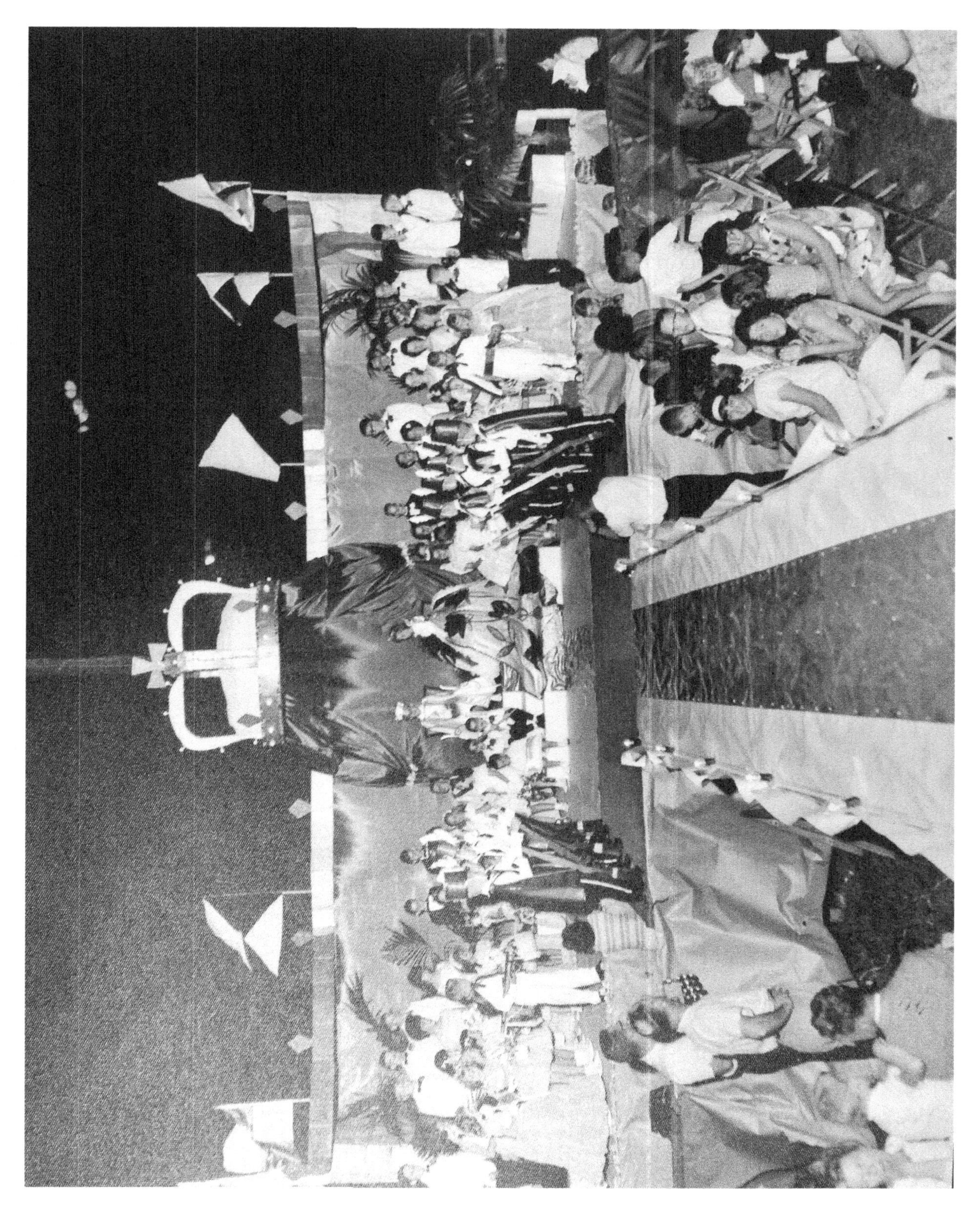

Churches - Our Lady of Lourdes Catholic Church

Riverside Baptist Church

1943 – present

The first members met in a tent

As more and more people moved into the area, a need for a Baptist church was felt by some residents, so much so that the first members of Riverside Baptist Church met in a tent pitched in the field between the home of Mr. and Mrs. Mac Davis and a little grocery store owned by Mr. and Mrs. Summers. The store is still standing at the fork in the road of Riverside Drive and Circle Drive.

A sketch of the original church that was on Riverside Drive in 1944 is above. Image courtesy of Rev. Ingram, Riverside Baptist Church.

After surveying the vicinity, the members decided that a physical building for the Baptist church was needed. Mr. and Mrs. Lindsey donated the land located at the corner of Riverside Drive and Valley Road next to their home to be the building site. Riverside Drive Baptist Church was organized October 23, 1943 with 16 participating members. In later years it was decided to leave out "Drive" from the name, making it Riverside Baptist Church.

Mrs. Lindsey vividly recalled the first Sunday services held in the new church before the windows had been installed. "A sudden rainstorm developed and the preacher had to wear a raincoat during the sermon." She also remembered how the people of the church would walk up the road singing as they went along Eloong Drive for the Baptism of members in Dog River. Later, when the baptistery was installed in the church, the water, piped from the Lindsey home next door, was heated by building a fire under the pipe while the water was running into the baptistery pool. Members worked physically to update the church: Mr. Lindsey and one of his sons put down the first well at the church.

In February of next year 1944, Brother Timothy Hottel became the first full-time minister of the church. In 1958, under the leadership of Pastor W.D. Simrell, the church purchased property on Dauphin Island Parkway owned by the Methodist Church. Ironically, one of the buildings on the property used to be a night club that was turned into a fellowship hall by the Methodists. In 1970, a steeple was added to the church and membership had grown from 16 to over 1,175. During the tenure of Pastor W. D. Simrell, the auditorium was completely renovated on the inside, and later, a bride's room was transformed "into a thing of beauty".

In the years since 1970, Riverside Baptist Church has added many other improvements to their Church facilities and grounds. But this church has not been an island unto itself. Under the leadership of Pastor Randall E. Ingram, it opens its doors on a regular basis for community meetings and events, most recently hosting voting rooms, and monthly community action group meetings where local citizens may keep abreast of events affecting them.

Above: A front-view sketch by a member of the original church that was on Riverside Drive in 1944. Image courtesy of Rev. Ingram, Riverside Baptist Church.

Facing Page: The Riverside Baptist Church, 2018. Image by Susan Rouillier

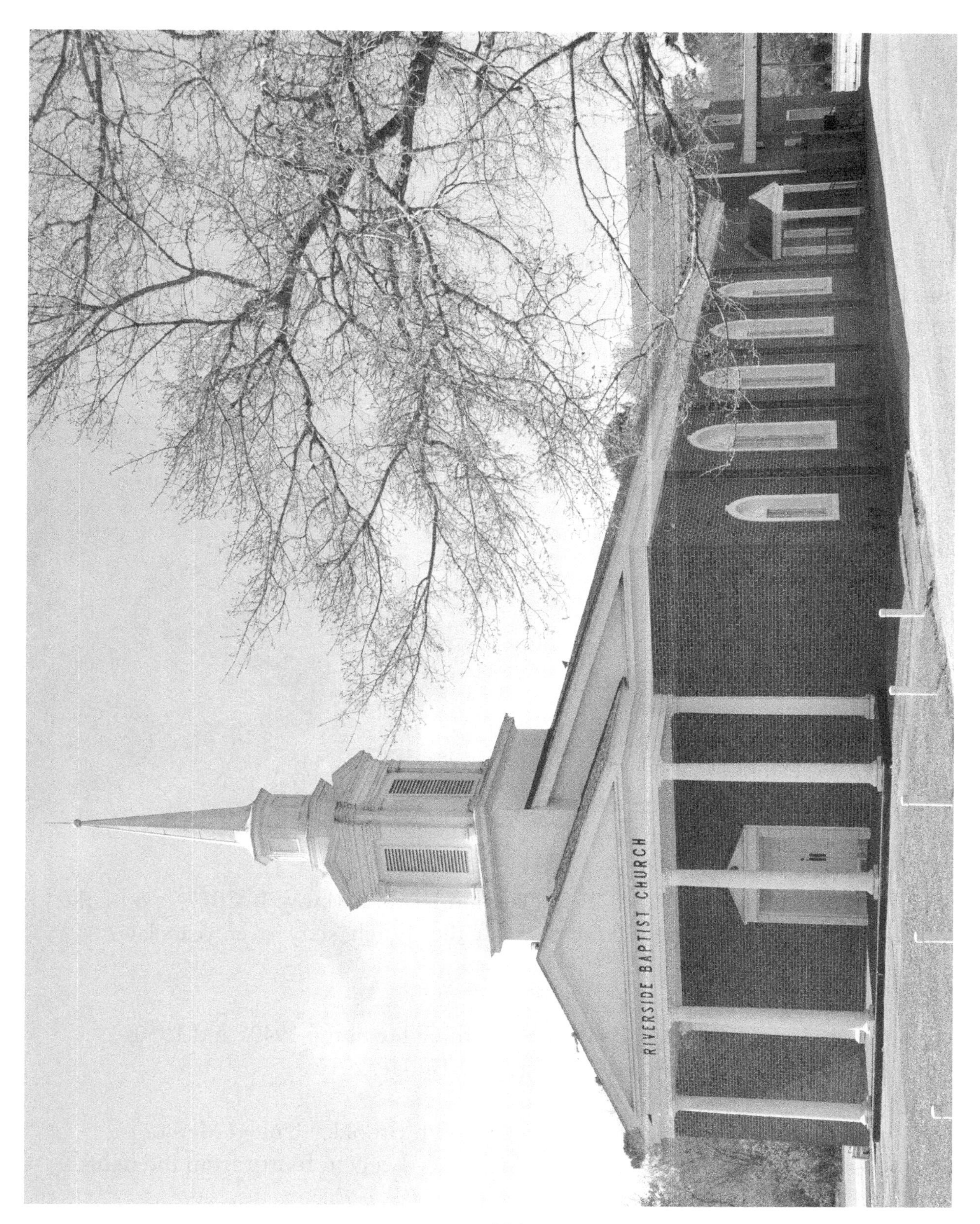

Churches - Riverside Baptist Church

South Brookley United Methodist Church
1950 – present

From a Slaughterhouse to a Night Club to a Church

In the spring of 1950, a group of people met to create South Brookley Methodist Church. At the first service, held in the slaughterhouse of Brill's Grocery Store, there was an overflowing crowd. After meeting in the slaughterhouse for some months, the church purchased a night-club called "Paul's Place", a building in front of the current Riverside Baptist Church to turn it into a sanctuary.

Harry Shaw, (image right with Harriet Dykes) recalled, "I can still picture Mrs. Imms scrubbing the floor getting the beer stains up." The first pastor was Reverend H. E. Palmes. Ten years after the first worship service, a newly built sanctuary opened it doors under the leadership of Reverend Lamar Brown. This church was sold and moved farther down Dauphin Island Parkway near Fowl River where it still rests. The newest and current South Brookley United Methodist Church is near Hannon Road at 3755 Dauphin Island Parkway. In 2017, two of the original fifty members were still members of the church, sixty seven years later.

Above: Harriet Dykes and Harry Shaw recall life in the 1940s and 1950s at the River Shack Restaurant by Dog River Bridge. 2016.

Facing Page: The original members of South Brookley United Methodist Church. 1955. Picture courtesy of Mrs. Lucy Leggett, fourth from the right.

St. Andrews Episcopal Church

1955 – present

As the area along Cedar Point Road was growing by leaps and bounds in the 1940s and 1950s, a group of Episcopalian laymen of Mobile County realized the need for a new Episcopal church in South Mobile. In 1955, Colonel John W. Morland was called to serve as chairman of the committee to establish the new congregation. Trustees were elected and the name "Saint Andrews" was chosen at the first organizational meeting. The first church service was held July 10, 1055, in the South Brookley Civic Club building.

After an intensive study and search for property, a plot of five acres was purchased on Staples Road, three blocks off Cedar Point Road. An army barracks building measuring 20 feet by 50 feet was purchased from a Methodist church and moved to the building site. To this was added a 20 by 25 foot room. The larger area was equipped as a chapel with donated church furniture and other furnishings made by members. The smaller room was fitted out with washrooms and storage for the twenty vestments hand sewn by members for the youth choir. The heating and water systems, a new roof, and various repairs were all completed by the members themselves. A reed pump organ was found and purchased in Tuscaloosa and installed just in time for the first service in the building on the occasion of Bishop Murray's visit on November 27. The total cost of the land was $4750, and the building with improvements was $3250.

Reverend Benjamin Bosworth Smith, formerly of Mountain Brook, Alabama, became the first Vicar of St. Andrews on May 1, 1956. The church continued to grow and on September 9, 1962, a groundbreaking ceremony was held for the construction of the present church, an elegant modern design of brick and wood with lofty heights inside the contemporary and comfortable interior. The first service in the new church was on Palm Sunday of 1963 under the leadership of Reverend Patrick Dunn. In 2017, sixty-two years after it was created, the original army-barracks church was salvaged. In its place, the parishioners built a labyrinth of stones for walking meditations as well as a flower garden.

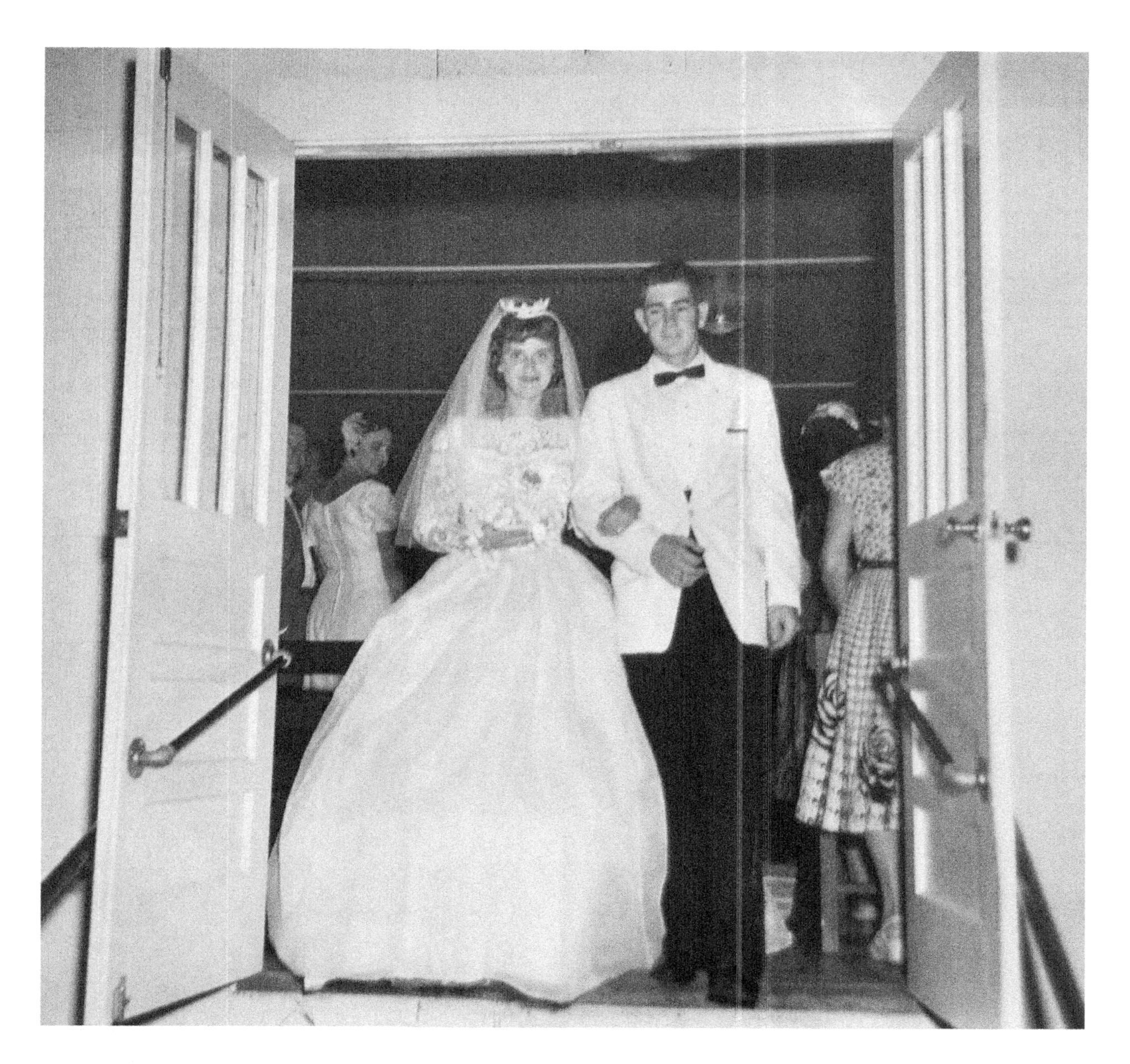

Harriet Dulaney weds Lyman Dykes in the first St. Andrews Church, a converted army barracks reconstructed into a church by members. 1950. Image Courtesy of Harriet Dykes.

Next Page: The original St. Andrews Church in 2016 before it was torn down and replaced with a meditative walking garden.

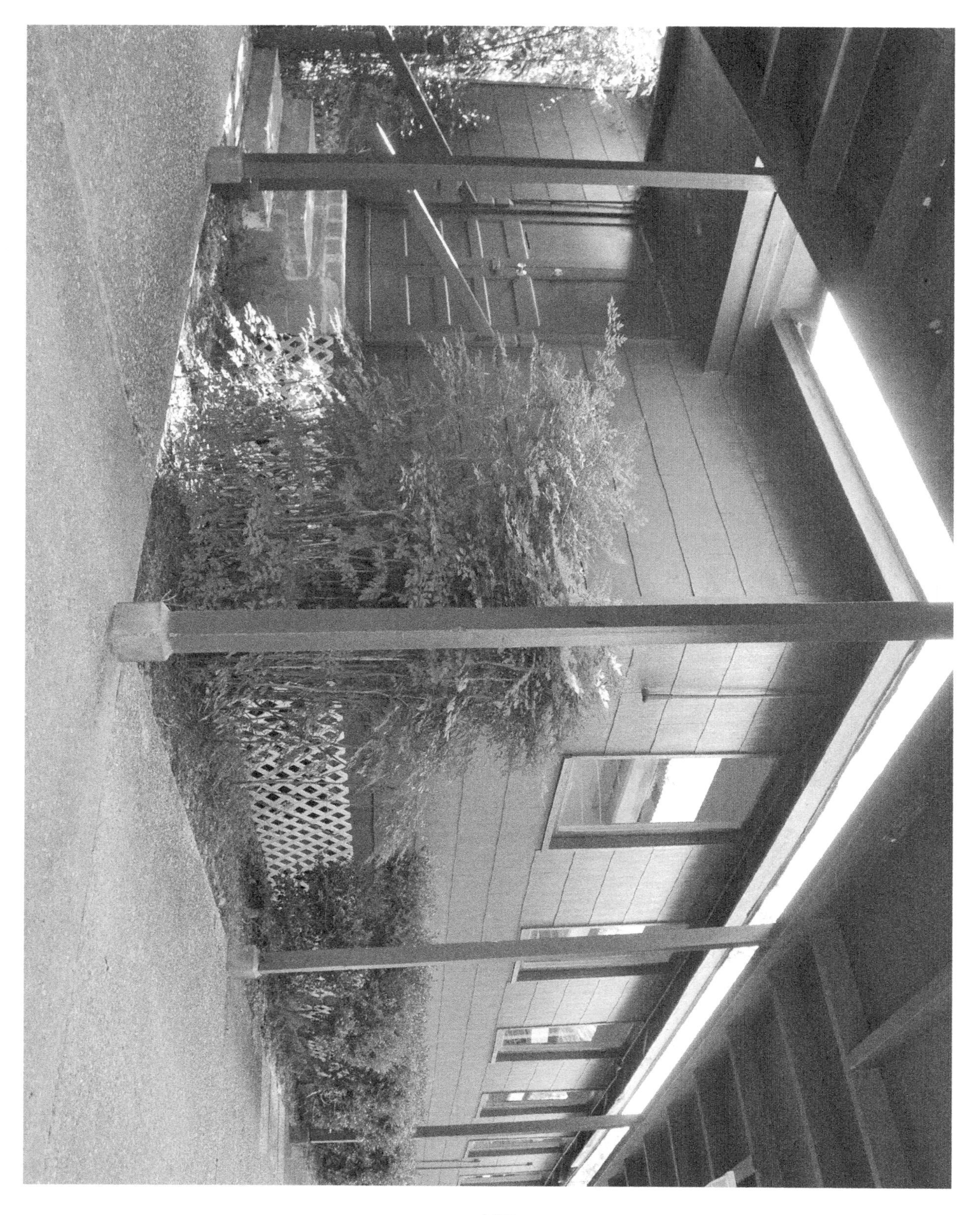

Churches - St. Andrews Episcopal Church

CHAPTER 26
Cemeteries

Casher Memorial Cemetery
1887

A visitor to the Casher Memorial Cemetery will drive down a narrow tree-lined passage off Clubhouse Road before entering a circular womblike oak-enclosed area where the small cemetery is located. A visitor feels unexpectedly transformed by the stillness of the space. Some graves are unmarked, some have hand-made markers, others have engraved granite markers and other graves of veterans have military markers. The entrance sign (shown below) is engraved with "donated in loving memory of Clifton C. Gatwood, 2006". Parishioners from New Hope Missionary Baptist Church were buried in the Casher Cemetery. Many early black settlers who made their living by farming are buried here. Some of the early settler's names are Rice, Bonner, Frazier, Singleton, Caster and Hagan.

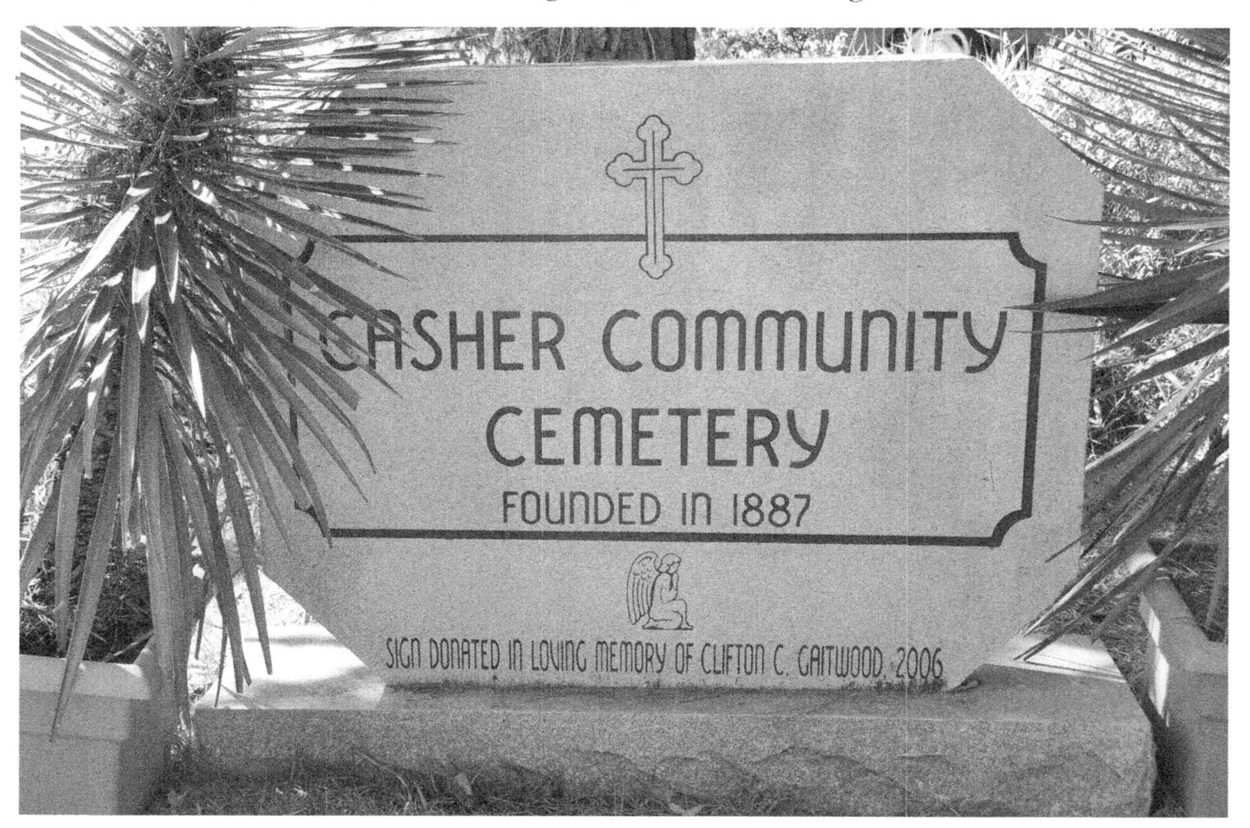

Lartigue Family Cemetery
Circa 1850 – Moved to present location 1939

The dozen or so graves of relatives in the Lartigue Family Cemetery were once family graves on land occupied by today's Brookley Complex. The graves were excavated and moved to their present location next to Brookley at the end of Cedar Point Road in order to make space for airplane runways for the WWII efforts. The oldest grave (shown below) in the cemetery is engraved in French: "Ici repose de la corps de Marie Joseph Legrand, espouse de Isidore Delvauy, nee a Assenois, Belgique, le 22 December, 1849 Decedee A Springhill Le 25 Aout, 1909" Translation: Here rests the body of Marie Joseph Legrand wife of Isidore Delvauy, born in Assenois Belgium on December 22, 1849, died in Springhill the twenty-fifth August, 1909.

Pine Crest Cemetery
1906 - Present

Pine Crest was originally located "out in the country", where there were no paved roads. For the first few years after its opening in 1906, the company operated a horse-drawn bus from the end of the street car line at the loop to the cemetery.

Greg M. Luce became president of the company in 1916 and remained in charge until his death in 1935. His son Jex H. Luce, succeeded as president until his death in 1958, and during his tenure established gardens and statuary in order to make Pine Crest one of the South's most beautiful cemeteries. He loved birds and created a bird sanctuary on the property. Ownership of Pine Crest Cemetery remained in the Luce family until it was sold to Stewart Enterprises, and later to Service Corporation International.

Located at the corner of Dauphin Island Parkway and Military Roads, Pine Crest was the first perpetual care cemetery developed in Mobile. There have been more than 14,000 families served and 39,000 burials on more than 140 acres of the cemetery's wooded land. In 1988, a crematory was built on-site. In 1994, Pine Crest Funeral Home opened on the grounds for funeral planning and cemetery services, including a chapel that seats 170 people.

Notable burials here include Senator Frank Boykin, C.J. Gayfer, Alfred Delchamps, Ernest Ladd, as well as the cemetery's early managers, Greg M. Luce and Jex H. Luce.

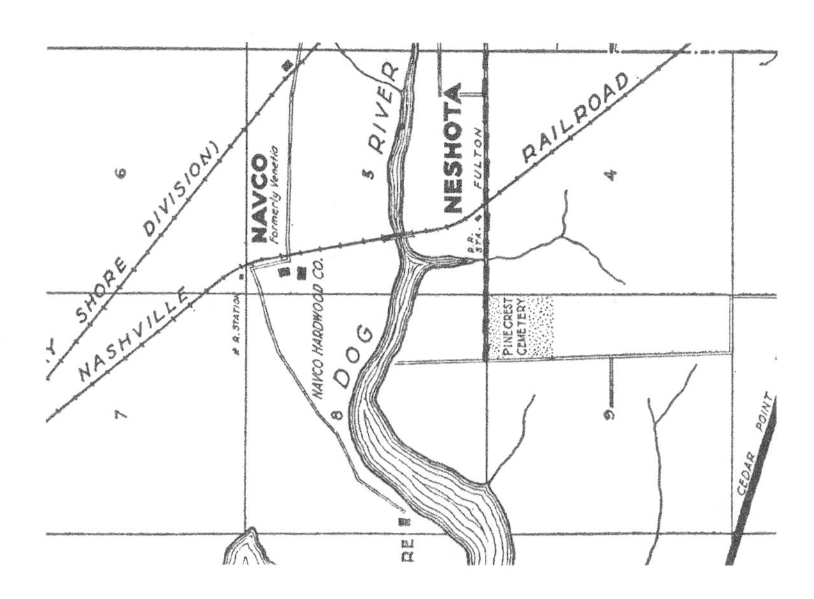

Pine Crest Cemetery in 1923, when it was "out in the country". Map image courtesy of the Local History and Genealogy, Mobile Public Library.

CHAPTER 27
Fishing

Fishing on Mobile Bay and Dog River

"The water was so clear we could see sting rays"
Peter Dais, III

Mobilians have always enjoyed fishing on the bay and in the river, whether from a boat, cast nets, seine nets, walking the bay with flounder gigs, or sitting on the banks of the river or bay with a cane pole, and crabbing for soft shell crabs or big blue crabs. Long-term residents describe abundant fish and crabs in the 1940s and as recently as the 1980s, while images solidify their descriptions as true. But there has been a distinct diminishing of seafood in the last few decades.

There are various suggested explanations. Some point to dredging for shells, and channel dredging which stirred up silt, coating the once sandy beaches with mud. Others say that today's large ships create unnatural large wave action that has disturbed and eliminated the grass-beds, where smaller creatures lived and fed the larger sea-animals and fish. Others point to pollution from industries through the air and water that settled into the ecosystem. Another explanation is that mullet roe became valuable and has been over harvested and sold to overseas markets. Yet another explanation is that the Bay has been over fished and over crabbed. Whatever the reason, our local seafood is greatly diminished.

Peter Dais III, who lived on Snake Road as a child (now Cedar Crescent) recalled that "*The Bay was the center of our life as kids. We were Catholic so we needed fish for Fridays. We were brought up to do things, so we'd do our chores first, then run to the Bay. The water was so clear that we could see sting rays clearly. There would be jubilees here too. If one was happening, people would blow their car horns driving around Snake Road to alert us.*"

A mullet net being thrown in Mobile Bay in 1907, right, and 2015 below. Catching fish with nets is a method thousands of years old, and was used by Native Americans in South Mobile.

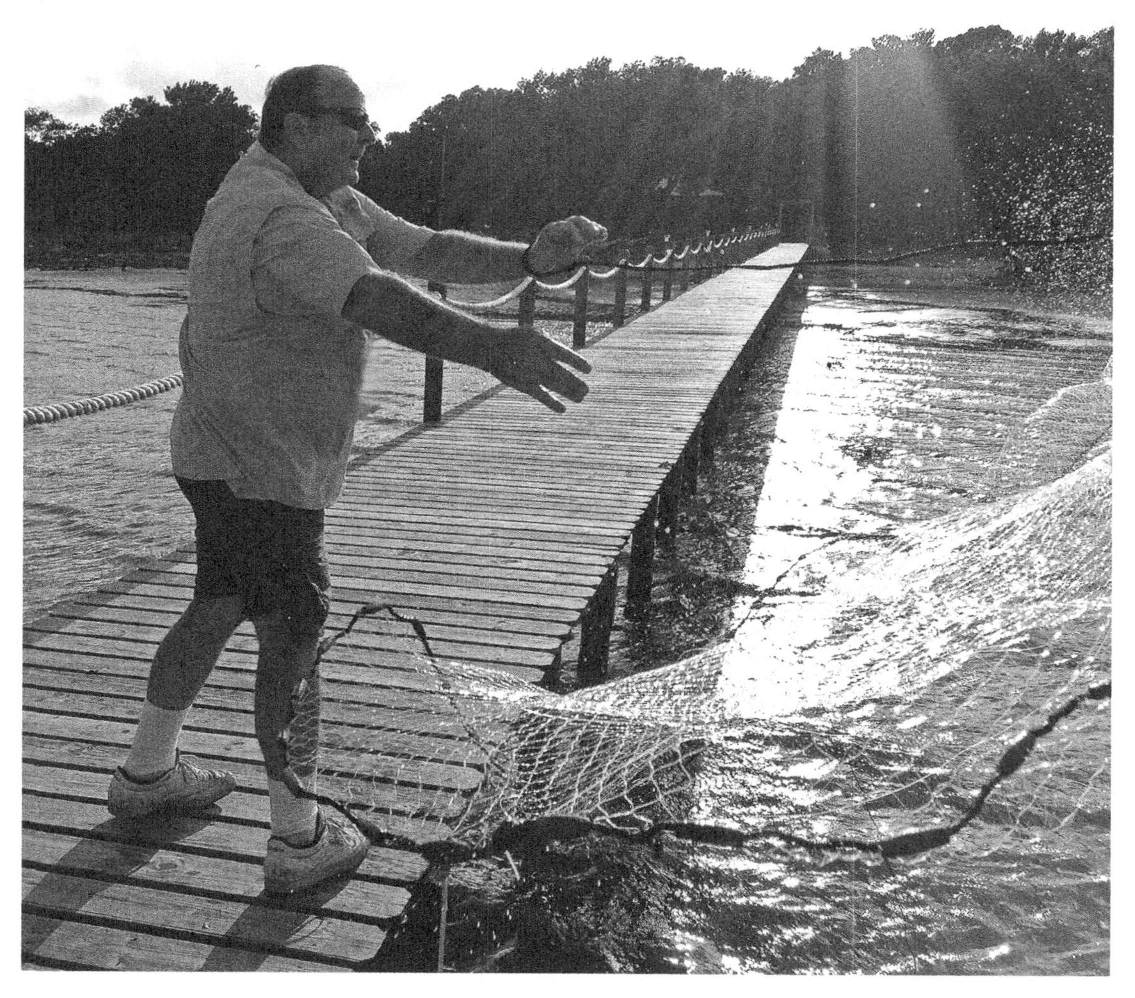

Lee Spafford throws castnet. 2015. Photo by Susan Rouillier

This Page: Dog River Fishing Rodeo. 1950. Image courtesy of Elmo Ziebach.
Facing Page: Hal Tippin's father, second from left, and friends enjoy a day of fishing.

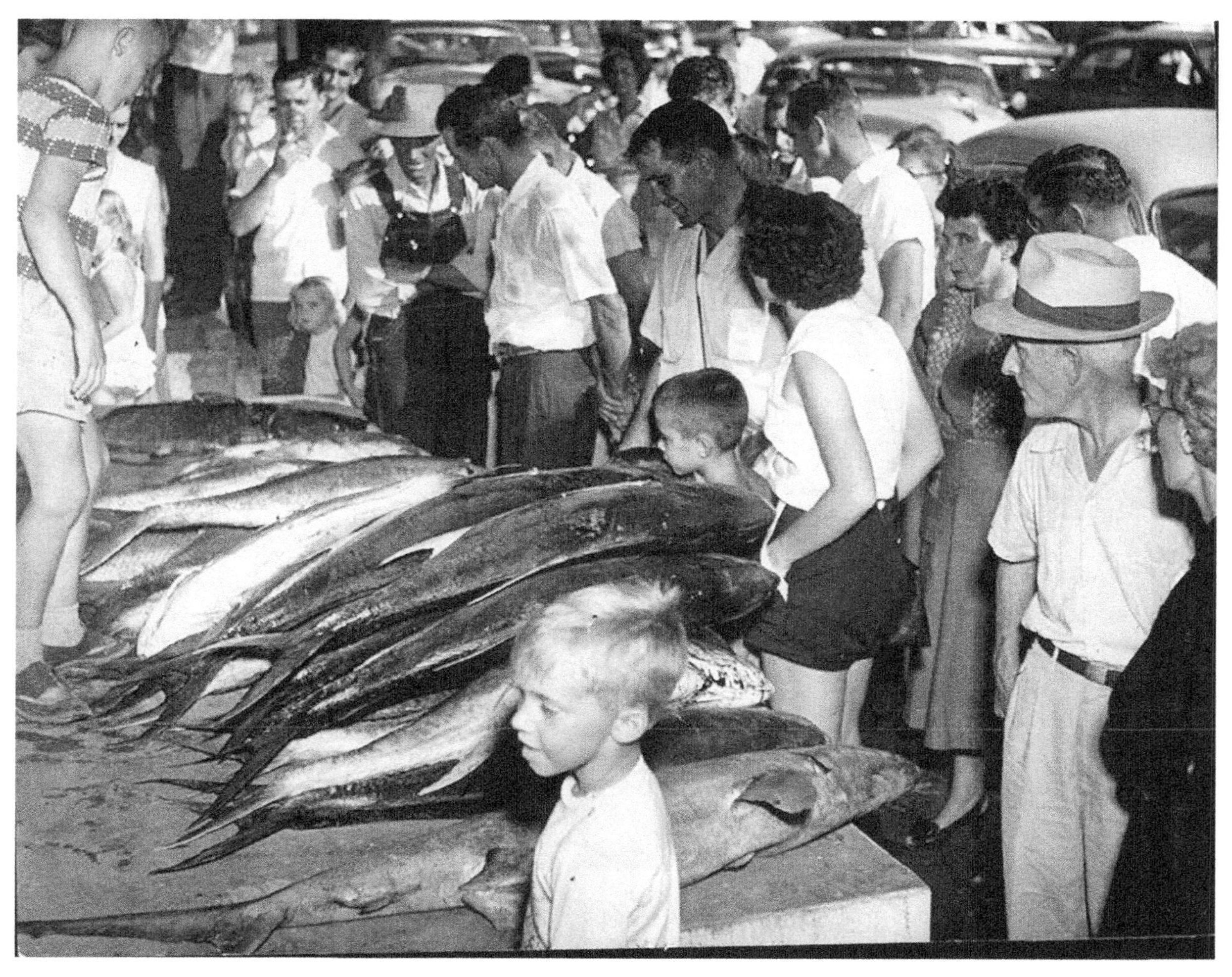

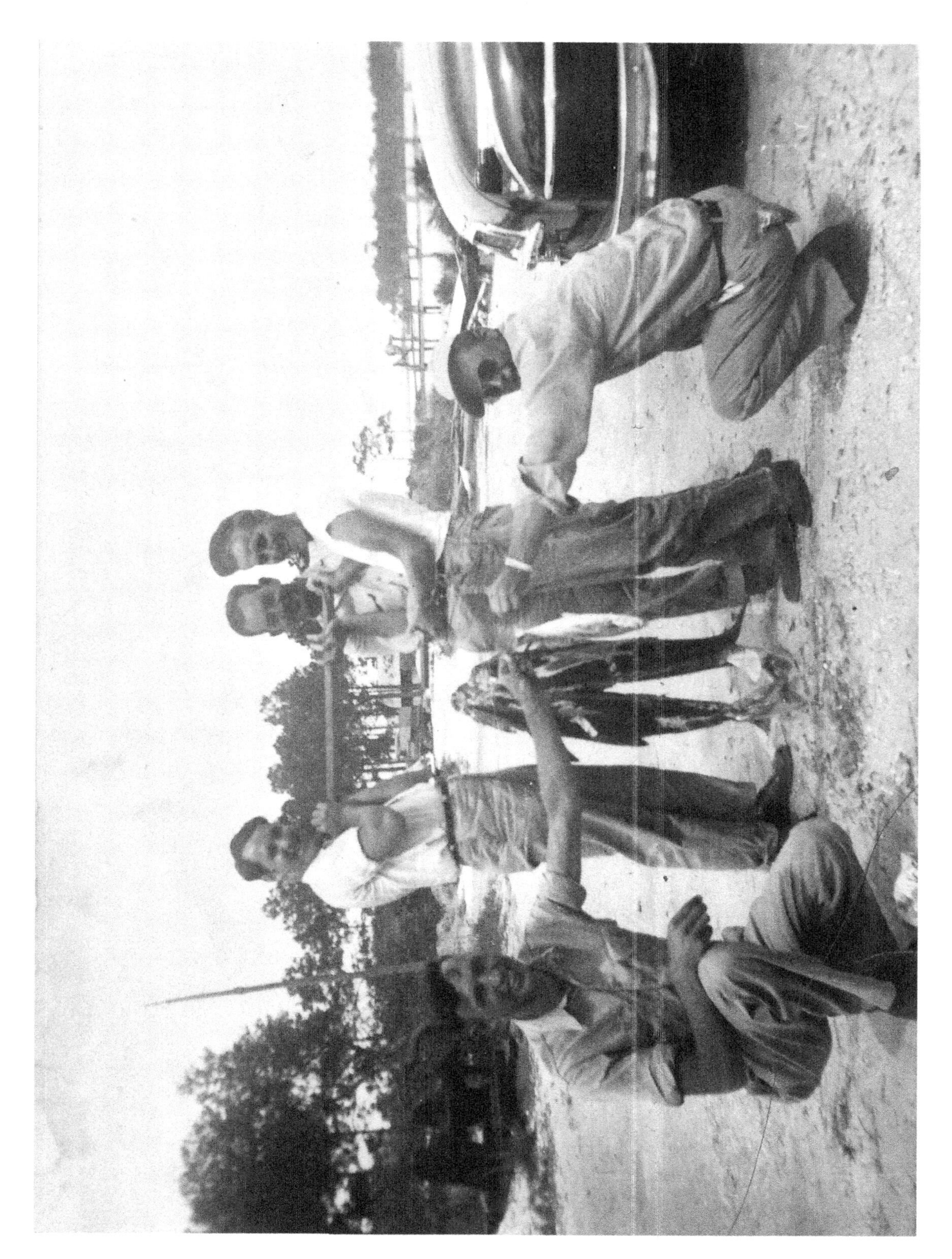

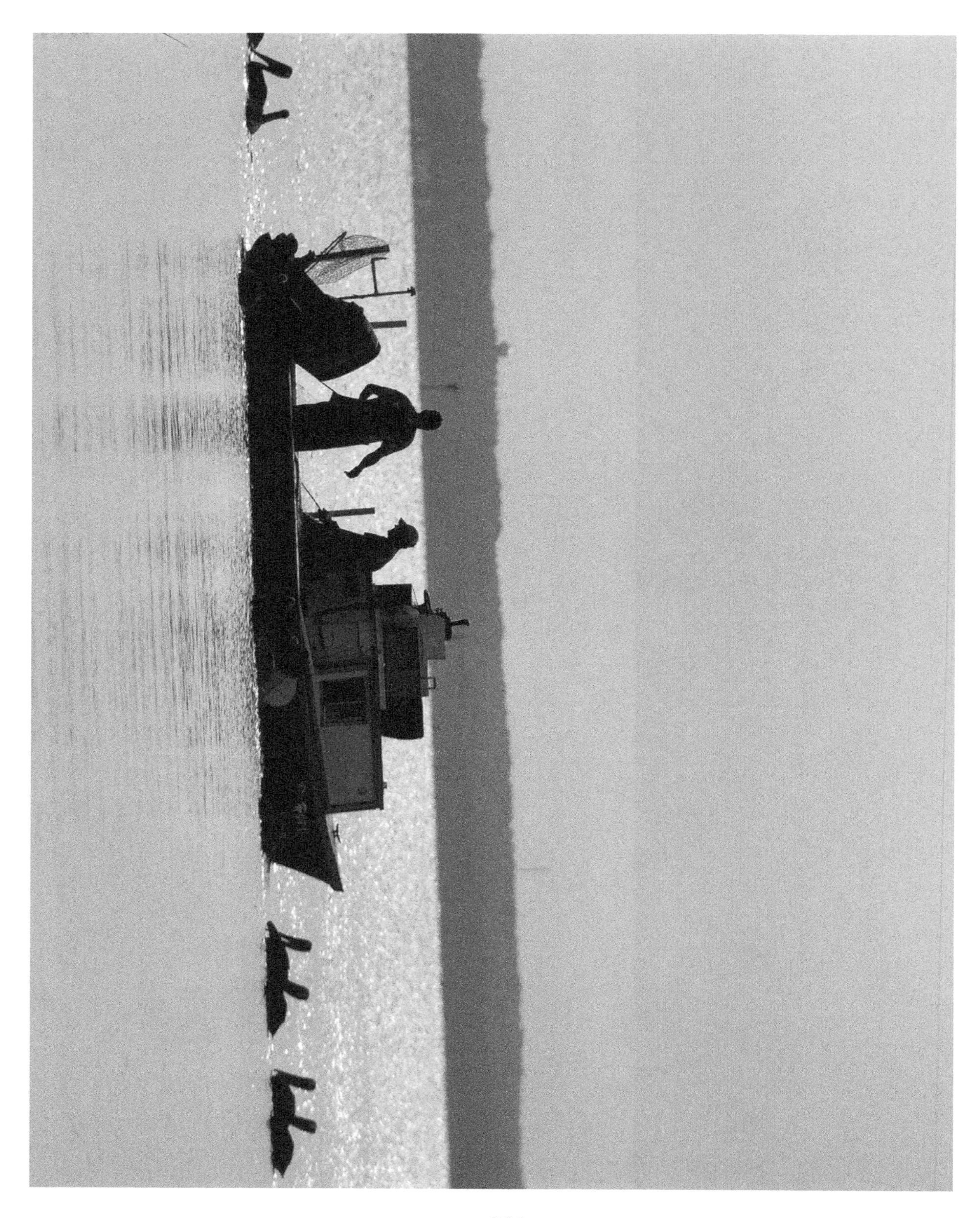

206
Fishing on Mobile Bay and Dog River

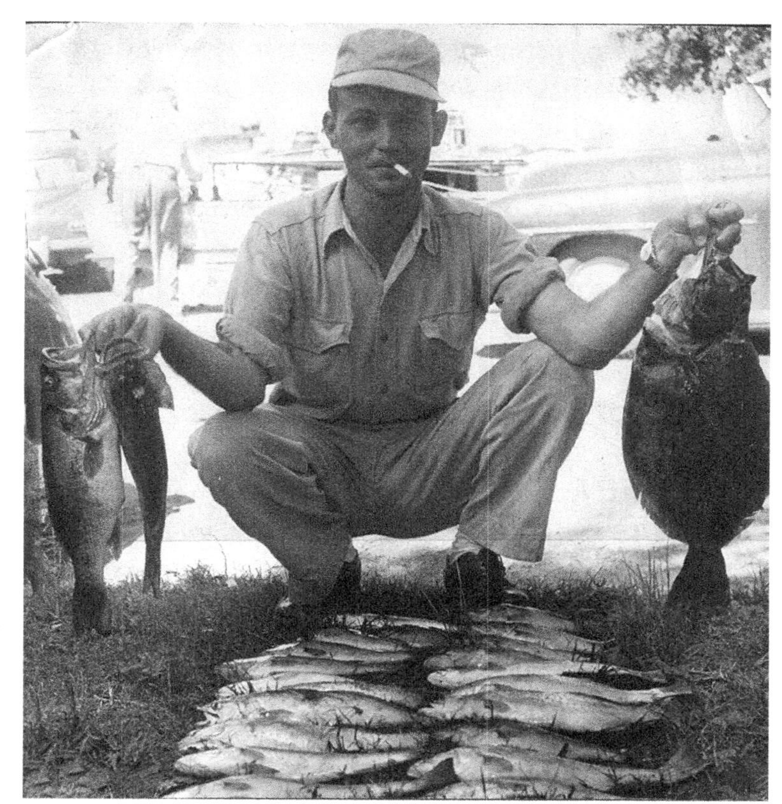

This Page: Dog River Fishing Rodeo. 1950. Images courtesy of Elmo Ziebach

.

Facing Page: There are very few Mullet fish boats, perhaps only one, left in Mobile Bay. 2017. Image by Susan Rouillier

CHAPTER 27
Oystering

"Oystermen were known to be fighters because they had big arms"

Lee Spafford owned an oyster boat and went oystering in 1973 with Teet Collier, a life-long oysterman on Dauphin Island. Mr. Spafford describes an oysterman's environment: "*The oyster reefs used to be open most of the year. There was much less competition and the reefs were not overharvested and the need to close the reefs was not as great due to pollution as it is now. Now there are restrictive seasons mainly to prevent over harvesting. Also there used to be no limit. Oystermen could keep all they caught. Now they must sell their oysters to a state authorized buyer. Today, a person can not buy a sack from an oysterman.*"

"*It's a slow boat ride from Dauphin Island to get over by the bridge on an oyster boat. An oyster boat is wide with a flat bottom often made by the oysterman himself. A flat bottom does not roll like a v-hull. It also has wooden decks to empty the oysters on. Often it had a small wooden cabin on the back to shelter the men from the rain or a storm. Cedar Point was the richest area for oysters. Usually a day consisted of about six hours. In the old days some oystermen would open the oysters at the shop behind their homes. Now the law regulates the processing of oysters. You must have a licensed oyster shop with an observer for sanitary reasons.*"

"*The oysters lie on a bed of old shells pretty loosely and usually are not attached to anything. Long rakes or oyster tongs about 16-feet long were used to easily get into water that is ten feet deep although most oysters come from water less than six feet deep. The tongs are hinged and similar to two garden rakes that rake together. It is literally like raking the bottom. It takes a hell of a strong man to rake and pick oysters up all day. Oystermen used to be known to be fighters because they had big arms. They raked up a big pile onto the deck of the boat. They would hammer off the small oysters and dead shells and put the good oysters into burlap sacks. Now, when they get to the dock they sell to an authorized buyer monitored by the Alabama Department of Conservation and Marine Resources. When a boat comes in, the buyers and representatives from AD-CMR check the harvest. Oysterman must have a tag for each sack that he sells to the licensed buyer.*"

"*The only time the oyster season has not been opened was in the years 2010 and 2011 due to high salinity which increased the numbers of oyster drills which thrive in salty water. They decimated the oyster population in south Alabama and in other areas. The drill bores a little hole through the shell and eats the oyster out of the shell. The reefs had to be rebuilt using old oyster shells and*

crushed rock. The bottom is layered in crushed rock and the oyster larvae attach to the crushed rock. After about four years the season has been reopened for about a month or two a year instead of all year. So now oystermen can't make a living as oystermen, because it is not an industry like it used to be. The oyster price has gone up and down over the years. The price is high now because the season is so limited. The oystermen used to find parts of cannon balls and mortar shells from the bombardment of Ft. Powell the day before the Battle of Mobile Bay. Fort Powell was just within the Cedar Point Reefs."

"There are no longer any professional oystermen who live on Dauphin Island because of the short season. There aren't any lifelong careers. The oysters would be caught during the cooler months, the "R" months when the water was cooler. They would make a living shrimping in the warmer months. Dauphin Island used to be a city of seafood families. There is only one shrimp boat and not even one classic oyster boat left on the Island. Now there are oil rigs and charter boats and so many regulations, that it is hard to make a living." (Note: the last shrimp boat on Dauphin Island was sold in 2016.)

Oystermen in Mobile Bay. 1911. Lewis Wickes Hine, photographer. Library of Congress, Pictures and Records Division.

Above: Oysterman in Mobile Bay. 1911. Library of Congress.
Below: Oystermen in Mobile Bay 1930s.

Oyster Boats in Mobile Bay. 1911. Lewis Wikes Hine, photographer, Library of Congress, Pictures and Records Division.

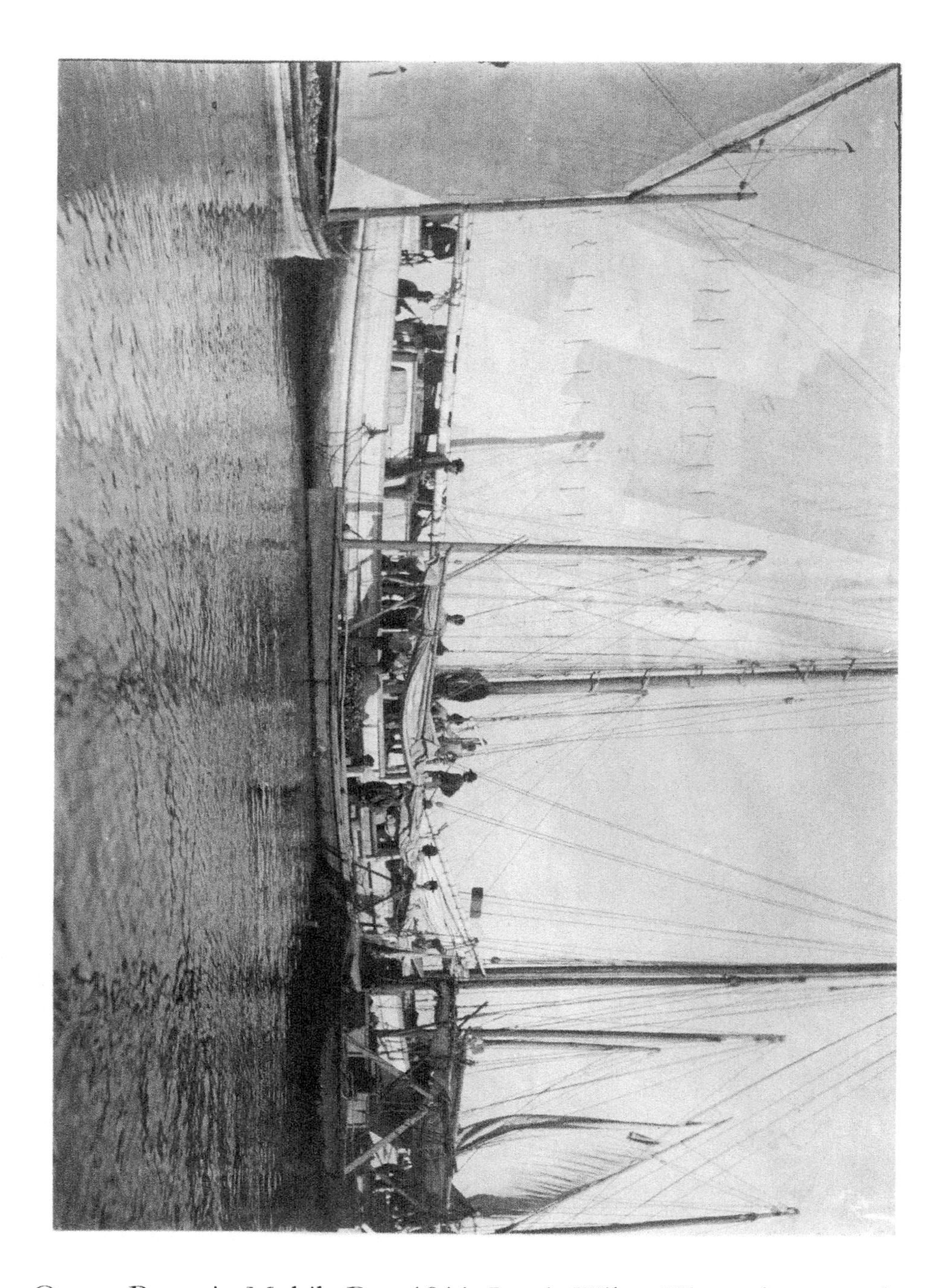

Oyster Boats in Mobile Bay. 1911. Lewis Wikes Hine, photographer, Library of Congress, Pictures and Records Division.

PART IV
PEOPLE

Edward Berger, Fire Chief

Rosa Boone

Gaines Frazier and Family

Jean Hopper Turner and Bond Hopper

The Lartigue Family

Teddy McGill

Mary McKeough

Katharine Phillips Singer

Frances Sirmon

Mandie Wade

The Cowboy

Priest

Katharine Phillips Singer

"We had a wonderful childhood full of fun"

The daughter of Sidney Phillips, the superintendent of Mobile Schools, Katharine was born in 1923 and grew up on Monterey Street. She was featured in Ken Burns' "The War" and was sister to Sid Phillips, the author of "You'll be Sor-ree! – A Guadalcanal Marine Remembers the Pacific War". Mrs. Phillips Singer shared memories of her life and times on the Bay front, and on Dog River.

"We had a wonderful childhood full of fun." She remembers the ice man coming to bring ice. *"Mother would put a plaque in the window signaling ten, fifteen or twenty-five pounds of ice. We would run out to the truck catch the ice chips when they would saw the ice. There was also a competition to see who could grow the best roses on our street. If a horse made a dropping, it was Sid's job to go and fetch it for the roses."*

"The first Country Club was on the Mobile Bay Front, south of Arlington Park."

"At Arlington Park they showed movies for ten cents, and Dad would drive us down there and we would open the doors and windows to cool down in the breeze. Then we would come home all cooled off. They would usually be cowboy movies."

"Bates Field was bought by Brookley and enlarged. Before it was sold there were large piles of dirt nearby and for ten cents you could drive cars over the dirt piles. People would come and drive over them for fun and thrills."

At the Gulf Hunting and Fishing Club, *"my friend Marie and I freely ran through the club and played off the wharf. We swam across Dog River. One time, here came a motor boat with a young man on skis hanging onto a rope behind. I didn't want to drown so to save myself I dived down as deep as I could and the boat passed over me. I swam back to the pier and the young man tcircled around and jumped off onto the wharf and asked if I was ok. It was D.R. Dunlap of the Dunlaps of the Dry Dock and Shipbuilding. He was a good looking young man, but he was killed in the war. Dunlap street is named after him. This would have been around 1936".*

"I was a member of First Baptist Church, and the Youth Group, BYU, would go and light bonfires south of Brookley because no one was there. There was a steep slope down to the water."

"During WWII two of my friends and I worked at the Red Cross Canteen that was at the end of Government Street. When the trains would come in with soldiers, we would serve them free coffee, spam sandwiches, which we doctored with pickle relish, and donuts. The Railroad switchman would come into the canteen and announce the arrival of troops. We walked out to the trains and lifted our arms up for the soldiers to take the food from us through the train windows. Sometimes they would hand us letters to mail for them. One night a train full of marines came in and came off the train and were trying to kiss us. We hiked up our skirts and ran inside the canteen, but Polly got caught, was surrounded and kissed. We were about 20 years old. "Will we tell our parents?" It turned out that these marines had served at Iwo Jima and had just come through the port of New Orleans and we were the first females they had seen since returning. We all tried to do our duty. I wrote to about eight servicemen. Almost everyone had a serviceman in their family."

"During the war, boys came from Pensacola. The cadets would come over and we would take them to the beach for a picnic. But it turned dark and someone slipped and dropped the food basket spilling all the food and another slipped and ended up with his legs wrapped around a tree. Kitty called and said she found the way, to come on. "Hell if I'm coming", one said. But they went anyway and one had a cigarette and a pack of weenies so they made a fire and roasted the weenies on sticks and had one of the most fun times ever. Later we received letters from these men from the Pacific that said that "it was more dangerous to go to dinner with us than it was to fight the Japs in the Pacific."

"I had a date with an officer who took me to the Brookley Officer's club. Remember that I was the daughter of a Baptist Minister. He gave me a quarter and told me what to do – to drop it in this machine. It hit the jackpot and quarters came flying out. I lifted my skirt to catch them all but he put his hat to catch them. We won about sixteen dollars."

"Grandview Park was built right before the war. Lots of soldiers from the middle states had never seen the water. We dated them and took them to the wharf. There was a juke box on the wharf and we could dance. It had a zoo with lots of animals even tigers. Daddy had a new Dodge and was particular about it. He would not let anyone drive it, but he did let Gene Haliburton, a Sergeant, my date, drive it. We drove to Grandview Park, but we had to be home by 12:00 p.m. There was a tall fence around the park and when we were leaving, the gate was locked and we couldn't get out. We waited and waited for someone to come by and help and finally someone did. A boy named Ollinger said he knew a way back through the swamp and woods, so he jumped the fence and we all drove and drove and finally came out at Hollinger's Island. Daddy believed the story."

"Frascati beach – Everything started there and went all the way to Dog River. Night clubs sprung up all along Cedar Point Road. The most famous night club was called the Airport Restaurant – real important dates were taken there – the other clubs were considered "joints" on Cedar Point Road. One night three of my girlfriends and four marines went to Club Rendezvous. They had not been too long from Guadalcanal. We settled in and danced. A sailor bumped into one of the ladies on the dance floor, and my date asked him to apologize to the lady. He refused. So they escorted us back to the table and said excuse us, we'll be right back. They took the sailor outside. He returned kind of swaggering. The sailor then had some of his friends join him to challenge the marines. They went outside again, only to return to challenge the marines once more. Then a Navy Chief came over, grabbed the sailor by his collar and said, "Haven't you learned your lesson? Leave those damn marines alone!" We felt it was our duty to entertain the boys."

Image on facing page: Katharine Phillips, shown on left in the image, entertains servicemen with friends on the Mobile Bayfront, 1943. Image courtesy of Katharine Phillips Singer.

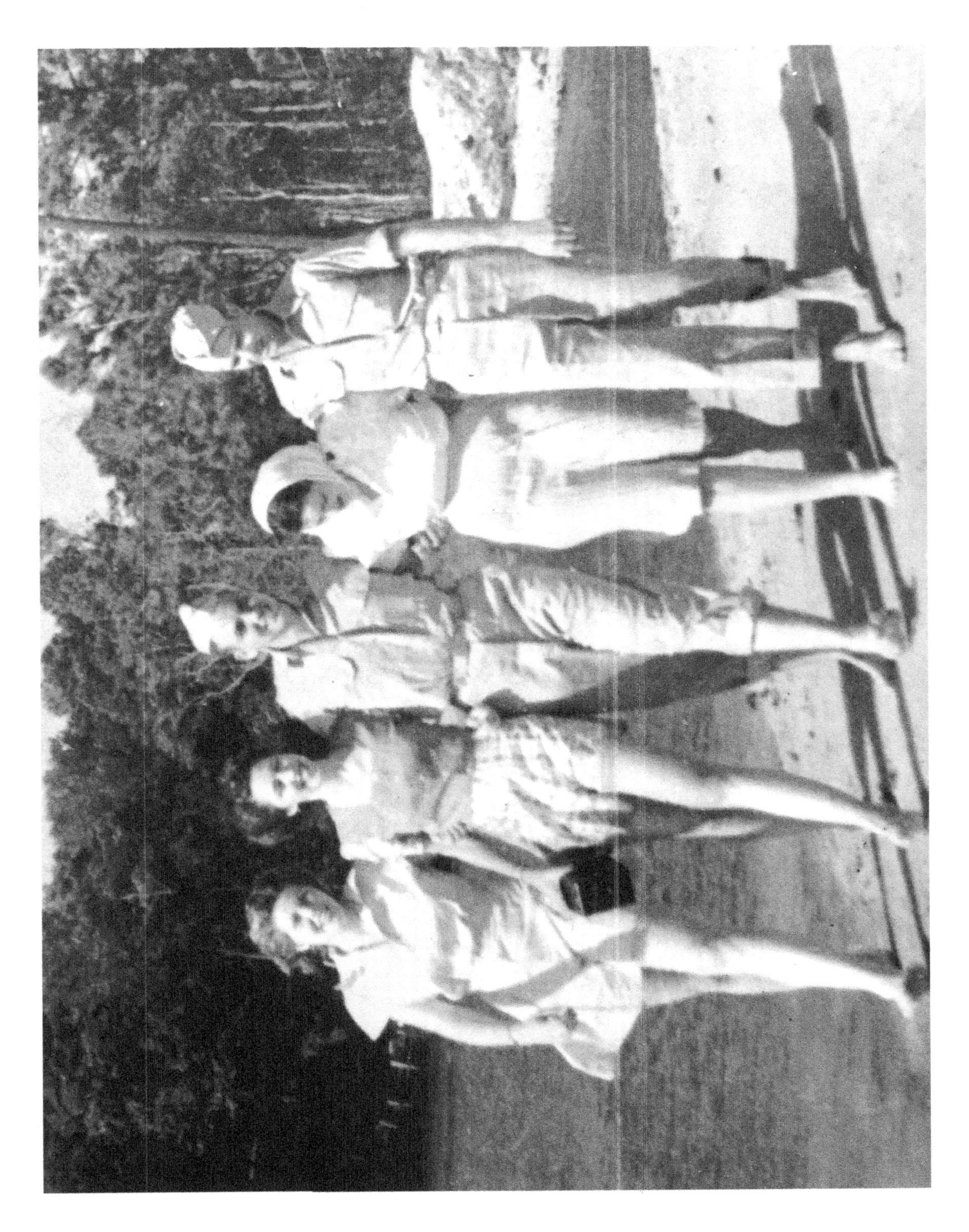

People - Katharine Phillips Singer

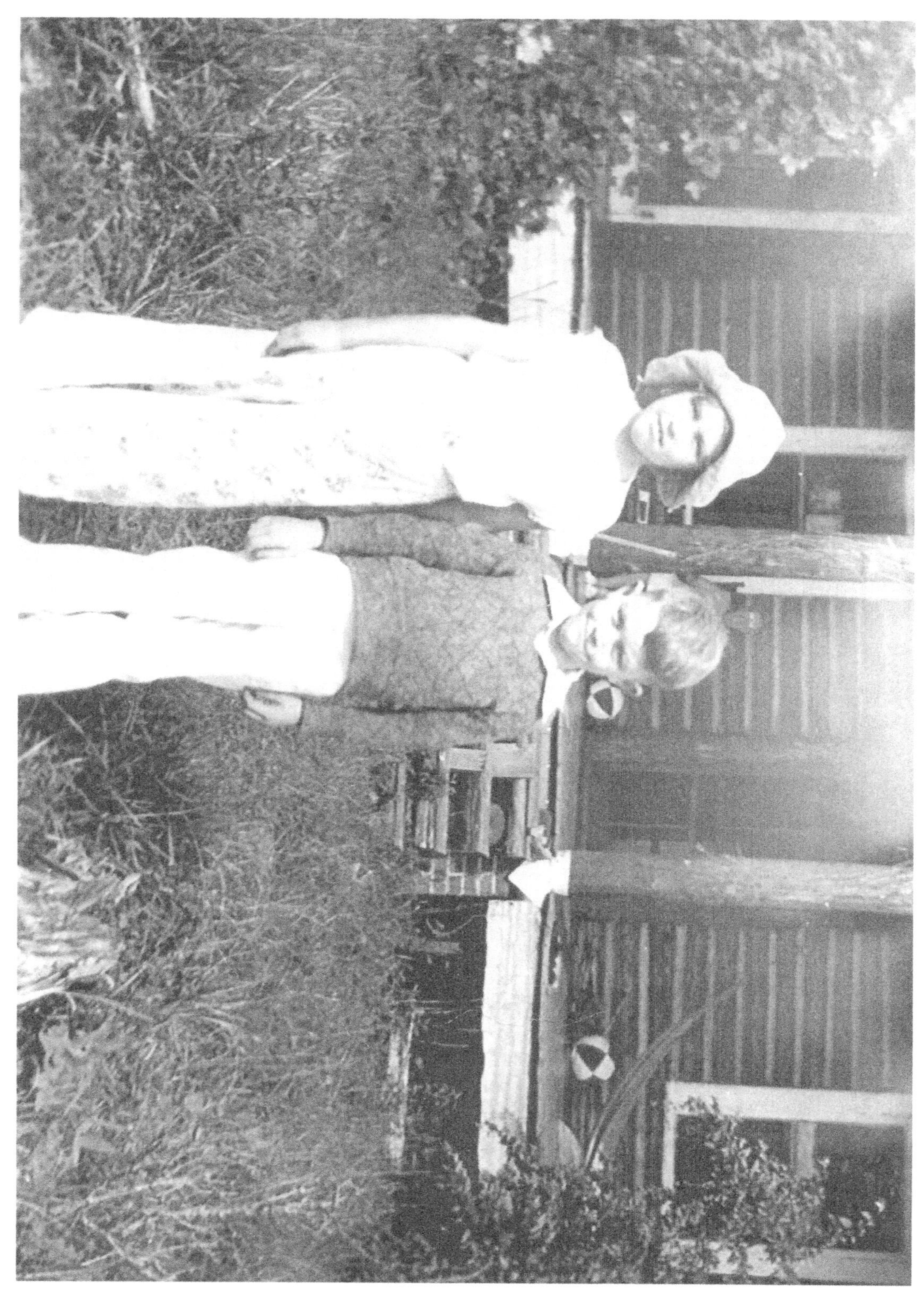

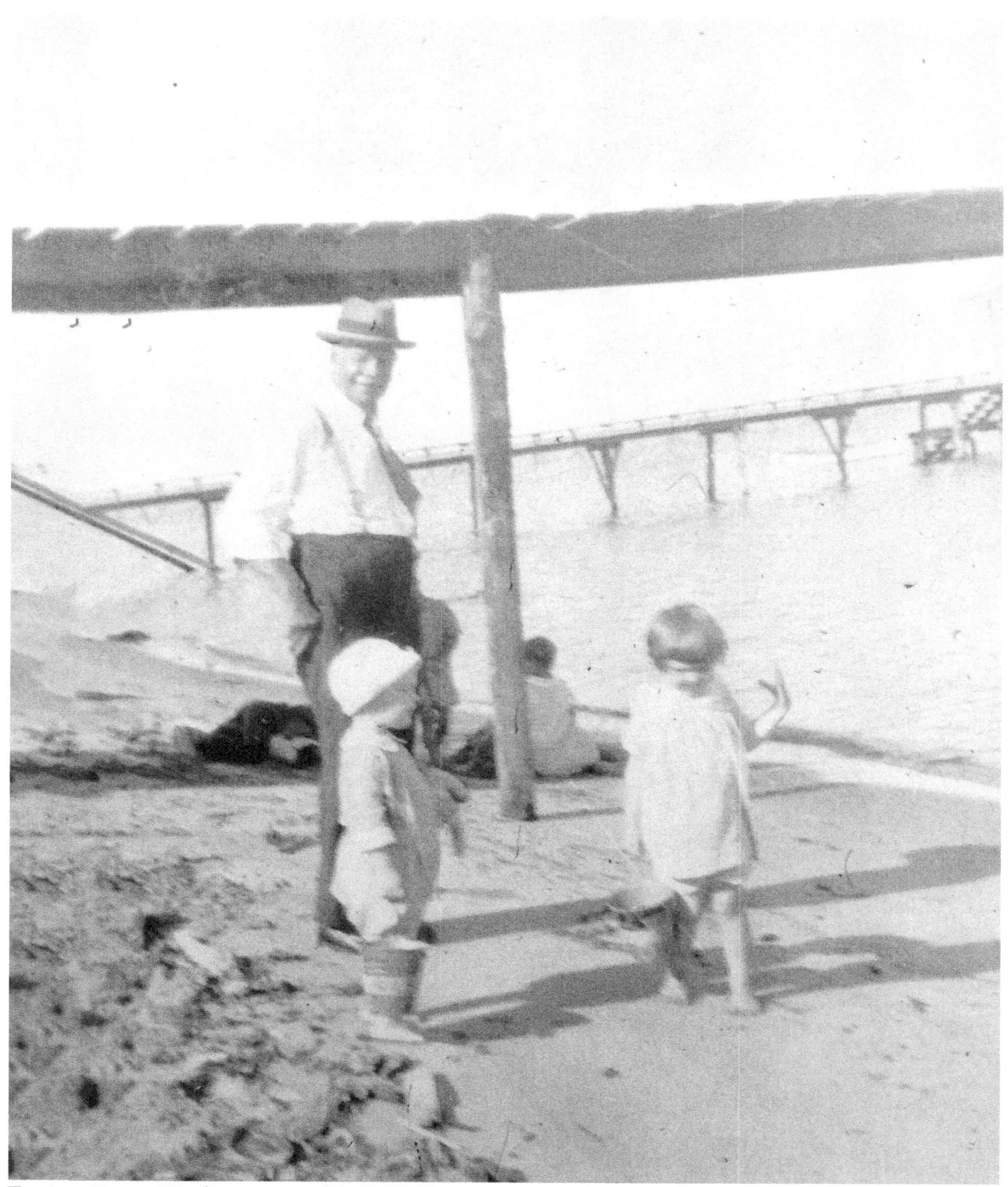

Facing Page: Katharine and Sid Phillips, at Foster's Beach, 1930.
Above: Sid and Katharine Phillips at Fosters Beach with Great Grandfather Luke Phillips who immigrated from England. 1925

Above: Katharine Phillips Singer's mother sailing on Mobile Bay, 1919.
Facing Page: Katharine Phillips Singer's mother swimming in Mobile Bay, 1919.

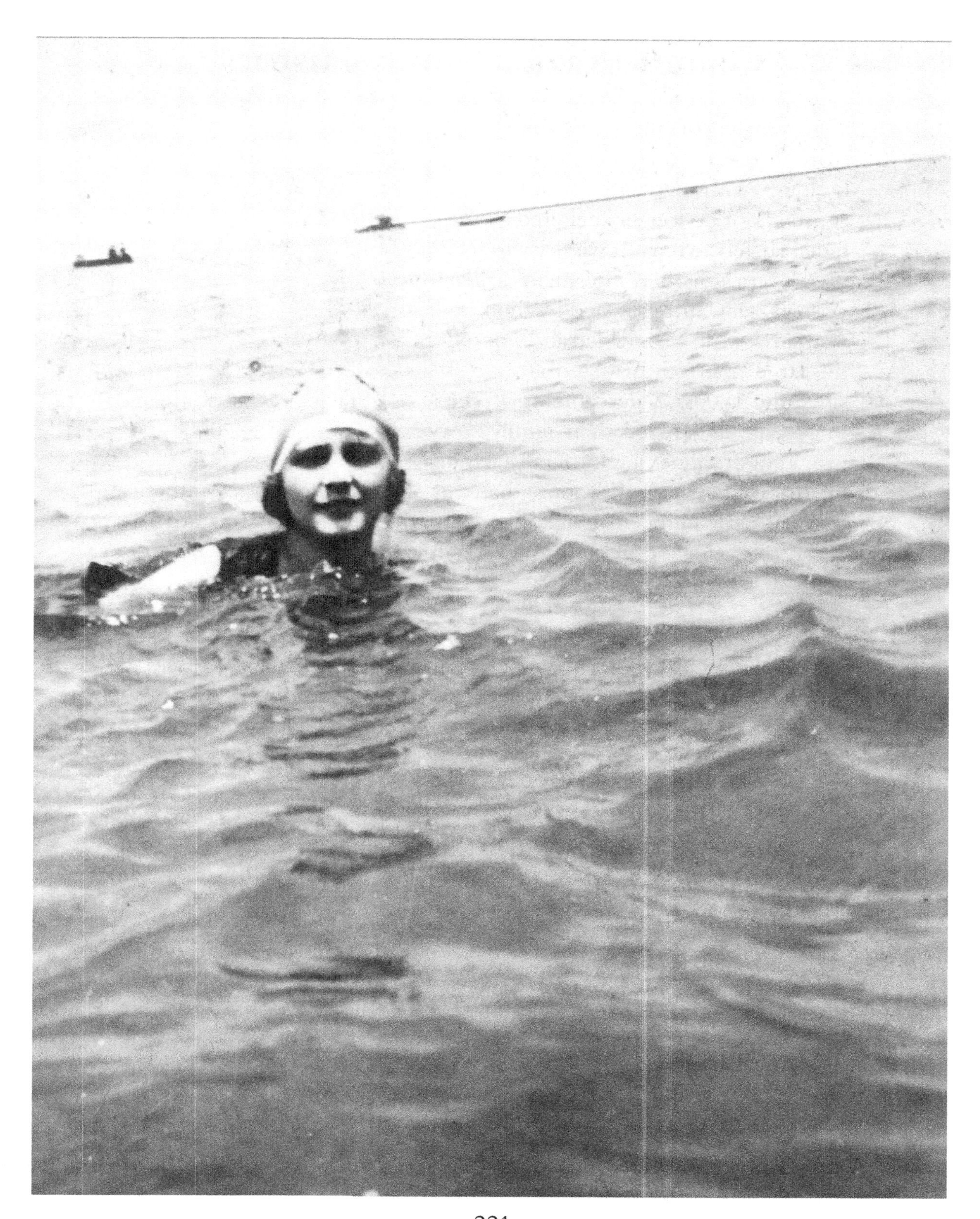

People - Katharine Phillips Singer

Gaines Frazier Family History

Frazier's Store, Cafe and house, 2000.

The remains of the uninhabited old store were haunting: a concrete block building with two large windows, a central door no longer sheltered by the faded rusted awning. It was easy to feel there was a story here. Residents said it was Frazier's Store, owned by the Frazier family who also owned and worked the large tract of farmland around it since the 1800s. A descendant of the Frazier family shared their family story providing a unique view into early farming life of South Mobile. But more than this, it is also the classical American story of early pioneers, demanding work on the farmland, of arduous struggles against oppression and accomplishments through generations.

Gaines Frazier, probably a slave, was born in 1848 in Autauga County, Alabama. He died on his farm in South Mobile in 1947 at age 99. He was the father to twenty-four children by two wives.

Ciby Herzfeld Kimbrough (1942-2012), granddaughter of Gaines Frazier, wrote the following Frazier Family History.

"Long ago in the southeast part of what is now the United States, there were many native tribes who set up villages and organized government. The Cherokee, Chickasaw and Chateau were living in southern Alabama when it became a state in 1819. They lived on farms and grew crops the way they had learned from their ancestors."

"Before the Civil War, many run-away slaves found refuge among these people and became members of their tribes. Just after the war, immigrants, natives, and free African American farmers lived together in the Cedar Point Road community. Gaines and Francis Frazier were descendents of these proud people. They spent most of their lives on their farm on Mobile Bay."

"When Gaines bought the Frazier Farm in 1878, it was mostly swampland and forest. He had to clear it for farming with his mule team. He built a home for his family and a barn for his farm animals. He planted many fruit and nut trees and grew vegetables. As he had sons, he taught them the ways of the early native farmers. To make money to support his young children, he became a dairy farmer. His farm grew to include an 18-mule team and a 138 dairy-cow herd. He even cut a road behind the farm to shorten the distance between Cedar Point Road and Old Bay Front Road so that he could get to town quickly. Today that road is called Doyle Avenue."

Gaines Frazier, his daughters Addie, Nettie holding Will L. Herzfeld, who would become internationally famous, and Juanita, about 1934.

"Our grandfather knew how to make things grow; and he had a mind for business. He enjoyed his work until he died on his farm in 1947 at the age of 99. I believe the farm kept him alive because, it gave him a purpose and lots of exercise."

"On this farm, our grandfather raised 24 children and many grandchildren. He taught them all to farm. Over the years some of his children moved away to make their own lives. To some, he gave land to start their own farms. Many of his children, like him, died on the farm."

"Back in the old days, the females in the family took care of the housework while the males took care of the farm. Older children took care of younger children and taught them do their work. At first this was the only school on the farm. Everyone had plenty to do and it kept them busy all day each day."

"Before the sun arose each morning, the females would prepare a big breakfast for the family. After breakfast the men and boys would leave to work the fields, tend the milk cows and peddle milk and butter."

"The females spent the rest of their day cooking, cleaning, making clothes, canning, washing, ironing, tending the garden, picking fruit and tending the yard animals. In the yard near the house there were chickens, goats, turkeys, ducks, and hunting dogs."

"The poultry was raised for eggs and meat. The goats helped to keep the grass cut; they also made delicious barbeque. The hunting dogs helped the men and boys find wild animals for meat to feed the family. The males hunted raccoons, squirrels, rabbits, deer, quail, duck and wild turkey to feed their large family. They also fished. With as many as twenty-five to thirty family members present for a meal, they needed a lot of food."

Leo Gaines and Neal Frazier, 1950s.

"Grandfather Gaines wanted his children to get an education but there were no schools in this area. Before 1900, he donated some land to his church and helped them to build Race Track Elementary School. (Note: See the Schools section for an image of Race Track School) His children went to school there with many other children in the community. For many years it was the only African American school in the Cedar Point Road area. Because there was no teacher in the area, he arranged for the school bus driver that took the white children to school in the city of Mobile to pick up Ms. Lee, a black teacher on the school bus in the morning and bring her to teach Race Track School. The bus driver would take her home each evening before he picked up the white children of the area to bring them back home. This continued for many years until Mobile County Schools took over the operation of the school."

"The Frazier farm was established before the tractor or trucks were widely used. Horse and wagons were used for the first fifty years of the farm. A pump was the only source of fresh water on the farm. Water was carried in buckets for every need in the house. There was no indoor plumbing. Trees had to be cut down and logs split for firewood. The firewood was used to fuel the fireplaces and the iron cook stove. There was no electricity! Every day was filled with work, work, work!"

"Frances Osborn Frazier, (in picture above) was the second wife of Gaines Frazier after his first wife died and many of his twelve children were adults. Together they had twelve more children who called her "Big Mama". When Gaines Frazier became very old, Big Mama's children continued to take care of the farm under her direction. From the early 1930's Big Mama ran the Frazier's grocery store next to the house. For a long time it was the main grocery store on Cedar Point Road. All summer long people came from miles around for fresh watermelons and ice from her icehouse."

"In the early 1940's, she had a café added the back of the store, so that she and her daughters could tend the store and cook for the family at the same time. They served family style meals each evening. It was not unusual for the meal to consist of five different meats, six or more vegetables and a soup made fresh each day. By 6:30 p.m. the café was filled with people who lived in the area who did not cook dinner. They were mostly farm workers, shrimpers and fishermen who lived in the Cedar Point area. This was during the time of segregation, but Big Mama's café was integrated. Black and white people would sit at the pink and blue tables together and enjoy their dinner and friendship. This was very different from the way of life in Mobile and the rest of the South."

"I spent a lot of time in the café with Big Mama and Aunt Juanita, watching them cook. I would mostly peel vegetables and help in the store. Sometimes I would wander out to the orchard and choose fruit to eat fresh from the trees. I had the most fun playing in water at the old pump. On a summer's day, getting wet allowed me to escape the heat for a time. We didn't have air conditioners."

"With a grandmother who owned a store, you could get cookies, sodas and ice cream just for the asking. My favorite treat was sugar wafers. I could only get them after suppertime in the evening. Before bedtime, I loved to sit on the wind-cooled front porch letting my sugar wafers melt slowly in my mouth as I watched the traffic on Cedar Point Road. Unlike my brothers, I found listening to baseball games and boxing on the radio boring. There were no televisions. The only music on the farm in the evenings were the sounds of the animals and the wind rustling through the shade trees near the house and store."

"My brothers followed our uncles about the farm as they worked. Our grand-father taught his sons to fish, hunt, plant vegetables, graft trees, tend milk cows, slaughter farm animals, store hay and corn, plow, harvest crops and many other tasks necessary for keeping the farm going."

"In 1940, just before World War II, the United States Government needed land for the runway of Brookley Air Force Base; they bought part of the farm that was on the Mobile Bay and closed off part of the road that our grandfather cut. Some of our uncles had to go to fight in the war in Europe. After the war, they returned to the farm determined to keep it going. They learned new methods to improve the farm's yield. By the late 40's, our uncles were able to manage the farm alone with tractors, refrigerated trucks, bush hogs, hay balers, combines, and other farm technology. With these advancements they doubled and tripled cropped the land to market produce all year round. Their days started before dawn and ended after dusk."

"My Grandmother and Aunt enjoyed new advancements with electric lights, a washing machine with a wringer, an electric iron, and a gas stove. Indoor plumbing brought them a kitchen sink and a bathroom. No more trips to the pump for water!"

"Before they were sold, vegetables were graded, washed, and packaged in the refrigerated truck for the grocery store shelves. For more than 50 years the farm produced many of the vegetables for Mobile area grocery stores. Delchamp's Supermarkets, Inc. was their best customer."

"The farm was expanded in the early 40's to include cattle, pecans and timber for sale. By the

1950's our uncles became scientific farmers who worked with Auburn University's Department of Agriculture on projects to prevent erosion and soil contamination. They also acted as consultants for the Agricultural Stabilization and Conservation Services (ASCS) and the Extension Services for Mobile County."

"In 1976, Jones and Kilpatrick wrote "Commercial Vegetable Farming, Mobile, Alabama", an article about the Frazier brothers, Neal, Gaines Jr., and Leo.
After my Grandmother died in in 1963, the Frazier brothers ran the farm with help from Dwight Frazier, while my Aunt Juanita took care of the business. My Mother helped in the house. The store and café were closed to customers but the family still used the café for meals."

Dr. William L. Herzfeld with Haitian President Jean-Bertrand Aristide

"Over the years our uncles taught us a lot about growing things. Farming was selected for them by their father many years earlier; yet it became their life's purpose. Growing safe healthy food became their mission in life. There were all kinds of trees on the farm; many were planted by our grandfather. Our uncles were masters of grafting trees. Many satsuma, kumquat, pear and and peach trees, as well as blue-berry bushes grew in a fruit grove behind the barn. There was also a pecan orchard near the house."

"When I had sons, I carried them to the farm to visit with my uncles and pick fruit. On my last trip to the farm, I picked figs with my granddaughter in the shade of the old pecan tree. That old pecan tree was planted next to the store for shade by my grandfather over 100 years ago. I believe that his spirit lived in it. We know that Mobile can get really hot in the summer. Well, it was never hot under that tree. At 100 degrees in the summer, it was 85 degrees under that tree. Twisted and misshaped by countless hurricanes with many broken limbs, it still bore pecans each year."

"While time stood still on the farm, Mobile, grew all around it. Our uncles got old, but the needs on the farm continued to be demanding. One by one they died. There was no one left to do the work because all the grandchildren had made their lives away from the farm. The last time I saw the farm, it was under demolition. The house, store and barn were gone. The shade trees had been uprooted. It was painful to see. Aunt Juanita was the last of the Frazier children to live on the land. She did not want to sell the farm, but she could not take care of it alone. She sold it to Mobile Public Schools because she felt that it would be good use for the land, since Grandfather Gaines believed in education."

Top Left: Dr. William L. Herzfeld with Reverend Desmond Tutu, Top Right: with Andrew Young, Above: on a humanitarian trip to India., and Right: with sister Ciby and brother on the Frazier Farm, 1946.

Maybe this is why success runs in the offspring of the Gaines Frazier family. Children and grandchildren of Gaines Frazier went on to highly successful careers.

Peter Dais Jr. was a grandson of Gaines. His maternal grandfather, General Gatewood, was a drayman, who hauled with a mule and wagon. He toiled for decades, like his father, as a furniture and piano mover. He supported four sons through college: a cardiologist in Washington, D.C., Dr. Kenneth A. Dais, a teacher, a postal executive, Peter Dais, III, and a computer programmer. He was well respected; even Liberace used him when he played Mobile. Peter Dais Jr's sister, Annie May (Dais) Allen raised four children, two of whom became doctors, one, a lawyer at the Corp of Engineers, and one was a successful real estate agent.

Two other grandchildren of Gaines Frazier, one who was born on the farm, gained national and international prominence working for the greater good of humanity:

Dr. William L. Herzfeld, the first grandson of Gaines and Francis Frazier, was born on the Frazier Farm. He earned a doctorate in Theology. After his graduation from seminary, he worked closely with Dr. Martin Luther King, and Andrew Young in the Civil Rights Movement of the 1960s. He was President of the Alabama Southern Christian Leadership Conference and later served as the President of the Association of Evangelical Lutheran Churches. He worked with South Africans to free Nelson Mandela from prison, and to end apartheid. He was elected the first African-American Bishop of the Lutheran Church in 1984. During his last trip to Africa to ordain the first female Lutheran pastor on the continent, he contracted brain malaria and died shortly after in 2002.

Dr. Ciby Herzfeld Kimbrough was an educator and civil rights activist. She was influenced to stand up for equality by her brother, Rev. William Herzfeld. In 1963, when she was 21, she picketed the segregated theaters and was arrested with about 50 other activists when they tried to enter one of the white-only theaters. In the spring of 1965, Kimbrough participated in three marches from Selma, including "Bloody Sunday," when protesters were driven back across the Edmund Pettus Bridge by police with tear gas, clubs and dogs. She later walked 53 miles to Montgomery from Selma, with several hundred demonstrators. In a famous photograph of King, Kimbrough can be seen following him and the Rev. Ralph Abernathy across the Pettus Bridge. She earned a doctorate in psychology, specializing in early childhood development, and worked for several private psychiatric practices.

She also taught in St. Louis public schools. She later became a psychology professor at Washington University and the University of Phoenix. Kimbrough traveled to more than forty countries. After meeting several women in Nigeria who were struggling to help children with developmental disabilities, she helped start an educational center for children there. Her life tragically ended in a car crash in 2012, at age 70.

Dr. Herzfeld speaking on the balcony where Dr. Martin Luther King was assassinated. 1968.

Mandie and Reggie Wade

An Immigrant's Story

"...the rabbit's belly was split open and it had a note inside"

Reggie Wade would cycle by my house at 8:30 every morning and we built a friendship over the years. We set a date to meet to discuss memories of South Mobile. It was meant to be an interview of a long-time resident to gather his memories of growing up in the area but it turned out to be that and much more.

Mandevillas bloomed on the arched entry into the well-cared for home. The living room was comfortable with two recliners facing a TV, and a leather couch. It was an uncluttered room with no photographs, or paintings. I noticed a little dog bed. Taking my seat on the leather couch, Reggie, his wife Mandie and I settled down for the meeting. What Reggie told me was reinforcement for what I already had heard from others: *"You would come to Joe McGovern's to crab in the 40'. I was ten or twelve. The Bay Front was a shell road. We used cast nets. Daddy would wade out and catch mullet and grass would be up to his knees. The whole neighborhood would go and catch the fish and have a neighborhood fish fry. People would get together and have a party."* His Christmas memory was equally familiar: *"If you got a toy you were doing good. We were given apples oranges and walnuts. You didn't complain either."*

It was then that I noticed that his wife Mandie had an accent. Where are you from Mrs. Wade? *"Belgium."* How did you meet Mr. Wade? *"We Met after the Korean war at the Girls City Club at a St. Patty's Day Party in Rhode Island - servicemen went there."* Was she the prettiest girl there, Mr. Wade? *"Oh yes!"* And was he the most handsome? *"Yes, he had black curly hair, and was soooo handsome."* "Was?" Reggie said with a twinkle in his eye. How old were you when you came to America? *"Sixteen."* I did the mental calculations, and asked, "So were you living in Belgium when the German's took it over? " "*Oh yes.*" "What was that like?" She began:

"The Germans came into Belgium and one night knocked on the door, came inside our house and told my father "Come with us". They took him to a German factory to work. All men 18 years

and older had to go to work for the Germans." How did you survive? "*Mother had to find a job. She worked in a place to make cakes. She put food on the table. My cousin who was a seamstress fixed our clothes to make them last longer. She made me a coat out of a gray blanket that was really nice and warm especially while we waited in line once a week for a little bit of potatoes or a little bit of something else. We waited for hours In bitter cold."* What did you eat for protein? "*Rabbits."* Rabbits? "*Yes. We raised them outside. Mother was working so I took care of them. I was allowed to keep one as a pet, but the others were for eating. It was understood."* What did you feed them? "*We scavenged the neighborhood for grass. They were skinny rabbits."* Who killed them? "*My Grandfather came once a week and killed one."*

"*At school, the Germans tried to force us to learn German, but our parents forbade us to learn it. We would just sit. My German teacher was nice and tried to teach us but we ignored her. She didn't get us in trouble for not learning and she was nice, really. She was not in the army just a teacher. She finally gave up and went back to Germany."*

Did you ever hear from your father while he was gone? "*No, Oh, yes, well one morning mother went outside. She found a dead rabbit in the backyard just lying there. When she picked it up to dispose of it she realized that the rabbit's belly was split open and it had a note inside! The note was left by my father and said that he and his three friends escaped from the German factory and went to France to join the resistance. While there, he went out at night to blow things up."* Did he ever tell you about being in the resistance? "*No, he told my mother though. She couldn't save the note because she said it might get them in trouble."*

During his three years away, German soldiers came into their house and tore it up looking for her father. They gave her chocolate to bribe her into talking one time, but she didn't know anything. "*Germans thought they owned this town. I got out of the way when I saw them coming. The Germans really took over. I saw a young girl chased by the soldiers. She was Jewish, and she ran to the third floor of a neighborhood house and jumped out to kill herself. Some people hid out the Jews in their attics. When they were found and taken away, the Belgians who hid them were taken away also and beaten almost to death. The children were left to the mercy of neighbors."*

Which city were you from? "*My home city was Mouscron, two hours from Brussels. It is right on French border. I could see it from my backyard. The river was the border - not a big river - a stream really. The children would go back and forth over the border quite freely, but now the Germans had a patrol by the river. They would walk back and forth with guns. They also patrolled with army trucks on my street."*

Did your father simply show back up after the war? "*A few months after the war he felt safe to return. He just turned up at home in 1945. I was 14 when the war ended. Father wanted to come to America. His brother, my uncle, had already come here. He left his wife and he never sent for his wife and children. Everyone wanted to leave Belgium because the times were so terrible. When father came to America he worked as a weaver of blankets. He worked in a mill in Providence, Rhode Island and he and I went to night school to learn to speak English for a year, then went on to regular night school. There were people from so many different countries in that class but we all learned to speak English."* What was your language? "*There are two languages in Belgium*", *she said, "Flemish and French. I spoke French. French was considered upper and Flemish was more for farmers or you might say "red-neck Belgians."*

Have you returned to Belgium for visits? "*Yes*", *she said, "but I don't want to go back now because everyone is gone."* Does this feel like home? "*Oh yes*", she said. "*She better say yes after all these years*", Reggie said smiling. This couple has endured war, the loss of their only son, and life's joys and sorrows, but the lines of wear sit gently on them because they still have a warm regard and deep connection to each other.

I left their home, feeling humbled for having had the privilege of hearing this couple's story. The week moved on, and I found myself complaining that I HAD to go to the grocery store AGAIN. Then I remembered the rabbits.

Mary McKeough

Growing up in South Mobile

My name is Mary Helen Butler McKeough. I was born to Richard (Dick) and Lucille Duff Butler in 1937. I had four brothers. We moved to Snake Road probably in the early 1940's. Our neighbors were Vaiden and Lucille Matthews and someone named Dumas . There were only three houses on Snake Road (now known as Shore Acres Drive) for a long time.

World War II was in full swing. Times were very hard for most people. Our house was always open for people who needed a place to stay. Sometimes we would wake up in the morning to find that a whole family of relatives had moved in during the night.

Neighbors were very close-knit. They shared food, wringer washing machines, clothes lines, money, a ride to the store and a shoulder to cry on.

Our house was big, but there were only two bedrooms and the kids all slept in one with mom and dad in the other. There were two porches and a huge swing on the front. When people came to stay, they bunked in the living room and dining room. Dad finally enclosed the back porch for his only daughter, me.

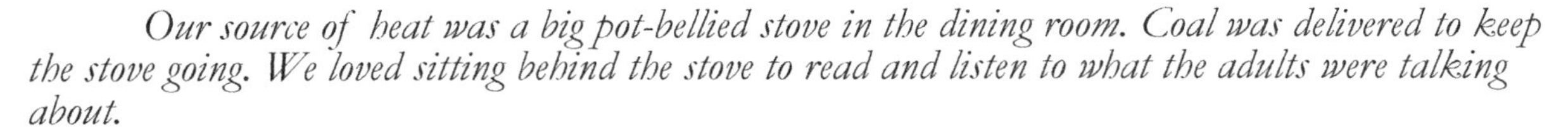

Our source of heat was a big pot-bellied stove in the dining room. Coal was delivered to keep the stove going. We loved sitting behind the stove to read and listen to what the adults were talking about.

Our yard was always a mess. Dad was a plumber and had all his supplies in the back yard. People did not care too much about flowers. If anything was planted, it was a vegetable garden.

We had chickens, hogs, dogs and cats - Our neighbors had cows and we helped round up the cows in the afternoon. The chicken coop was the best place in the world to hide because no one would think of looking for you there. If we had fried chicken, Dad would go out and count his chickens to be sure none of them was in the pot.

Dad was a gentle, kind hearted man who loved kids, animals and everyone else.

Dad worked all day, and Mom was busy cooking, washing clothes, sewing and taking care of kids and being pregnant again. Mom made all of our clothes, underwear included. All of my dresses had those stupid puffed sleeves and I looked like a sissy. I kept those sleeves tucked in. God forbid the elastic broke in your drawers if you were somewhere besides home. I would stand for hours by *momma while she sewed.*

One of my first recollections of the war was looking out of the window at night and seeing the soldiers marching in the fields of grass next to the house. You could see the moon shine on the bayonets. We could see them and hear them tramp through the grass, but never heard them speak a word. Mom and Dad assured us that all was ok. One morning, we found a helmet in the yard and Mom called the Army and they came and picked it up.

Our Uncle Joe was in the Army and he trained at Brookley. One day he came from the woods in his uniform. His uniform was covered with "Beggar Lice" and we picked them off before he returned to the woods. He stood in the yard and Mom was so proud of him.

Every night Mom and Dad listened to the news on the Radio. We had to be very quiet. We did not understand but we learned a lot of new words like — Japs, Kamakazi, Germans, Pearl Harbor, B—29, B—50, invasion, Hitler, Nazi and Frank Boykin.

Our Grandmother who lived with us, was a German immigrant and was very angry that her sons were fighting in the motherland. She would take us in the closet and make us say "Heil, Hitler". Momma would be really mad at her. We liked her because she kept chocolate hidden and shared it with us.

Things like sugar and chocolate were rationed and we did not get much candy. We loved sandwiches made of condensed milk and peanut butter. What did we really like? butter bean sandwiches.

At night, we had to keep the shades pulled down and the top half the car head lights were painted black so the lights would not shine up. Daddy was an air-raid warden and he would leave the house sometimes at night and walk to the Bay .

Snake Road traveled straight to Bay Front Road. At the corner of Bay Crescent and Snake Road there were 4 brick columns that reminded me of entering a mansion. Roses mixed with honeysuckle lined both sides of the road and they smelled sweet and seemed to bloom all year long.

We did not have a Catholic church and on Sundays, we walked down Snake Road, to the mansion and went to Mass in the basement of Dr. Zieman' s house.

Bay Front Road was beautiful. There were side-walks in some places and the road as made of red brick. Red Bricks lined the road in front of some homes. Before the military base was made, Bay Front Road went all the way to Mobile and Arlington Park. There were homes on Bay Crescent filled with many children.

Some houses on Bay Front had been vacated, the windows were broken and were really scary. We call them "haunted". One of the houses was call "The Villa".

After the war was over, my brothers had free rein of the Bay Front. They and their many friends stayed on the Bay from early in the morning until dinner time. They were typical boys: they made carts and wagons, had trapezes in trees, fished, crabbed, rowed their boats, rode bikes, searched for alligators, made bikes from spare parts and probably borrowed bikes. They rode horses if they could find one and got in trouble more than once.

The roads were not paved, of course, and they were sandy and white like the gulf sands. When you drove, you had to stay in the ruts and move over when you met an oncoming car. When it rained, the sand and dirt turned to slick mud and it was easy to get stuck.

Momma bought milk from a farmer on Cedar Point Rd. and we loved to drive to pick it up because the roads were so bad and we could slip and slid and sometime end up in the ditch. We were never hurt in our accidents in the ditch.

Sometimes at night, there would be a knock at the door and the person would tell Dad that they were turning around and got stuck in the mud. Dad would always go with them and (usually about mile in the woods) and pull their cars out. Momma and Daddy always laughed at the excuses the men would give for being in the middle of the woods with their female friends.

The boys and their friends were always finding stuff on the beach. One day after the war was over, they found a bomb and brought it home to mom on a wagon they had made. They were excited and could not understand why Momma was upset. The bomb rolled off the wagon, rolled into the ditch and they kept putting it back. They managed to get the bomb to the garage and took one of dad's large wrenches and took off the large nut on the front of the bomb. Green stuff oozed out of it. It smelled funny and momma called the Army/ Air Force. A big truck and a lot of soldiers and firemen came and took the bomb and even took the boys to look for more. Supposedly the bombs were routinely dumped overboard when they were no longer needed.

The K-Rations they found, never compared to the bomb. Many days, they had K-Rations that had washed up on the beach for lunch.

The girls, of course, had different activities. We played paper dolls, rode our trikes, and later, produced plays. Momma and Mrs. Lucille made us costumes out of crepe paper, with ruffles and bows. The plays were the highlight of the neighborhood. Everybody had to come. We made our younger brothers play with us and they hated it.

As we grew older, the girls ventured to the Bay and were able to fish and crab just a well as the guys. We would row a boat almost to the ship channel and swim in in bluest water you ever saw. The bay was beautiful, you could see fish and crabs, with sea weed flowing in the waves.

The sand on the beach was as white as snow and the water very clear. Logs floated from wherever to the beach and we would pick out a perfect log and pull it out of the sand into the water and played for hours on logs.

We walked everywhere we went and the pavement/ bricks were so hot, your feet would blister. It was funny to see us running from one patch of cool grass to the other to keep our feet from burning. My brothers would compare "toe jam" with each other each night and insist that they did not need a bath. By the end of summer our feet were stained, scarred and cruddy. If we got a cut, someone would pour kerosene on the cut. It burned like the dickens but never got infected.

We had bonfires on the beach, cooked fish and shrimp and pears borrowed from the Zieman' s yard.

The woods around the bay held many treasures: there were paths to camping sites, roads to "lover's lane" and moonshine stills, cable rides from treee, over creeks to the ground and fishing in the creeks. We also found foundations of homes that had been destroyed years before.

We had a lot to entertain us. We read a lot, swam, rode bikes, fished, crabbed and hung out with friends. I think that sometimes we may have had fights. At night we played "kick the can" with all the neighborhood friends. During the summer, my uncle had a movie projector and every weekend he showed movies to the kids on the side yard of our house. We saw the Little Rascals, Frankenstein, and all the cowboy movies. We all sat on the ground and fought the mosquitoes.

Churches were very important to us, we had Riverside Baptist, Our Lady of Lourdes and others. Many continue to serve their members.

School was something else. Before Our Lady of Lourdes was opened, we went to school in town. We got there either by bus or cramped in a one-seater car. We sometimes rode in the back of a truck to get home, rain or shine. Later we rode the School bus provided by Our Lady of Lourdes Church. Bernie Knowles drove the bus and I think he was not much older than us. When Our Lady of Lourdes school opened their doors, we walked to school or rode our bicycles.

If we needed to go to town, or come home from town, we could ride the Bayou La Batre Bus. The bus traveled down/up Cedar Point Road to Fulton Road to Government Street and then to the bus station by the Bankhead Tunnel. If you missed your school bus, you had to ride the city bus to the Greyhound Bus station and wait until 5:45 pm to catch the last bus home.

Then of course, we had plenty of places to shop! Perry's Store was on the corner of Bay Crescent and Cedar Point, (It was there that we got our first taste of a chile dog) then Jackson's Store on Hannon Road and Cedar Point and Brill' s Store on Club House and Cedar Point. There was also a small store, run by the Crocketts on Cedar Point. They sold vegetables and Hot dogs. Most important was Zip and Vic' s Service Station owned by the Lartigues who did so much and continue to do so much for the community.

Of course, there were the night clubs: The Happy Landing, a dance club with huge neon lights where by Rite Aid is now. Then there was the Radio Ranch made famous by Curtis Gordon and Elvis even appeared there once. Our parents took all the kids there to dance at an early age (drinking and all). On Cedar Crescent, there was the Club Star Dust. They had parties every Saturday night and we could hear the music all the way to our house.

Later we were blessed with Mr. Mac's Dairy King, Colonel Dixie, Greer's and Robinson's Five and Dime, Parkway Pharmacy with Dr. Oliver, and Trimmier Park.

We did grow up, some of us went on to high school, graduated and got jobs at Brookley, then married. Others quit school in high school and went into the military.

Mrs. Frances Sirmon
At her home on Park Road

"Back then, this was out in the country and we could sit outside in our panties and bra"

"My earliest memories are when my Aunt would bring us down to Alba beach. I was five years old and we would take a ride down Cedar Point Road to Alba beach which was also called Barrett's Beach. Captain Alba left the land to the people to enjoy plus an easement for them to walk through. In 1930 there was a pavilion at Alba Beach built there by Mr. Buchannan."

"Daddy owned a motor boat called the "Big Launch" and he kept it at the foot of Eslava Street where Southern Fish and Oyster is now. We'd go in the boat over the causeway to his camp house in Spanish Fort. We'd stay there 3 or 4 days, drink beer and barbeque and come back."

Mrs. Sirmon was born in 1925 at the corner of Washington Avenue and Savannah Street downtown. She married in 1942 at age 17, and moved to Park Road on the bayfront where she lived for 75 years. *"J.D. Lyon built this house for $3800"*, she remembered smiling. Very shortly after she was married, her husband joined the Merchant Marines to serve during World War II. *"One of my happiest memories is on one Sunday afternoon when my husband was at war, I asked my friend to "walk the bay". We got our cigarettes and gigs and went out. My neighbor said you'll never catch anything in the daytime. We caught so many crabs we filled the basket. Oh, that was fun! We liked to use the crabmeat in omelets. We'd chip up onions and bell pepper and a little garlic and flour with eggs. Soooo good. I make a good gumbo…I put crabs and shrimp in mine."*

"I loved crabbing. We'd go out when the water was calm and wade out waist deep because that is where the crabs were. We would bring in tubs full, sometimes coming in at three a.m. We'd boil them and clean them the next day. We'd use a big wash tub and set that into an inner tube and go out with a crab light. We'd catch so many crabs we couldn't pull any more in because they were so heavy. We'd gig them and scoop them up. We didn't use a net. Sometimes we went "depression crabbing". That means we'd use a ball of chicken bones tied up with a string, weighted down with some washers or bolts. We would wade out there in our clothes, no bathing suit, and just scoop them up. We had parties down here. We'd have a "Rock-ola" that played '78 records, boil shrimp and dance. We all smoked cigarettes. Everybody smoked then.

"Back then, this was out in the country and we could sit outside in our panties and bra, because we could hear the cars coming and we could run in and put clothes on." When asked what was the happiest day of her life, she answered, *"When I retired!"* And to the question, how do you keep your complexion so beautiful? *"Ponds. Every day. And I leave a little on at night"*. (Mrs. Sirmon, at right on her pier in 1942, passed away at her home in 2017.)

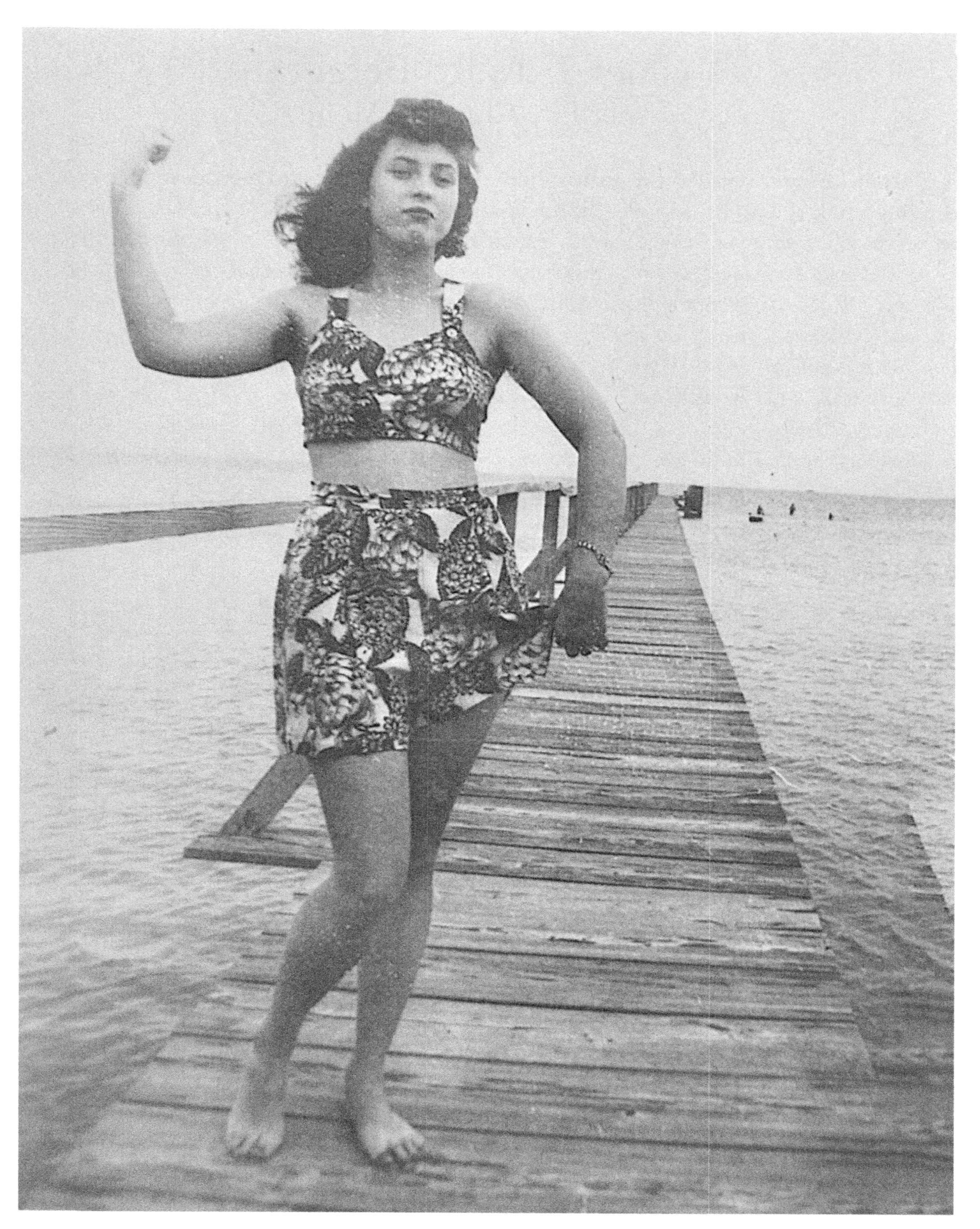

People - Frances Sirmon

Chief Edward Berger
Former Fire Chief of Mobile

Edward Berger recalled the atmosphere of life as a child and teenager while growing up in the South Mobile: *"We went duck hunting near where the Yacht club is now to a marsh island about twenty by twenty feet in size. We'd also go out in a boat by the blinds at Brookley or by the Radio station on Bay Front Road and wade out in hip boots and put cane out for a blind. We went before daylight because that is when they flew away. We shot diving ducks, canvas backs, and blue bill scaup…greater and lesser scaup and a few mallards. Sometimes there were so many ducks that it sounded like WWIII. We would be about 200 feet away from them. The worse the weather was the better for duck hunting. We would put out the decoys and get behind a log and shoot them with a double gage shot gun. If I went alone, I'd carry two bags of decoys and a gun, throw out the decoys and hold on to the gun, get behind the blind and freeze to death. Mom would cook them but the flavor was so strong I didn't eat them."*

In 1954, Edward was on the baseball team coached by Mr. Dulaney. T-shirts were donated by Brill's grocery store. Even though they were a "home grown" team, they went on to play in Bay Minette and other places and tcompeted against little league groups.

"Movies were held in the backyard on a screen at Mr. Pedersen's house down the road on Riverside Drive. He would charge ten cents per child under twelve years of age to see the movies. I rode a mule one time to the show. Some boys would watch from the side yard without paying while eating the neighbor's scuppernongs."

The Bolton family owned property on clubhouse road. They built a pool, (shown below) had a lake and a pasture with cows. People in the neighborhood would come and enjoy their facilities.

Edwards father, Edward Buddy Berger, was a talented pianist known by many who played at the Happy Landing Club in the 1940's and at many other venues in Mobile. Edward also has musical talent and played in a band at Grand View Park at dances for the Catholic Youth Organization of Our Lady of Lourdes Catholic Church.

Edward's family, like many in the area owned a boat in dog river. He recalls that "*there was a monkey on a chain next door. We were told to stay away from it, but one day my brother pushed the boat too close to the monkey and as my brother jumped out of the boat, the monkey jumped in and attacked me. I still have scars on my leg and arm.*"

The Plane Crash: "*We heard about the airplane crash after school when I was a senior at Murphy in 1959. So when we came home, we jumped in the boat and went up the river. We saw a place where everything was knocked down where the airplane had crashed. We waded into the river to look for it, but fuel was in the water burning our legs, so we had to get out. I stepped on something and reached down and gathered a small piece of the plane. The pilot landed farther away. The seat landed on Keeling Road.*"

Jean Hopper Turner and her brother Bond Hopper

"I saw palm trees for the first time and could even taste the salt in the air"

Decades have passed, but the warm memories of life in South Mobile are still vivid and cherished by Mrs. Jean Hopper Turner, and her brother Mr. Bond Hopper.

WWII brought he Hopper family to Mobile, Bond said. "*We came from the country in Tennessee during hard times. We heard from a relative that there were jobs here at the shipyard. We left Jackson, Tennessee at midnight and rode The Rebel train that ran from Mobile to St. Louis. After riding all night, stopping in every little station on the way we arrived in the most beautiful station. I saw palm trees for the first time, and I could even taste the salt in the . The water was safe to swim in then and we lived in our bathing suits all summer. The first flounder I caught was shocking…a flat fish with eyes on one side…but our neighbor said, "Boys, you got a good one!*"

Mrs. Turner was only eighteen when she started teaching at South Brookley Elementary School after one year of training. of training. "*During WWII you couldn't get teachers, but I went on to get a Master's degree and more later. Lillian Becton (the principal) was mean but she made a teacher out of me,*" she remembered. Mrs. Turner taught at South Brookley for fifteen years before working at Barton where she served in Human Resources for twenty years hiring teachers.

Her brother Bond remembered the coronation which was every year at South Brookley in May with maypole dances. "*Mrs. Becton made me walk with a girl in the maypole dance who no one wanted to walk with.*" Mrs. Turner recalls sewing a decorative dress for a student who wanted to be in the coronation, and couldn't afford it. "*We all helped each other*". "*South Brookley also had a Mardi Gras parade inside the building with little wagons decorated with crepe paper that went up and down the hallways. The school was heated with a coal-burning furnace. Volunteers students would go out and carry in the coal.*"

Mrs. Turner worked at Brookley for one year during the War in 1944 balancing the rotors that went into flight indicators. Before that she assembled ball bearings for the flight indicators. The assembly room had to be dust free so there were no windows. "*One day the lights went out and we were completely in the dark. After the war ended we weren't needed anymore.* "

Mr. Bond Hopper, brother of Mrs. Turner recounted how the neighborhood off park road was enjoyed by residents: "*Mr. Barrett gave the right of way across front of Park Road which was called Alba Beach Road back then. Teenagers would go to Foster's beach, a hangout for teenagers with a juke box. Mrs. Foster made everyone behave. There was a right of way all the way to Dog River. Families swam there. Mr. Barrett left the Alba beach area for all to enjoy but a Miss Buchanan put up a building and a wharf and sold popcorn and drinks and charged twenty-five cents to park a car. Mr. Newman took her to court and Mrs. Buchanan had to tear out her structures. Later when Mr. Newman would walk the beach, Miss Buchanan would yell, "There goes Hitler!"*"

"*Most women stayed home and got together for lunch. You didn't lock your door. When they asked their father why, he said "because someone might want to come in"*.

"*When we were little our neighbor told us to "make tracks" along the bay front. "Our little feet would make indentations in the bay mud for the soft-shell crabs to hunker down into. Then they could be found more easily.* "

"*When we first came here in 1944 people had row boats because there was no gas for engines due to the war. We built our boat. We were lucky we didn't die because we had no life preservers and rowed out to the ship channel and came back in with a boat full of fish. One of our neighbors always was waiting for us with an empty pan to get her share. Mobile was good to us.*"

"*My father was the manager of Grand View Park. The Government owned the park and used it as a recreation area for military people. The Pavilion had a dance floor and a PX for beer and cigarettes. MPs stood at the gate and there were a few slot machines for servicemen to play on, but not for civilians. There was a big walk-in safe where the slot machines were stored on Sundays. My father, Mr. Hopper ran the park for two years until the war ended. Joe Paluchi bought Grand View Park from the government and added the famous carousel. There was a house, an artesian well, civil war cannons for display, a small lake, horses to ride and a zoo. You could rent bathing suits for men. They were thick and made of wool because polyester had not been invented then, and cotton was too thin.*"

Later Mr. Hopper's father "*worked at Warehouse 13 and 14 on Brookley, the largest in America, and transferred to Warner Robbins after Brookley closed.*"

The Lartigue Family

Because it looks like a lonely unpretentious grave in in the small Lartigue family cemetery on Cedar Point Road, no one could ever guess the life journey of Marie Joseph LaGrand who lies below this marker, the oldest grave in the cemetery. She was born in 1840 in Belgium and became the wife of Dr. Isadore Joseph Delveaux.

Their Life in Europe:
Dr. Delveaux practiced medicine for a while with his uncle in Belgium, but his heart did not lie in medicine. His true love was horses, having been around the horse breeding business his father and grandfather owned. When the pandemic equine influenza broke out in the 1870s, Isadore begged his father to treat the horses and managed to save 90% of the stock. His father then agreed to let Isadore go to Veterinary Medicine School, where he obtained another degree. Isadore and his father worked together in the family horse business, in which he was a partner, but he was disinherited when he told his parents that he would marry a commoner, Marie Joseph LaGrand. Marie and Isadore had ten children in Belgium, seven boys followed by three girls: Joseph, Adrian, Constance, Edmond, Albert, Emile, Leopold (Paul), Sidonie, Leocadie (Aunt Kitty) and Marie Agnes, the youngest. The notorious King Leopold of Belgium required that any family with seven boys born in succession had to name the child Leopold and give him to the Palace for education as consort to the King and Queen. Dr. Delveaux did not want to break up his family so he decided to leave Belgium.

Marie Agnes was three when her father left the family business in Belgium, moved to Reims, France and partnered with a Marquis to raise and sell pedigreed horse and show horses. They even sold Ringling Brothers their first show horses. Agnes spoke of living in a large stone house, all meals in a dining room, and a seamstress who made all the clothes for the children. She attended school at age three being carried by her older brothers three miles to school. The family still owns her first French primmer. The boys helped with the horses and sang in the choir at Reims Cathedral. Albert, a prankster, decided to sing in the choir with only ½ of his face shaved which created such a commotion in the choir loft that ended his church pranks. Fortunately for Albert, Dr. Delveaux did not believe in corporeal punishment.

Marie Joseph had severe migrane headaches and although she went to many doctors, she did not get relief. She decided to walk ten miles from their home to Lourdes, hoping for a cure. She took her youngest child at the time, Adrian who could not yet walk. With blistered feet after the long walk she waded into the Lourdes stream, bathed her face in the water and held Adrian with his feet in the water. He walked from that time on, and Marie Josephine never had another headache.

Kitty and two of the boys caught smallpox in Reims. Dr. Isadore requested two interns from a Paris hospital to attend to the children in an isolated room at home. The interns withdrew serum from the pox papules on their faces. All three children survived, but Agnes slipped into see what was going and ate an apple on the table to the family's dismay, but she did not get small pox to everyone's surprise.

Agnes recalled her father talking about a special formal black-tie and tail dinner to entertain business associates. The Marquis' spoiled little boy was told to stay in his room upstairs, but he slipped down unnoticed, and with scissors, cut off the tails of the dinner guests. (This same little boy later came to the states to visit the Delveauxs when they lived in Springhill, Alabama.)

The move to America:

A French Count convinced Dr. Delveaux to come to America to start a horse breeding business since there were few good horse breeders at the time. He had already traveled to America selling horses and believed the pastures were greener and decided to leave France even though his wife and business partner, the Marquis of Reims were against the move. One daughter, Sidonee suffered a bad hip injury skiing before the family came over on the Isle de France, a passenger-freight ship. They brought six of their horses and barrels of china and cut glass, all stolen on the passage. The family jewelry was also stolen even though it was placed a cigar box hidden in bed with sick Sidonee. Upon arriving in New York, Sidonee went to doctors but did not respond to treatment, and died shortly thereafter, possibly from osteomyelitis. Antibiotics had not yet been invented.

The family and horse business settled into Mt. Clemmon, Michigan, and they found other French people across lake Michigan to socialize with including a gentleman friend who had a vicious growth on his tongue. He had been to New York and did not respond to their treatment so he asked Dr. Delveaux to treat him since he was both a veterinarian and an M.D. Dr. Delveaux didn't have a medical license to practice in the U.S., but he agreed to treat the friend with the understanding that no money was to be involved. The man became healthy again and became a staunch friend. One of the older boys, Emile, developed Typhoid Fever while working in Detroit as a chef in a hotel. He died and his body was shipped home. Then Katie and Agnes developed typhoid. Agnes had a mild case, but Kitty was at death's door and lost consciousness. One night a vagabond slipped into the barn to sleep for the night, smoked cigarettes and caught the barn on fire. The horses burned and the house was threatened. In the course of the excitement, Kitty in her delirious state wandered outside and was found in a ditch in front of the house. Her doctor said she could not get well, but slowly, she did recuperate.

After the great fire in Michigan, and against many of their friends wishes, the family headed for Mobile, Alabama, but by mistake the train put them off in Chunchula. The family thought, "What a desolate place". Madam Delveaux wanted to go back to France. Someone finally routed them to Mobile which was also a disappointment, but they quickly made friends. They had hoped to find a lot of French speaking people in Mobile but found very few. They rented a large home with acreage from Mr. Clay King where Dr. Delveaux practiced veterinary medicine with the help of his oldest son, Joseph, as interpreter. Later the family moved to Springhill near the Convent of Visitation.

Below is a brief account of what happened to the remaining Delveaux children:

Adrian became a chef in Kansas City hotel, and was later the manager there. He married a Swedish woman, Christine, and had one daughter, Blanch.

Joseph Delveaux and his wife Leonee had two children, one named August.

Constance Delveaux had five children, but three died with diptheria. Only Edmond and Jeanie Dunklin survived.

Albert married Jennie Lartigue, the sister of Louis Paul (grandfather of Zip and Vic). They had no children and lived in Kansas City, Missouri where Albert worked in a meat packing company. Albert met his death walking into an open elevator and fell six floors.

When Mrs. Delveaux died in 1910 in Springhill, Agnes moved to Kansas City and lived with her brother Leopold. She attended college and worked in a design and dress making shop until Leopold died in an auto accident while returning from a baseball game. Her father encouraged her to return to Mobile to live with her sister Kitty, and him.

This story was summarized from the family history by Marie Louise Lartigue, who was the daughter of Marie Agnes Delveaux, and the grand-daughter of Marie Joseph LaGrand, (buried at the Lartigue Family cemetery)

Above: Barbara Lartigue Smith's wedding in the original Our Lady of Lourdes Catholic Church, 1961. Photo courtesy of Barbara Lartigue Smith.

Facing page: Great Grandfather of Lou Lartigue, Zepra Lartigue and Molly Greer, about 1880. Photos and family story courtesy of Lou Lartigue.

Teddy McGill

Born on Riverside Drive, 1937

"We wanted to win the marbles. No girls were allowed to play"

At South Brookley School, all the boys would play marbles. There were five or six circles drawn in the dirt at any time. We'd play before school, during recess, and after school. We wanted to win the marbles. No girls were allowed to play. It was the first gentlemen's only club, I suppose. The school was heated with a coal furnace. I volunteered to carry the coal into the school because I was always dirty. It was like a family.

"I joined the Boy Scout troop for $1.00. We met at Our Lady of Lourdes. At the first meeting they gave me a flag and told me that I had to carry it down the hallway. The school looked as though it was an old army barrack with a long hallway down the center. So, I took the flag. They turned out the lights. What they didn't tell me was that they were going to beat me all the way down the hall. That was my first and last boy scout meeting."

"My friends and I used to walk across Riverside Drive and cut through the woods. There was an old cemetery there. (Casher Cemetery) One night we were walking home and I accidentally stepped into a freshly dug grave and sank up to my waist. I got out and I don't remember my feet ever touching the ground I ran so fast on the way home."

"I used to go to Mr. Peterson's movies that he showed in his backyard and charged all the kids a dime. When he raised the price to a quarter, I'd climb the scuppernong tree next door, eat scuppernongs and watch the movie for free."

"Father Donald from Lourdes Catholic Church would drive a bus all through Riverside and pick up kids to go to Lourdes to play baseball. The truck broke down many times, and we would get out and push. The Shaw boys, Joe Pounds, the Fields all played. Our team was called the "Clubhouse Foxes" which is probably why we never won a game. But so what? We had a good time."

"There was a holiness preacher who planted a large field of sweet potatoes across from Allen Court on Riverside Drive. At harvest time he'd hire some of us boys to pick up the sweet potatoes he had plowed up with a mule and sled. We had to pick up the sweet potatoes and throw them on the sled. He gave us a quarter if we filled the sled. Sometimes he didn't give us anything. So we would kick out some sweet potatoes onto the ground and take them home to our mamas."

"We fished and hunted and stayed in the woods. We would duck hunt off Bayfront Road. We paddled over Robinson's bayou to hunt in the woods. One day, they cut roads into the woods and we were mad. (Sherwood Subdivision) They messed up our hunting grounds. Once I found a hornet's nest. I thought all the hornets were gone, but a few weeks later, the larvae hatched and they were back! "

"One of my first jobs when I was twelve was working for Mr. John O'Brian at his boat dry dock and repair business on Allen Court. He was a former ship captain on the Mississippi and had some good stories. My job was to scrape barnacles off the boats bottoms. I painted some too. Shrimpers would bring their boats to him for repairs."

"There was a British boy who moved down here and he wore wool even in the summer. He had an accent and was different from us and we didn't like him. He took a lot of hits. He'd call us "bloody rot" and then we would hit him some more. He turned out ok, though, and owned a nice business."

"There were some really poor people here then. One family lived in a tar-paper shack. We didn't have to worry about getting robbed. Everyone got along."

Rosa Boone (1916-2017)

"I do not regret being poor at all. Being poor brings out things that you might not know you had."

A resident of South Mobile since World War I, Mrs. Boone was age 98 at the time of our interview.

Her father was from Spain and had lived and worked in Bauxite, Arkansas, where aluminum ore was being mined to build planes for WW I. He moved to Oakdale known then as the "the south part of town" in 1920, fell in love, married and the newlyweds returned to Arkansas where their only child Rosa was born. After World War I the family returned to Mobile when Rosa was two.

When she was four her family lived on Cedar Point Road in a house next to a store they ran near Cedar Crescent. She recalled, "*There were Gypsies who lived in woods behind the store. They wore colorful clothes and the women had long hair and they always had good transportation. They came south every year in wintertime, and came in our store and bought things. They didn't bother anybody. They had their own cars and they lived in tents in the woods behind the store near the bay. They led a traveling life.*"

Rosa recalled that "*there were only dirt roads and woods down here in the early 1920s. The big crop here was satsumas. Fields and fields of them were planted as far as you could see. Theodore had a train stop, important for shipping the satsumas. One winter there was a horrible freeze and every single satsuma froze and instantly the industry was gone. It hurt the people.*"

"I had a good education in the Catholic Schools. Anybody who would look into that would see that they teach things that are neglected in some homes. Mixing religion with education is a good thing, and it was free when I went to the old St. Vincent's Church and Academy until the 8th grade. After that I went to Bishop Toolen High School for girls which had Sisters of Loretta from Kentucky. I'd play the mandolin for the girls to dance to during lunch."

"My mother was an angel and she ironed everything she could get her hands on. She washed the clothes by hand too. She was a worker. My parents never even said "Damn". We had a T-model Ford. During the war everything was rough because you couldn't buy much. No sugar, but we managed. But being poor has its advantages because you are more serious about life. Being poor brings out things that you might not know you had. I do not regret being poor at all. My mother cashed in an insurance policy to pay for my graduation and she bought me a pair of white high-heeled shoes, and a white graduation dress with the money. When times were hard, Daddy and I entertained ourselves by singing and playing the mandolin. We had a lot of years playing music together. We'd sit on the porch and sing songs like "Blowing Bubbles, La Paloma and The Swallow". Evidently the neighbors liked it too because they didn't complain."

"I can still do the Charleston. I had some cousins who were flappers, and when I moved into the big Linzey house on Bay Front Road in the 1950', one of my cousins said, "I'm glad these walls can't talk. I think they served booze here". Mrs. Boone lived in the Linzey's house for ten years and had ten children. "I lost one who is buried at Pine Crest. I was asleep for all ten children. My babies were all born behind the Providence Hospital where there was a special place just to have babies. My first baby was born in 1939. Now my youngest child is 56. Once I came home after giving birth and cooked supper. The Dr. called and fussed at me".

Mrs. Boone's children went to Little Flower. "*Before Lourdes*", she related, "*Catholic children went to Little Flower. Father Burns was at Little Flower. In those days his car had running boards and he always had boys on the running boards...he dedicated his life to boys and sports. He was an excellent person. He took them to ballgames."*

"Being an only child, I had to entertain myself so I read a lot and I wasn't interested in dolls. I loved words. Words to me are like people. I went to Bishop State when I was in my 70's, for nine years. I took history, and I took everything they had to offer and I loved it. I went back again and again and even took painting which I loved. I learned about Haiku and I wrote a Haiku poem that was published in Japan. It was the only one published from the United States."

The last time I saw Mrs. Boone, she was standing in the voting line for the 2016 Presidential election. "*Let me go ahead*", I overheard her say. "*I am a hundred years old,"*

As I escorted her to the front of the line, and when I asked how she was, she told me, "*I still* go *to mass every morning.* (At Our Lady of Lourdes) *It is a part of my life. Everyone thought I would become a Nun. I've been lucky. The Lord has been good to me and my faith has helped me. I had a wonderful life, undoubtedly one of the most happy lives.*" Mrs. Rosa Boon passed away in 2017 at age 101. Below and on the next page is one of her many wonderful poems.

A Summer Day in Mobile

Dawn's goddess wears her fairest gown

And wanders softly through the town,

But cruel wench, in cool deceit,

Hides grim Apollo's fevered heat.

The golden ball ascends the sky

And when at noon the sun hangs high,

Each ray a white-hot burning brand

That leaves its mark, your summer tan.

Don't think, too soon, the worst is through,

The very breath of Hell's at two;

Like dragon' fiery flames it sears,

It burns the eyes too dry for tears;

Purgatory's expiation

Measured out in perspiration!

Go seek your icy eaves of home

'Til evening's cooling breezes come.

And when at twilight's peaceful call,

You lean upon some garden wall,

Where curling fingers wildly climb

Of blooming honeysuckle vine

You smell the Rose of Cherokee

That clings to picket, lazily.

Remember these are summer's boon,

Now dare you curse the sun at noon?

Doug Allen
The Cowboy

A very interesting thread in the fabric of South Mobile for decades has been Doug Allen, known simply to all as "The Cowboy". He can be seen riding his bicycle daily in most neighborhoods and is friendly to everyone. No one seems to know his story, but his presence is a reassuring constant and reminder of the intriguing people

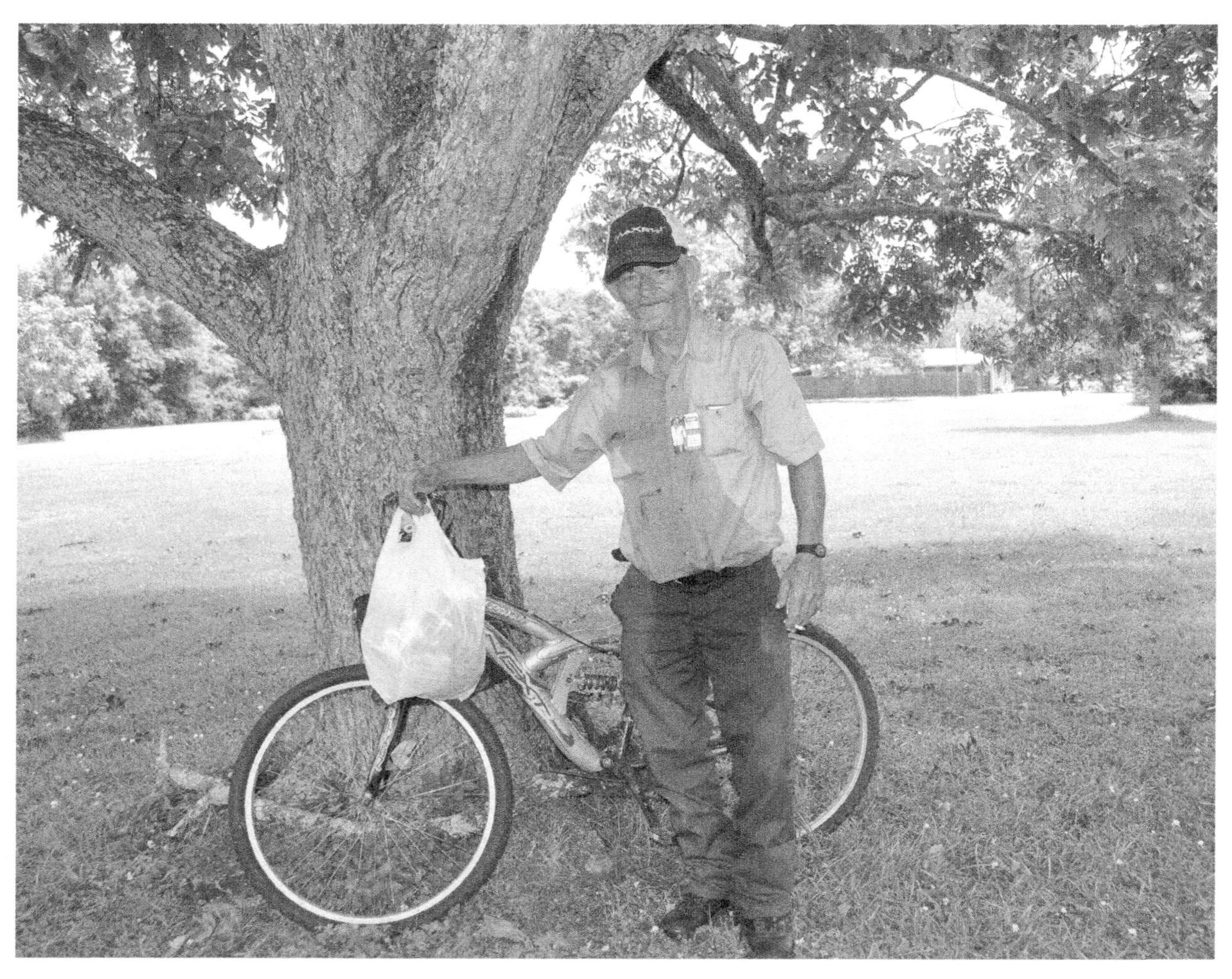

Above: Doug Allen in 2014. Facing page: Doug Allen in the 1980s.

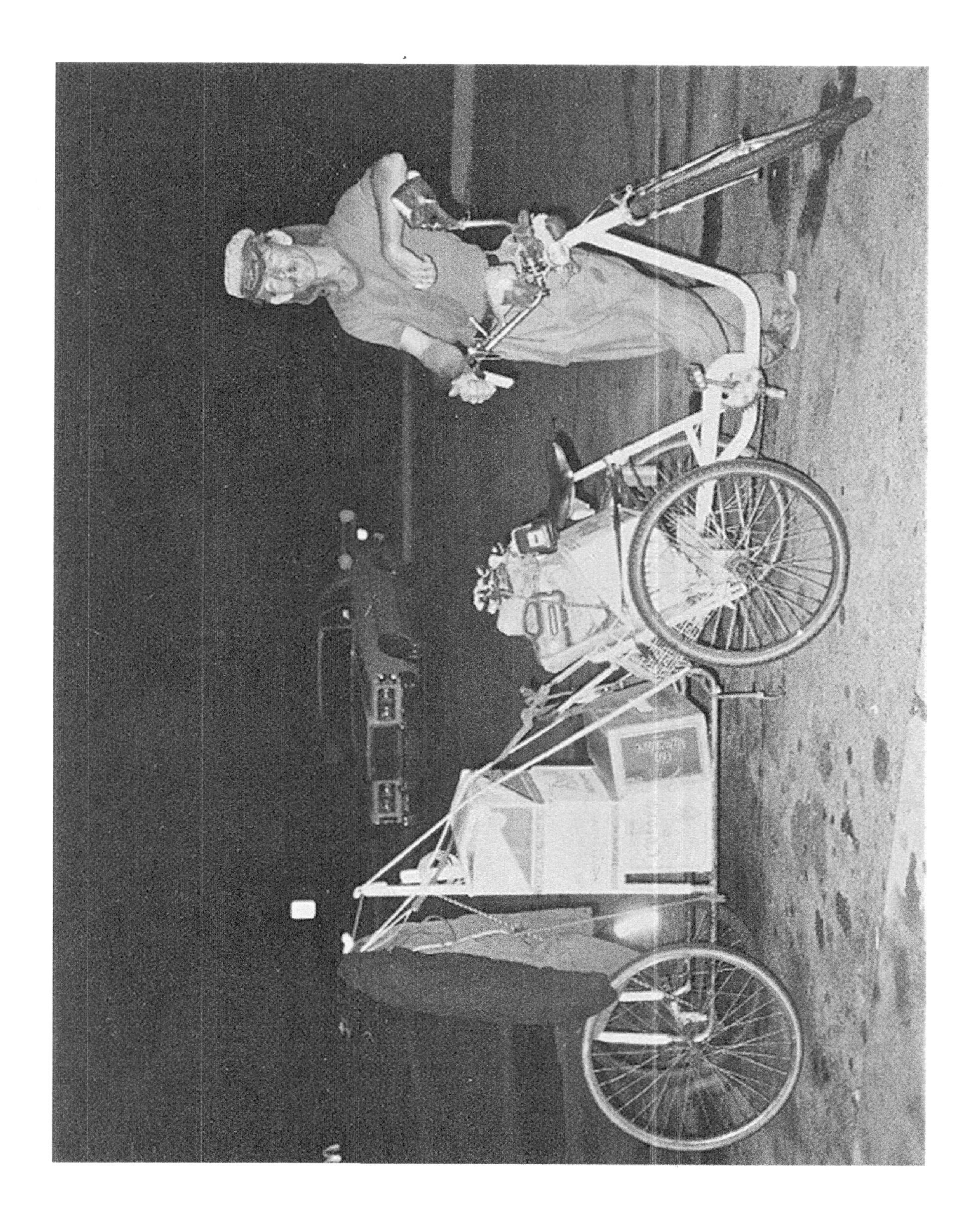

People - The Cowboy

Priest, Street Artist

A well known street artist from a small fishing village in Alabama is known for his stencil work seen around the Mobile and New Orleans areas. Priest's political voice speaks loudly through his work as he takes on and locally relevant topics. He brings recognition to harsh truths and proof that humor can be found in even the darkest of street corners. He has given our vicinity three of his artworks: the "Little Boy Watching TV" on the abandoned filling station at 1715 Dauphin Island Parkway, the "Night Watchman" on the Dog River Bridge, and the often-photographed "Feed the Hungry" work on the sunken boat that was near dog river.

The artist Priest's "Night Watchman" that was on Dog River Bridge.
Facing Page: "Feed the Hungry" that was near Dog River on DIP.

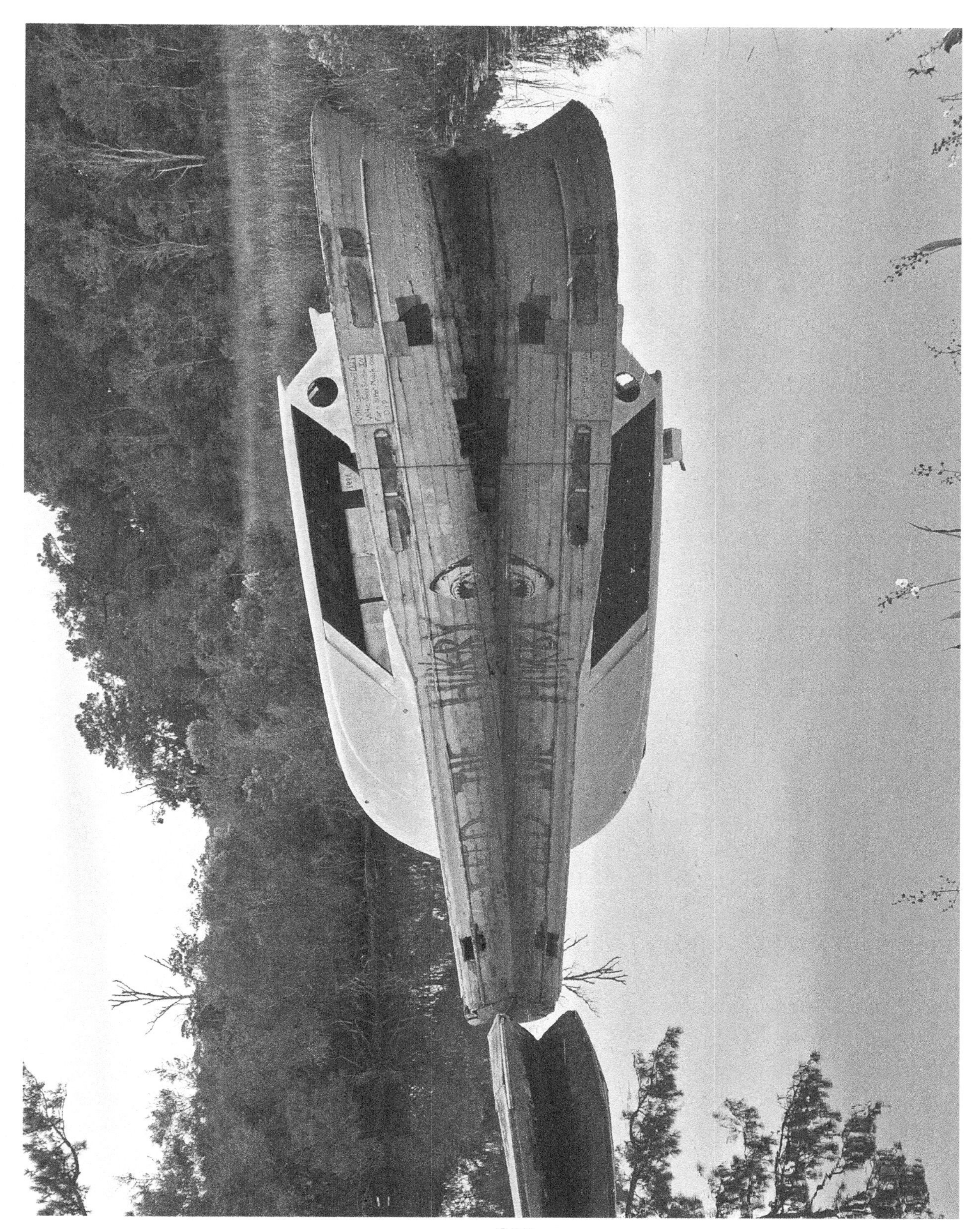

259

People - Priest

Afterword

Jane Botter Capsis

Seventy-years of Friendship and a Reinactment

The young girl looked so charming in her Easter Bonnet and lacey outfit in the image below, taken in 1949 that was submitted for *South Mobile*. When I looked more closely, I realized that the image had been taken in my backyard in front of the old shed and garage that is still there.

Thinking that it would be great fun to reenact the image, I set about to find her. Harriet Dykes found Jane Botter Capsis. She was alive and healthy, living and working in Baldwin County, as a well-known piano teacher. Jane agreed to pose and the rein-actment date was set. Four of her childhood friends that she grew up with along Bay Front Road heard about the event and also attended. Our good Councilman, C.J. Small came for the reenactment event. David Ladnier found an antique car similar to the one in the original image, Annette Stewart brought her well-trained dog, "Bear", Jane Capsis donned some accessories similar to what she wore in 1949, and the photos were taken. Afterwards, the childhood friends from 70 years ago enjoyed reminiscing about their time growing up together in South Mobile, three of whom never left. Experiencing the camraderie of these long-term friends reminded me what I already knew. So to end this book with the first words in the foreword: "There is just something wonderful about one's home dirt".

Above: Councilman C.J. Small, the attendees and contributors for the reinactment.

Below: Sue Shaw Pitts, Harry Shaw, Jane Botter Capsis, and Mary McKeough, friends for seventy years enjoyed reminiscing growing up in South Mobile.

Acknowledgements

South Mobile would not have been possible without Harriet Dykes, a resident in South Mobile since 1948. For years, we would spend every Wednesday together, talking with residents, combing through archives, all of them, and sometimes fearlessly taking risks. She could be seen on her hands and knees looking through dusty old shelves in library closets or driving through scary unknown trails and up to doors of people she knew, or knew of, who might have something to contribute. She was able to get us into the doors of many residents who were happy to share their stories, and who graciously opened their family albums. Her tenacity and interest drove this project and she always had a smile. I share credit for this book with Harriet. Thank you. It was a lot of fun.

Harriet Dykes

I also want to thank the following people for their assistance with and contributions to *South Mobile*: Devereaux Bemis, William Benbow, Edward Berger, Ivan Boatright, Rosa Boone, Jane Botter-Capsis, Jan Botts Lindsey, Edilea Bullen, Sharon Carter Cain, Chilton Coulson, The Cowboy, Peter Dais, III, Zoe Donalson, Dr. Michael and Laura Doran, Harriet Dykes, Marion Firle, Ben Glover, Nick Hain, George Hall, Gayle Hall, The Hillcrest Writers, Bond Hopper, Randall Ingram, Eugene Jackson, Myrt Jones, Linda Kennedy Jones, Collette King, Kenny and Amy Kleinschrodt, Lou Lartigue, Lucy Leggett, Fred and Joan Lorge, Homer McClure, Teddy McGill, Mary McKeough, Sonny Middleton, Eugene Moseley, Tracy Neely, Kathy Odom, Peter Palm, Sue Shaw Pitt, Priest (Street Artist), Martha Pringle Kidd, Dr. and Mrs. Dan Reimer, Harry Shaw, Katharine Phillips Singer, Frances Sirmon, Barbara Lartigue Smith, Councilman C.J. Small, Father Sophie, Lee Spafford, Robert Stewart, Tim and Desiree Tate, Sharon Tharp Lindsay, William Hal Tippins, Chuck Torrey, Jean Turner, Reggie and Mandie Wade, Reginald Washington, Oliver Washington, and Mel Washington. It took a village.

Susan Rouillier

References

Alabama and the Borderlands: from Prehistory to Statehood, Clayton, Lawrence A. 1985.

Archaeological Investigations on Dog River: An experiment in Public Archaeology, by Stephen Lau, Noel R. Stowe and Richard S. Fuller, Jr. University of South Alabama Archaeological Research Laboratory, Mobile, Alabama, 1978.

Back Home: Journeys through Mobile, Hoffman, Roy, 2001.

Brookley Spotlight, June 27, 1969; Mobile Press Register, May 7, 1957.

Bulletin of the Mississippi Valley Collection. John Willard Brister Library, Memphis State University, No. 6, Spring, 1973.

Colonial Mobile, Peter J. Hamilton, (1897), p. 71.

Creoles of Color of the Gulf South, Dormon, James H. 1996.

Cotton City: Urban Development in Antebellum Mobile. Amos, Harriet, 1985.

Craigheads Mobile, Delaney, Caldwell, The Haunted Bookshop, 1968.

Excavation Photos from the Dog River Plantation Site (1MB161), Mobile County, Alabama.. Gregory Waselkov, Bonnie L. Gums, George W. Shorter, Jr., Diane Silvia. Mobile, Alabama: University of South Alabama Center for Archaeological Studies. 1994.

First Peoples, PBS, 2015.

Highlights of 100 years in Mobile, 100th Anniversary, First National Bank, 1865-1965.

Historic Indian Towns in Alabama 1540-1838, Wright, Amos J. Jr., University of Alabama Press, 2003.

History of Our Lady of Lourdes Parish, Mobile Alabama, 1939-1979, Fr. Joseph Couture, S.S.E. edited by Edwin Benson.

History of Riverside Baptist Church, 1943-1998, Catherine Snow.

Library of Congress, Pictures and records division.

Local History and Genealogy Library, Mobile Public Library, Mobile, Alabama.

Lost Villages and Ancient Kingdoms, Sierke, Ted, 1980.

Mobile Aviation, by Billy J. Singleton.

Mobile Register Archives, Local History and Genealogy Library, Mobile Public Library, Mobile Alabama.

Mobile County, Alabama Department of Archives and History.

Mobile Bay Monthly, April 2008, p.108, McGehee, Tom.

Mobile: The Life and Times of a Great Southern City, Milton McLauren, Michael Thomas.

Mobile Alabama's People of Color: A Tricentennial History, 1702-2002, volume one Bivens, Shawn A., 2004.

Old Mobile Restaurants, Steiner, Malcolm, 2009.

Poor But Proud: Alabama's Poor Whites, Flynt, Wayne. University of Alabama Press, 1989.

Records and Archives, Probate Court of Mobile County, Alabama.

Romances of Mobile, Issued by Louisville and Nashville Railroad, 1923.

Sacramental Records of the Roman Catholic Church of the Archdiocese of Mobile, Volume 1, Section 1, 1704, 1739.

Smithsonian Report, S. Gaines and K. M. Cunningham, 1877, pp. 290-291.

Ten Year Faculty Reevaluation Study, B.C. Rain High School, 1989-90.

The Mobile Indians, Prieur Jay Higginbotham, 1966.

The Story of Mobile, Caldwell Delaney, HB Publications, 1994.

Things I Have Thought, J.R. Culpepper, Nall Printing Co.

Travels of William Bartram, William Bartram, Mark Van Doren, editor, 1928.

Treasured Memories: The Beginning of an Era. Mobile Alabama's Historic Black Churches, 1806-1945. Paulette Davis Horton, 2012.

Urban Emancipation: Popular Politics in Reconstruction Mobile, 1860-1890, Fitzgerald, Michael W., 1956.

The Author

Susan Rouillier has an degree in Microbiology from the University of Melbourne where she was a Commonwealth Scholar, and a Master's Degree in Computer Science from the University of South Alabama. She taught in Australia, Japan, and the United States. Rouillier set up a joint ecological project between Meiji Gankuen High School in Kitakyushu, Japan and The School of Math and Science in Mobile, Alabama, funded by the Fulbright Master Teacher Program.

Rouillier founded and has led the Hillcrest Writers in Mobile for the past eight years. She is the author of *Japan: Vignettes by a Southern Lady Abroad,* and *Video Call Activities with Children,* both available on Amazon. She also compiled and published a book of selected works: *Hillcrest Writers: Visions in Words.*

Her motivation for this book is that the rich history of South Mobile is preserved for future generations.

The author, her brother Bobby, and friend Mixon Keller on the shores along Bay Front Road in South Mobile, 1953.

Made in the USA
Monee, IL
22 May 2023